Tim McCarthy

AutoCAD Express

With 122 Figures

Springer-Verlag
London Berlin Heidelberg New York
Paris Tokyo Hong Kong

Timothy J. McCarthy, PhD
Lecturer, Department of Civil and Structural Engineering,
UMIST, PO Box 88, Manchester M60 1QD, UK

ISBN 3-540-19590-4 Springer-Verlag Berlin Heidelberg New York
ISBN 0-387-19590-4 Springer-Verlag New York Berlin Heidelberg

British Library Cataloguing in Publication Data
McCarthy, Timothy *1952–*
AutoCAD express,
1. Microcomputer systems. Software package: AutoCAD
I. Title
005.369
ISBN 3-540-19590-4

Library of Congress Cataloging-in-Publication Data
McCarthy, Tim, *1959–*
AutoCAD Express/Tim McCarthy.
p.   cm.
ISBN 0-387-19590-4 (US:alk. paper)
1. AutoCAD (Computer program)   I. Title
T385.M3776   1990   90-9607
6209.00425902855369—dc20   CIP

Typeset by MJS Publications, Buntingford, Herts
Printed by The Bath Press, Bath, Avon

2128/3916-543210   Printed on acid-free paper

To Grace

ACKNOWLEDGEMENTS

I would like to express my deep gratitude to all those who helped me with this project. I am indebted to my colleagues in the Department of Civil and Structural Engineering at UMIST, in particular Ray Heywood and Bob Gowans. Thanks also to the undergraduate students from whom I have learned so much and to Philip Windle of Autodesk in London.

My special thanks to my wife, Grace, for everything.

September 1989   T. McCarthy.

Trademark acknowledgements

ADE, ADI, AEC, AutoCAD, AutoLISP, AutoShade, AutoSolid and DXF are registered trademarks of Autodesk Inc. PC-DOS, OS2 and IBM are registered trademarks of International Business Machines Corporation. Postscript is a trademark of Adobe Systems. MS-DOS and Microsoft are trademarks of the Microsoft Corporation. Ventura is a trademark of Ventura Software Inc. PC-WRITE is a trademark of Quicksoft. Wordperfect is a trademark of Satellite Software International. Logimouse is a trademark of Logitech. Hewlett-Packard is a trademark of Hewlett Packard Inc. Epson is a trademark of Epson America.

Further software products are listed by company in chapter 12.

CONTENTS

Chapter 1 **INTRODUCTION**

What is AutoCAD?

With well over 200,000 copies of the program sold, AutoCAD is the world's most popular computer aided drafting package for the personal computer (PC). It is a fully functional 2D CAD program. Full 3D wire frame representation was incorporated in the program with the launch of Release 10 in 1988. Its popularity has made AutoCAD the de facto industry standard for PC-CAD with a host of other program developers providing application software conforming to the AutoCAD format.

As a fully functional drafting program, AutoCAD can achieve anything that can be drawn on a drawing board. The main benefits of CAD come more from being able to edit and exchange drawing information rapidly rather than simply replacing the drawing board. Starting to use AutoCAD is a difficult step as it requires a certain amount of new skill development. Once you have made the commitment to learn how to use the program and implement it in your everyday work the benefits will soon accrue. You will quickly discover that there are many things that you can do with AutoCAD that you could never do with a drawing board.

With AutoCAD your drawings become more than just black lines on a white sheet of paper. The AutoCAD drawing is a database of information. Some of this is indeed graphic information, but AutoCAD knows the length of every line on the drawing. It knows what symbols and parts have been included on the drawing and it can output this information to design programs or spreadsheet programs for bill of materials and cost analysis.

The aims of the AutoCAD Express

The main aim of this book is to introduce AutoCAD users to effective CAD drawing techniques. This is done through structured exercises that demonstrate the AutoCAD drafting principles clearly. The commands are dealt with in this context as tools to make the job easier. It is also hoped that you will have fun doing these exercises and creating some of the pretty pictures.

The AutoCAD Express is suitable for new users as it covers the program from the very basics right through to advanced techniques. Occasional users will find it a useful and quick refresher, while even seasoned users will discover novel aspects to old commands. Not only are the commands fully described but AutoCAD drawing techniques are explored with many examples.

The book has been written for AutoCAD Release 10 with ADE3 and the Advanced User Interface. It covers all the important aspects of the version with full descriptions of the 3D functions and dynamic viewing. It is also suitable for Release 9 users with differences between the old and newer versions highlighted. The operating system used is MS or PC DOS. References to the operating system are kept to a minimum, so users of OS2 and UNIX should not be distracted.

Because it is so flexible, AutoCAD can seem unwieldy to the new user. The exercises in this book follow each other logically along a well defined learning curve. Each chapter represents a stage along this curve, and at each stage the user can pause to consolidate the skills obtained, or proceed to the next stage. To overcome the sheer size of the AutoCAD program and the number of facilities available, the user is directed through the most appropriate path to complete the example drawing. You will never be overwhelmed by lengthy descriptions of abstract concepts and myriad command parameters. Rather you will learn things when you need to know them. By the end of the book there will be little left about AutoCAD that you will still need to know.

The Express route through AutoCAD

The AutoCAD Express is designed as a tutorial guide to the varied facets of the world's most popular computer aided drafting package. The emphasis is on *doing* the various commands and *achieving* results. Chapters 2 to 8 each present instructive drawing exercises which call on AutoCAD's drafting facilities in a logical order. Each chapter has a broad theme with useful asides included where appropriate. Each new command and facility is introduced in the context of solving a particular drafting problem.

Chapter 2 provides a quick introduction to the essentials of producing a drawing file. Chapter 3 gives a complete description of line drawing in AutoCAD with detailed examples of the user–AutoCAD interface. In Chapter 4 the Express takes to the skies to introduce the bulk of AutoCAD's drawing commands. Your first encounter with the program's editing facilities also happens in this chapter. In Chapter 5 the AutoCAD Express lands in Paris to explore more advanced editing features and construct Gustav Eiffel's famous tower. It's back to the steamy kitchen for Chapter 6 where you will learn how to make and manipulate AutoCAD blocks and create a library of symbols. These symbols are used to help AutoCAD Express Kitchens Ltd. to quickly design new fitted kitchens with automatic bills of materials. Their competitors must be worried! Chapter 7 covers automatic dimensioning and a few other high level commands. The world tour continues in Chapter 8 from the unlikely start back in the kitchen. This particular leg of the journey covers isometric projection and a 2.5D view of the Big Apple before visiting the pyramids of Giza in glorious 3D colour. All the major new facilities introduced for 3D drafting are described with relevant examples covering 3D drawing and visualisation.

The second part of the book concerns AutoCAD output and methods of getting that bit more from the program. Chapter 9 deals with aspects of printing and plotting your drawings and how to get the right output at the first attempt. The benefits of customising AutoCAD to your own situation are discussed in Chapter 10. You can speed up even the AutoCAD Express with bespoke menus and command macros. This chapter shows you how to write your own screen and pull-down menus. The profits of AutoCAD Express Kitchens Ltd. are further boosted when you make a pull-down icon menu for their symbols library. Chapter 11 provides a quick introduction to AutoCAD's built-in programming language, AutoLISP. Here you will learn how to write simple labour saving programs to do calculations and draw graphs as well as picking up a few good one-liners. The final chapter shows how to get others to do the programming for you. This contains descriptions of programs available as add-ons to AutoCAD. The first part of the chapter covers routines distributed free by Autodesk. These include some handy text editing software. The second part of Chapter 12 gives an overview of the commercial software available to enhance you CAD productivity.

Finally, there are a two appendices covering technical aspects of AutoCAD. Appendix A describes how to configure AutoCAD on a new computer. Appendix B provides a useful list of hints and hiccups to look out for when running the program. After the appendices you will find glossary of CAD and computer terms. You will find a comprehensive index at the back of the book.

Conventions used in the AutoCAD Express

The style of presentation is fairly simple. There are no distracting icons or hieroglyphics. Plain English is used through out and where jargon cannot be avoided it is clearly explained. There are a few computerese phrases used in the text which have helped me in writing the book and, I hope, will help you in reading it. Here they are:

RETURN or ENTER?

These are two words that mean the same thing. AutoCAD will frequently tell you that you must "Press RETURN to continue". Now, most keyboards don't have a key called "RETURN" but do have one with "ENTER" or one with ↵.

All three mean to "enter" the line by pressing the key and "return" the cursor to the left margin. In this book the symbol <ENTER> has been used to signify this. You will also find references to <SPACE> in the book which mean "hit the space bar".

Presentation of user–AutoCAD dialogue

What you have to type is shown in bold text. The AutoCAD prompts are shown in normal text. Some points are referenced in diagrams and in the dialogue. These references are presented in the text in brackets to the right of dialogue. For example:

> Command: **LINE <ENTER>**
> From point: **35,40 <ENTER>**   (V)

This means that AutoCAD will display the word "Command:" and you have to type the word "LINE" followed by pressing the ENTER key. AutoCAD will reply with the prompt "From point:" to which you reply by typing the two numbers and pressing the ENTER key. The "(V)" indicates that this corresponds to the point marked with a "V" on the nearby diagram. You should not type the "(V)".

Control keys

One of the keys on the PC keyboard has "CTRL" written on it. On some keyboards the word is spelt out in full, "Control". When this key is held down simultaneously with other keys special computer commands are executed. AutoCAD uses the control key in conjunction with a number of letters to execute different commands. These are given in the text as, say, "CTRL B" or "^B". This means to press the "Control" key and while holding it down also press the "B" key.

Menus

From time to time Autodesk issues improved screen menus. With each new issue, the display details change. Because of this, there may be small discrepancies between the screen menus displayed in this book and those that appear on your screen. The menus used in the AutoCAD Express are those distributed as ACADUK.MNU. These menus are considerably better than the standard ACAD.MNU file originally issued with Release 10. The differences between various versions of the menu file are highlighted where appropriate in the text.

Other conventions

Some of AutoCAD's commands require more care than others. Those commands where errors can give disastrous results are preceded by "HAZARD WARNING!". Less dangerous commands are accompanied by a brief "Warning!". Don't avoid these commands. Just follow the safety procedures given with the warnings.

The final note is not about jargon but is timely advice. Be careful not to confuse 0 (zero) with the letter O (Oh), and 1 (one) with l (lower case L).

Enjoy the book and soon you will be enjoying the benefits of productive AutoCAD drafting!

Chapter 2 STARTING AUTOCAD

Preparation

This chapter assumes that AutoCAD has been installed on the computer and is ready to be used. If this is not the case you can follow the procedure outlined in Appendix A of this book. Most dealers will install the software for you when they deliver it. It is good practice to request this service so that your purchase can be fully tested while the vendor is present.

Clear your work area so as to give comfortable access to the computer, keyboard and mouse. An area of about 20mm by 20mm (9in. by 9in.) should be adequate for the mouse. Switch the computer on and wait for it to go through its automatic self test and "booting" procedures. This will take approximately 30 seconds. When the computer has booted, change directory to the one containing AutoCAD. If it is located in a directory called "ACAD" this can be done from DOS by keying **CD\ACAD** followed by <**ENTER**>. You are now ready to start computer aided drafting.

Starting up and shutting down

When the DOS prompt C:> or C:ACAD> appears on the screen type **ACAD** <**ENTER**> to invoke AutoCAD. The screen display will go blank for a few moments and then display a message screen similar to Figure 2.1. Press <**ENTER**> to clear the message and the screen should display the AutoCAD main menu (Figure 2.2). This gives eight options and appears at the start and end of an AutoCAD session. The first three menu options are the most important for day to day use. Selections are made by keying the appropriate number and then pressing <**ENTER**>. To begin your new drawing, type **1** <**ENTER**> or to exit AutoCAD and return to DOS type **0** <**ENTER**>. If the drawing already exists and you wish to see it or to make some changes to it then type **2** <**ENTER**> at the main menu.

```
                A U T □ C A D
Copyright (C) 1982, 83, 84, 85, 86, 87, 88, 89 Autodesk, Inc.
Release  10  (3/20/89)  IBM PC
Advanced Drafting Extensions 3
Serial Number:  12-345678

Thank you for purchasing AutoCAD

If you have a full copy of AutoCAD be sure to
return the Registration Card if you haven't
already done so.  Registered users receive notices
of updates.

This message is in the file ACAD.MSG.  You can delete
it or replace it with a customized version if you like.


Press  RETURN  to continue:
```

Figure 2.1 AutoCAD message screen

```
                A U T □ C A D
Copyright (C) 1982, 83, 84, 85, 86, 87, 88, 89 Autodesk, Inc.
Release  10  (3/20/89)  IBM PC
Advanced Drafting Extensions 3
Serial Number:  12-345678

Main Menu

    0.   Exit   AutoCAD
    1.   Begin  a  NEW  drawing
    2.   Edit   an  EXISTING  drawing
    3.   Plot   a  drawing
    4.   Printer  Plot  a  drawing

    5.   Configure  AutoCAD
    6.   File  Utilities
    7.   Compile  shape/font  description  file
    8.   Convert  old  drawing  file

Enter  selection:
```

Figure 2.2 AutoCAD's main menu

Creating a drawing

Drawing identification

Having entered **1** in response to the main menu prompt you will then be asked
to name the drawing file as follows:

Enter NAME of drawing: **EXPRESS1 <ENTER>**

The bold text is what you type in. The name can be from 1 to 8 characters long and can have letters or numbers. Lower case letters and upper case letters are fully interchangeable (a is equivalent to A etc.) but no full stops or blanks are allowed. AutoCAD appends the file extension .DWG onto the drawing name so that the full name of the file to be stored on the disk is EXPRESS1.DWG. The user never specifies the ".DWG" part of the name when using AutoCAD but you would need to specify it if you were using DOS on its own, say for disk tidying. Never use the name ACAD for your drawing as ACAD.DWG is used for special purposes by AutoCAD. The drawing name can be preceded by a valid DOS pathname. For example by responding to the "Enter NAME.." prompt with a drawing name "C:\ACAD\EXPRESS1" you can specify that the drawing is to be stored on disk drive C: (the hard disk) in the directory ACAD.

Once you have named your drawing, AutoCAD enables the drawing editor program and the drawing file is opened on the disk, ready to receive data. The screen display changes to show the blank drawing area. The program then takes a few moments to load in the menus and the ACAD.LSP file.

The drawing screen

When the menu is loaded it should appear in a column at the right of the screen with the word AutoCAD at the top (Figure 2.3). The command prompt area is located below the drawing area. This is where commands that you type appear along with the appropriate responses and prompts from AutoCAD. A status

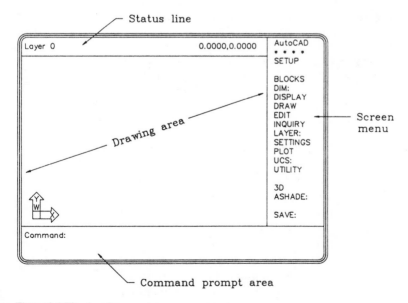

Figure 2.3 The drawing screen

line is shown along the top of the screen. This gives you information about the current layer, what drafting modes are active and also the position of the cursor. Initially, the screen should appear as shown in Figure 2.3. Some extra words (eg "SNAP") may appear on the status line. These will be described fully in Chapter 3.

The two little arrows at the lower left of the screen drawing area are AutoCAD's coordinate system icon or symbol. They point to the directions of the coordinate axes. In this case X is the horizontal axis and Y is the vertical and to locate a point four units to the right and three units up you would use the coordinates "4,3". (A third axis, Z, is available for 3D work and is perpendicular to the screen.) The "W" indicates that the WORLD or global coordinate system is active. This just means that when you give a pair of coordinates such as "4,3" that the location is calculated relative to the drawing's origin, which always has the coordinates "0,0". You need not worry about the intricacies of coordinate systems; the default "X,Y,WORLD" is all that is required until Chapter 8. The coordinate system icon is on the screen as a reminder to the user, but it is not part of the actual drawing and so does not appear on prints out or plots. If you are using any version of AutoCAD earlier than Release 10, the world coordinate system is the only one available and no icon is displayed.

As you move the cursor out of the drawing area at the right hand side of the screen it changes into a highlighting bar. When the bar is at a screen menu item it is highlighted, and may be selected by pressing the pick button. Most digitising devices and mice have more than one button. The "pick button" can be found by trial and error, though it is usually the first button or the left-hand one. If you pick a menu item the display will change to a new menu. To revert to the original menu, pick the "AutoCAD" at the top of the screen menu. If you now move the cursor into the status line area at the top of the screen it changes into the menu bar. As the cursor is moved left or right the various key-words on the bar will be highlighted. Picking one of these causes a pull-down menu to appear from which various commands can be executed (Figure 2.4). This menu bar and the pull-down menus are available only with Release 9 and later and only with certain types of screen. The most common types of display devices (Hercules, EGA and VGA) are catered for, though some less common high resolution boards are not. If in doubt consult your AutoCAD dealer.

At any stage during the AutoCAD editing session you can save your drawing, exit the program and come back to it later. When you wish to do this go to the section "Saving the drawing" towards the end of this chapter.

AutoCAD's menus and Advanced User Interface

It is possible to type all of AutoCAD's commands using the keyboard. What you type appears on the command line and is executed when you hit <ENTER>. However, to save time and typing errors and also to remind the user of the commands available AutoCAD has a system of menus and submenus. These provide convenient groups of similar commands.

Depending on which version of AutoCAD you are using there may be some slight diffrences between the menus displayed in this book and those that

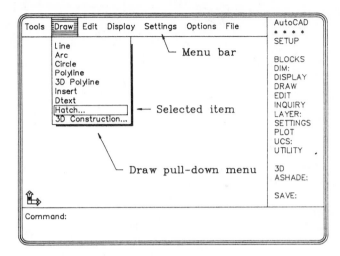

Figure 2.4 Pull-down menu (ACAD.MNU)

appear on your screen. The menus used in the rest of the book are from the file ACADUK.MNU which is located in the \SOURCE sub-directory on one of your release disks. If your menu displays only some of the features used in the exercises and you have a copy of ACADUK.MNU on one of your release disks, then this file may be copied into the main AutoCAD directory to replace the standard menu file, ACAD.MNU. Be sure to make a safe backup of the standard menu onto another disk before attempting this. Use the DOS RENAME or COPY commands.

The screen menu at the right of the drawing area consists of a tree structure of menus and commands (Figure 2.5). At the end of each branch is a command. The initial menu that is displayed is the root menu from which all the menu branches can be reached. The menu items ending in a ":" are executable commands, while those without the colon are the names of sub-menus. As an example, move the cursor so that the "DRAW" lights up and press the pick button. The menu changes to show a number of drawing commands arranged in alphabetical order. At the bottom of the menu the word "next" indicates that the DRAW menu extends over more than one page. To access the second page pick the "**next**" and the remainder of the commands are shown. Return to the first page of DRAW by picking "**previous**" and then pick "**LINE:**". As this is a command it will be executed. The LINE sub-menu will be displayed and at the bottom of the screen the prompt line will display

Command: LINE From point:

and will wait for you to input the coordinates of one end. Move the cursor into the drawing area and press the pick button. This is taken as the start of the line and the prompt changes to

Command: LINE From point: To point:

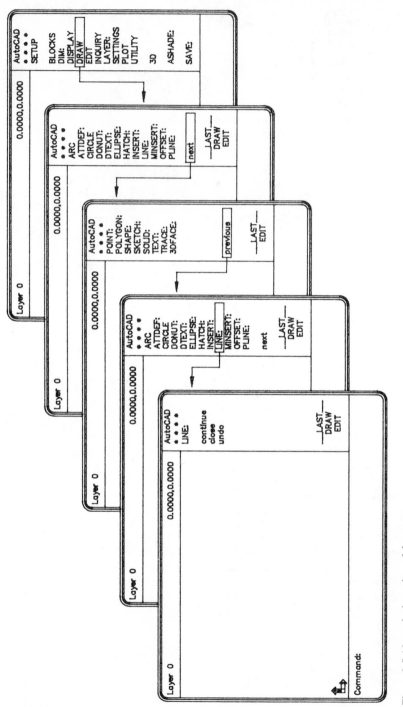

Figure 2.5 Along the branches of the menu tree

waiting for the other end point to be input. Pick as many points as you want to create a series of connected line segments. To exit from the LINE command simply press <ENTER>. Picking ___LAST___ returns you to the DRAW menu and picking **AutoCAD** at the top gives the root menu.

This has been a quick squirrel hop along one part of the menu tree. Tasty morsels are also to be had along the other branches. As you use AutoCAD you will become familiar with the menus and the most useful commands. If you get lost on the menu tree, picking **AutoCAD** will always return you to the root. Remember, all commands can be typed at the keyboard irrespective of what menu is displayed.

The Advanced User Interface is a powerful way of communicating with AutoCAD. Some of its pull-down menus duplicate the functions of the screen menu and some make extra features available. The main difference between communicating via the screen menus and the pull-down menus is that the latter employ graphics, pictures and dialogue boxes in place of the simple textual prompts of the former.

As an example, select a command from the screen menu and then from the Advanced User Interface: pick **DRAW** from the AutoCAD root menu at the right of the screen. Now pick **HATCH:**. The command prompt at the bottom of the screen displays

> Command: **HATCH**
> Pattern (? or name/U,style)<>:**?** <ENTER>

Pressing **?** <ENTER> gives a long list of patterns on the screen (Figure 2.6). In

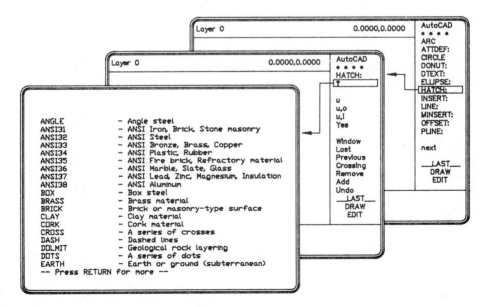

Figure 2.6 HATCH patterns from screen menu

doing this the screen also jumps into text mode. This is quite normal. Keep pressing <**ENTER**> until the full list as been displayed and at the "Command:" prompt, press the **F1** key of the grey function keys. This redisplays the graphics screen. The pattern list is long and the names of the styles are difficult to remember. However, help is at hand.

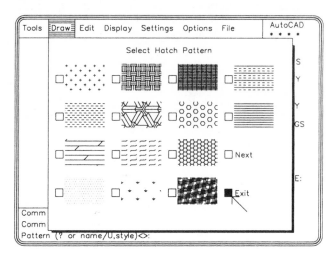

Figure 2.7 HATCH pat'ern icons

Now move the cursor to the status line above the drawing area. The menu bar will appear and you can pick **DRAW** followed by **HATCH** from the pull-down menu. This causes a pop-up icon menu showing actual pictures of the various hatch styles (Figure 2.7). Moving the cursor (now transformed into an arrow) into the box beside the desired pattern and pressing the pick button makes selection or pick **Exit.** To delete the icon menu and return to the drawing press, the **ESC** key.

HAZARD WARNING!

HATCH is a dangerous command. HATCH is used to fill in an area of the drawing with a given pattern. Do not fill large areas as this uses a lot of computer memory and disk space. In response to the prompts "spacing between lines" or "scale for pattern", reply with large values. A small value of spacing or scale causes the pattern to be repeated too many times. It is possible to fill a 30Mb disk with one inappropriate HATCH command. To abort an embarrassing HATCH press Ĉ (CTRL and C). Follow the guidelines given in Chapter 4.

Setting up the drawing environment

Now that you know how to communicate with AutoCAD, why not execute some commands and embark on some controlled CAD? The emphasis here is on your being in control and not accepting any old rubbish the computer might tempt you with in the name of "convenient defaults". The default drawing environment contains all the settings somebody somewhere found suitable for his or her own application. You can be sure that they were not meant for you. Even if it is acceptable for one drawing the environment may need changes for the next.

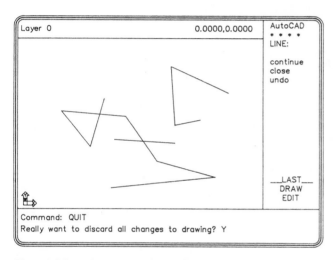

Figure 2.8 Dumping an unwanted drawing

For this section you will need a clear drawing, so if you have already drawn some lines, follow the procedure below (Figure 2.8). If your drawing is empty, then skip to the "Drawing size" paragraph. The QUIT command can also be found in the UTILITY sub-menu or in the FILE part of the menu bar.

Command: **QUIT** <**ENTER**>
Really want to discard all changes to drawing? **Y**

This will discard the current drawing, exit the AutoCAD editor and return to the main menu. Now select **"1"** and press <**ENTER**>, as below.

Enter selection: **1** <**ENTER**>

Enter NAME of drawing <EXPRESS1>: <**ENTER**>

This starts a new drawing, again called EXPRESS1.DWG. If the drawing already exists you will get a warning message asking if you want to overwrite it. Type "**Y**" to overwrite.

Drawing size

All AutoCAD drawings are made to *full scale*. One of the principal reasons for this is so that when you use AutoCAD's automatic dimensioning it will give the correct lengths rather than scaled ones. Thus the drawing size will depend on the size of the items being drawn. It will also depend on the working units. For example, to draw the architectural layout of an office measuring 23.8m by 15m you would choose a size big enough to contain the whole floor, plus other items such as margins and title boxes. A good drawing size in this case might be 29.5 units wide by 21 units high. If you were using millimetres as the base unit rather than metres, then the drawing size would be 29,500 by 21,000. (Note that this is approximately the same ratio as an A4 sheet and other sizes in the A series.)

For the drawing EXPRESS1 you will require it to be 65 units by 45 units. The LIMITS command allows us to do this. Pick **SETTINGS** from the main menu and then **LIMITS:**

> Command: **LIMITS**
> ON/OFF<Lower left corner> <0.00,0.00>: <**ENTER**>
> Upper right corner <12.00,9.00>: **65,45** <**ENTER**>
> Command: **LIMITS**
> ON/OFF<Lower left corner> <0.00,0.00>: **ON**
> Command:

Pressing <**ENTER**> in response to the lower left prompt means that you accept the default setting of positioning that corner at the WORLD origin, 0,0. AutoCAD always displays the default values between angular brackets, < > and any time you wish to accept this value simply press <**ENTER**>. If you wish to over-ride the default then key in the desired values as in the upper right prompt above. If the defaults offered by your computer are different from 12.00,9.00, don't worry. Simply replace whatever the values are by **65,45** <**ENTER**>. The second execution of LIMITS is to turn the limit checking facility on. This prevents anything being drawn outside the limits by mistake.

At this point if you move the cursor around the drawing area picking points, you will notice that the coordinate read-out is giving similar values as before. So, even though you have changed the drawing size the display shows the old size. To display the whole of the new drawing size type

> Command: **ZOOM**
> All/Centre/Dynamic/Extents/Left/Previous/Window/<Scale(X)>: **A**

The response to the type of zoom required can be truncated to whatever AutoCAD displays in CAPITAL letters, in this case "A" for "All". This command can be found by picking **DISPLAY** from the root screen menu and then **ZOOM**. It works like a zoom lens in a camera allowing magnification and demagnification of the image. ZOOM is fully described in Chapter 3. Now, if you move the cursor around, the coordinates will reflect the current drawing size.

While it is important to consider the drawing size before you embark on an AutoCAD drafting session, it is not essential. You can alter the drawing size at any time during editing, but it's more efficient to get it right first time!

The next choice you have for the drawing environment is the system of units to be used. The standard AutoCAD default settings use decimal units and decimal angles. If the coordinates on the status line are in decimal format then you can skip to the next section, on "Layers". If it is in feet and inches, or you are not sure, then use AutoCAD's UNITS command. This is on the second part of the SETTINGS sub-menu. Pick **SETTINGS** from the root menu, then **next** and **UNITS:**. Follow the screen prompts and give the responses outlined below.

Command: **UNITS**

System of units:
    1. Scientific
    2. Decimal
    3. Engineering
    4. Architectural
    5. Fractional

Enter choice, 1 to 5 <default>: **2** <**ENTER**>
Number of digits to right of decimal point (0 to 8) <8>: **4** <**ENTER**>

You will then be asked to define the units for angular measurement and the number of decimal places.

Systems of angle measure:
Enter choice, 1 to 5 <>: **1** <**ENTER**>
Number of fractional places for display of angles (0 to 8)<>: **2** <**ENTER**>
Enter direction for angle 0 <>: **0** <**ENTER**>
Do you want angles measured clockwise? <>: **N** <**ENTER**>
Command:

This procedure should ensure that the examples in this book match the displays on your screen.

Layers

Having decided on the size it is now worth considering how your drawing is to be organised. Using AutoCAD's LAYER facility is the most efficient way of doing this. The layers of a drawing can be considered as a series of transparent sheets each containing parts of the drawing (Figure 2.9). Whole layers can be manipulated to change the colour or linetype for all the objects on a particular layer. Layers can also be made invisible when they are not relevant to the current task, and then they can be made visible again later. For example, you might use one layer to contain all your construction lines, one layer for text and drawing margins, one for floor plan and another for the wiring diagram. Unlike a conventional paper drawing there is no need to delete your construction lines, simply make them invisible. In this way, when you come to edit the drawing or add in a plumbing diagram, all the original constructions are available.

Because of the importance of layers in the organisation of drawing information and the increasing need for drawing exchange via CAD, most users adopt some convention for using layers. For construction drawings, British Standard 1192 Part 5 (in preparation) sets out recommendations for naming layers and what kind of information should be on them. Because some CAD systems have only a layer numbering facility the Standard recommends the names summarised in Table 2.1. This process is still evolving and highlights the importance of adopting a logical approach to organisation of information in CAD. Adherence to a common standard allows engineers using different CAD systems to communicate effectively.

When you start a new drawing AutoCAD always has a minimum of one layer called "0" (zero). Extra layers can be set up at any stage during the drawing but it is advisable to decide on the structure of the layers before commencing actual drawing. In older versions of AutoCAD only one linetype and one colour per layer were possible. Thus each layer has associated with it a colour and

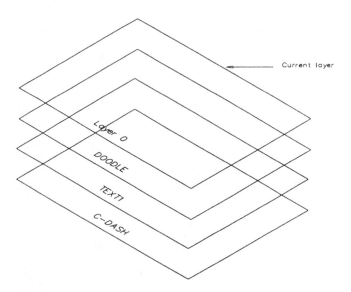

Figure 2.9 Layers as transparent sheets

Table 2.1 Recommended layers in construction drawings

Layer name	Type of information
1	General drawing sheet – lines, arcs, circles etc.
2	Margins and title block
3	Building grids
4	Hatching
5	Text annotation
6	Details to be plotted at larger scales
7	Dimension lines etc.
8	Empty
9	Empty
10 to 19	Foundations of building
20 to 29	Main structural elements
30 to 39	Secondary structural elements
40 to 49	Finishes
50 to 69	Services
70 to 89	Fittings
90 to 99	External elements

Based on British Standard 1192 Pt5, November, 1989.

linetype. Release 10 allows multiple colours and linetypes on a layer but still allows you to give a layer specific default settings.

As an example, our drawing, EXPRESS1, will contain some doodling as you try out some drawing commands, some text, and some construction lines. You will use dashed lines for the construction layer and call it "C-DASH" and then assign the colour blue to our doodles. The following sequence gives the AutoCAD prompts and your responses.

> Command: **LAYER <ENTER>** (or pick it from the screen menu)
> ?/Make/Set/New/ON/OFF/Colour/Ltype/Freeze/Thaw: **N <ENTER>**
> New layer name(s): **DOODLE, TEXT1, C-DASH <ENTER>**

The options within the LAYER command are given in the line "?/Make...". Again you can truncate the response to whatever is given in capital letters. The "N" allows you to define the names and then creates them within the drawing. Layer names can contain letters and numbers and have up to 31 characters, though it is advisable to restrict them to as few as practicable. The names should be descriptive or follow some conventional numbering or acronym. New layers can be added at any time. Having created the three new layers, the default properties can be altered and AutoCAD returns to the "?/Make..." prompt. Initially all layers have CONTINUOUS linetype and the colour white (colour number 7), so here goes with the changes.

> ?/Make/Set/New/ON/OFF/Colour/Ltype/Freeze/Thaw: **L <ENTER>**
> Linetype (or ?) <CONTINUOUS>: **DASHED <ENTER>**
> Layer name(s) for linetype DASHED <0>: **C-DASH <ENTER>**
> ?/Make/Set/New/ON/OFF/Colour/Ltype/Freeze/Thaw: **C <ENTER>**
> Colour: **BLUE <ENTER>**
> Layer name(s) for colour 5 (blue) <0>: **DOODLE <ENTER>**

AutoCAD's standard palette of colours consists of red, yellow, green, cyan greenish blue), blue, magenta and white. These colours may be referred to by name, as above, or by their numbers (1 to 7 in the order listed above). Further colours with numbers 8 to 255 are also available but are dependent on the type of screen you are using. Obviously, the colours are only meaningful at this stage if you have a colour display. However, even if you have a monochrome screen, colours can be assigned anyway, and it is possible to get multi-colour plots. On some displays the screen is "paper white" and so AutoCAD's "white" lines are shown as black. White lines normally convert to black lines when plotted on paper. Now you must tell AutoCAD which layer you wish to draw on. This is equivalent to taking the transparent sheet named DOODLE and placing it on top. To draw on the doodle layer use the "Set" option.

> ?/Make/Set/New/ON/OFF/Colour/Ltype/Freeze/Thaw: **S** <**ENTER**>
> New current layer <0>: **DOODLE** <**ENTER**>
> ?/Make/Set/New/ON/OFF/Colour/Ltype/Freeze/Thaw: <**ENTER**>
> Command:

Note that AutoCAD always returns you to the LAYER options prompt after each selection. To exit from this prompt line simply press <**ENTER**>. Of the other options that are available "Make" combines the "New" and "Set" operations; OFF causes a layer to become invisible while ON makes it visible again; Freeze is similar to OFF but in addition it causes AutoCAD to completely ignore the frozen layer while Thaw brings it back. The ON and OFF options are really relics of early AutoCAD versions and are not worth bothering about. Using Freeze to ignore layers that have a lot of information can significantly increase your drawing speed.

You can check that all the layers are set up correctly by using the "?" response to LAYER.

> Command: **LAYER** <**ENTER**>
> ?/Make/Set/New/ON/OFF/Colour/Ltype/Freeze/Thaw: **?** <**ENTER**>
> Layer name(s) for listing <∗>: <**ENTER**>

Layer name	State	Colour	Linetype
0	On	7 (white)	CONTINUOUS
DOODLE	On	5 (blue)	CONTINUOUS
TEXT1	On.	7 (white)	CONTINUOUS
C–DASH	On	7 (white)	DASHED

Current layer: DOODLE

On single screen systems the display will flip into text mode to display the layer information. All the layers are initially ON.

To get back to the graphics display press **F1** or type **REDRAW** <ENTER>. For screens that support the Advanced User Interface, this information can be obtained by moving the cursor to the menu bar at the top of the display and selecting **"Settings"** or **"Modes"** followed by **"Modify Layer"**. This should give you a pop-up dialogue box with all the above information. All the LAYER command options can be input via this dialogue box by moving the arrow cursor to the relevant part and pressing the pick button. You will then be asked to confirm any selections. To do this pick the **"OK"** box. To get back to the drawing screen pick **"CANCEL"** or press **ESC**. This dialogue box is very useful for beginners but becomes cumbersome if the drawing has a lot of layers when keyboard entry is recommended. More of this in Chapters 3 and 4.

If your layer information is different from that given above go back into the LAYER command and make the necessary alterations. If your display has the correct information but also has some other layers present you can freeze them. For example to freeze a layer named "TEXT1" use

> Command: **LAYER** <ENTER>
> ?/Make/Set/New/ON/OFF/Colour/Ltype/Freeze/Thaw: **F** <ENTER>
> Layer name(s) to freeze: **TEXT1** <ENTER>
> ?/Make/Set/New/ON/OFF/Colour/Ltype/Freeze/Thaw: <ENTER>
> Command:

Note: Freeze will only work if the layer to be frozen already exists. Since AutoCAD ignores items on frozen layers, you cannot freeze the current layer.

Drawing lines

Having done all that work on setting up the drawing environment, you are in a position to do some controlled drafting. The workhorse of any drawing is the humble line. Indeed, ultimately, every drawing entity can be reduced to a series of straight lines (curves consist of a very large number of tiny straight lines).

The AutoCAD LINE command allows you to construct any number of independent line segments. To draw a square 15×15 type the following:

> Command: **LINE** <ENTER> From point: **5,5** <ENTER>   (A)
> To point: **20,5** <ENTER>   (B)
> To point: **20,20** <ENTER>   (C)
> To point: **5,20** <ENTER>   (D)
> To point: **CLOSE** <ENTER>   (A)

AutoCAD's first response to the LINE command is to ask for a start point and then the end point. The program assumes that you want to continue drawing

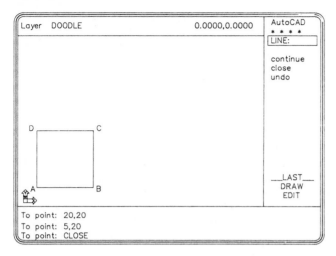

Figure 2.10 Drawing a square

lines until you tell it otherwise. By typing **"CLOSE <ENTER>"** you cause AutoCAD to join the end point of the last line segment to the very first point input. Now draw a line along one of the diagonals of the square from A to C in Figure 2.10. These letters won't appear in your drawing, they are just used to clarify this text.

>   Command: **LINE <ENTER>** From point: **5,5 <ENTER>**   (A)
>   To point:

If you move the cursor around the drawing area the line "rubber bands" and extends from the point 5,5 to wherever the cursor is located. You can now pick the point at the other end of the diagonal or type the coordinates.

>   To point: **20,20 <ENTER>**   (C)
>   To point: **<ENTER>**

As mentioned above, AutoCAD keeps replying with the prompt "To point:". When you are finished inputting lines you can exit the LINE command by pressing **<ENTER>** without giving any point. Alternatively, you can hit the space bar on the keyboard instead of the ENTER key. In most AutoCAD commands it is possible to interchange use of the space bar and the ENTER key. As the former is much larger it is much easier to locate (or harder to miss!). A third way to get out of the LINE command (and indeed any other AutoCAD command) is to CANCEL it. Press ^C (CTRL and C) to cancel the current operation and return to the "Command:" prompt. Remember ^C as it can get you out of trouble when things go wrong. CANCEL also appears in a number of screen menus, ready to come to the rescue.

What if you want to draw two lines which are not connected? Use **LINE** twice! This is easy and AutoCAD gives some assistance to make it easier. To draw the two parallel lines, EF and GH, type

Command: **LINE <ENTER>** From point: **5,25 <ENTER>**   (E)
To point:**20,30 <SPACE BAR>**   (F)
To point:**<SPACE BAR>**
Command: **<SPACE BAR>**
LINE: From point: **5,30 <ENTER>**   (G)
To point: **20,35 <ENTER>**   (H)
To point: **<ENTER>**

Instead of typing "LINE" the second time you can make use of the AutoCAD command memory. Since AutoCAD remembers the last command to be executed it offers that command again if you press <ENTER> or <SPACE BAR> at the "Command:" prompt without typing anything else. This is an obvious time saver when doing such repetitions.

Using the LINE menu

The LINE menu is reached by picking **DRAW** from the screen menu and then picking **LINE:** and is shown in Figure 2.10. This also causes the command line at the bottom of the screen to display that LINE has been activated.

Command: LINE From point:

Working from the top of the screen menu, LINE: also activates the command. One advantage of picking LINE: from the menu is that it first issues a CANCEL. This means that if you are in the middle of another command it will be automatically terminated before LINE: is executed. This facility could be used to draw the unconnected lines JK and LM in Figure 2.11. First pick **LINE:** from the menu, then move the cursor to the approximate position of J (**25,42**) and pick the point. Now, rubber band the line so that the cursor is approximately at K (**26,30**), pick the point and move to the screen menu and pick **LINE:** again. Then pick the two points near L (**25,25**) and M (**28,21**). Having picked point M, exit the LINE command by picking **CANCEL**. If your LINE menu doesn't have a CANCEL option you will have to press ^C or <SPACE BAR> to exit the command. The drawing should now look like Figure 2.11. Remember, don't draw the letters. They are just to make referencing the points from the text easier.

The second option on the menu is "continue". This is used to connect the new line to the end point of the most recently drawn line or arc (arcs will be covered in Chapters 4 and 5). This is of limited use as it is not always easy to remember what was the last line to be drawn. However, for the enthusiast, here is an example to draw a line from point M to a new point N (see Figure 2.12). Pick **LINE:** and when the prompt "From point:" is displayed, pick continue.

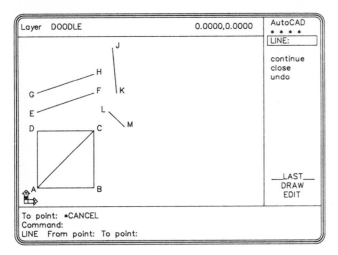

Figure 2.11 Adding some lines

This should cause the automatic selection of M as the first point of the new line. Now pick the point N (**28,10**) and pick **CANCEL**. If you have drawn any other lines after LM, your new line will be from the last end point of your last line.

We have already covered the "close" option. It makes a closed polygon of the lines by joining the most recently input point to the first point (ie. the "From point:") of the sequence. Close, which can be abbreviated to "c", will only work if more than one line has been drawn in the current LINE operation. The "current LINE operation" means all the inputs from *one* pick of LINE:.

Another sub-command that only works within the current LINE operation is the undo option. If, while drawing a sequence of connected line segments, an incorrect "To point:" is picked, you can immediately undo the last pick and re-input a new point. To illustrate pick the **LINE:** command and then the points P, Q, R and S (see Figure 2.12). Without leaving the LINE command pick **undo** from the screen menu. The point S disappears and you are prompted for a new "To point:" and can pick the points S′ and T.

Command: **LINE** <ENTER> From point: **35,5** <ENTER>	(P)
To point: **35,10** <ENTER>	(Q)
To point: **40,15** <ENTER>	(R)
To point: **45,15** <ENTER>	(S′)
To point: **undo**	
To point: **40,20** <ENTER>	(S)
To point: **35,20** <ENTER>	(T)
To point: <ENTER>	

You can undo all the line segments back to the point, P, in this manner but only if they are all part of the same LINE operation. A line segment can also be undone by typing "**u** <ENTER>" in response to the "To point:" prompt. There is another UNDO command in AutoCAD which can reverse any

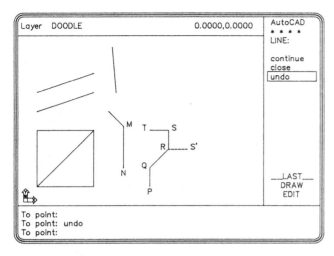

Figure 2.12 Continue and undo

previous command. The one within the LINE command only works for back-tracking the line segments. If you type UNDO at the "Command:" prompt it will back track the previous command or commands. This is described further in Chapter 4.

Linetypes and scales

When setting up the drawing layers earlier you set the linetype of C-DASH to DASHED. This means that all lines drawn on that layer will consist of a series of dashes. To see this working change the current layer to C-DASH and draw some lines.

> Command: **LAYER <ENTER>**
> ?/Make/Set/New/ON/OFF/Colour/Ltype/Freeze/Thaw: **S <ENTER>**
> New current layer <0>: **C-DASH <ENTER>**
> ?/Make/Set/New/ON/OFF/Colour/Ltype/Freeze/Thaw: **<ENTER>**
> Command:

Now draw the lines U to V to W to X to close as shown in Figure 2.13.

> Command: **LINE <ENTER>** From point: **60,40 <ENTER>**   (U)
> To point: **35,40 <ENTER>**   (V)
> To point: **35,30 <ENTER>**   (W)
> To point: **60,30 <ENTER>**   (X)
> To point: **C <ENTER>**

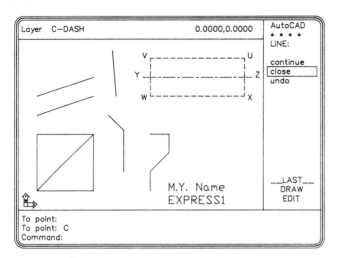

Figure 2.13 Dashed lines

Did the lines come up dashed? If not, this may be because the dashes are too close together to be displayed individually. You can control the size of the dashes by altering the linetype scale, or as AutoCAD calls it, the LTSCALE. Initially the LTSCALE has a value of 1. For the DASHED linetype this means that you have one dash and one space per drawing unit. For consistency with Figure 2.13 set the LTSCALE to 2.5. This command can be found by picking **SETTINGS** from the AutoCAD root menu.

> Command: **LTSCALE:**
> New scale factor <1.0>: **2.5 <ENTER>**
> Command: **REGEN <ENTER>** (This may happen automatically.)
> Command:

The REGEN command forces AutoCAD to re-calculate all the lines using this new linetype scale. Depending on your default settings this regeneration may occur automatically after LTSCALE. The larger the drawing size the larger LTSCALE will require to be so that the dashes are visible.

One other factor that controls whether the dashes are visible is the view resolution setting. To save screen redrawing time AutoCAD allows you to alter the resolution with which curves and different linetypes are displayed. The cruder the resolution the shorter the redraw time. At low resolution settings curves appear on the screen as a series of straight lines and dashed lines appear continuous. To set up the optimum resolution pick **DISPLAY** from the root menu and then pick **VIEWRES:.**

> Command: **VIEWRES**
> Do you want fast zooms? <Y>: **<ENTER>**
> Enter circle zoom percent (1-20000) <default>: **100 <ENTER>**
> Command: **REGEN <ENTER>**
> Command:

Choosing a value lower than 100 percent will give circles that look like polygons. They are still circles and will be plotted correctly.

DASHED is only one of a set of linetypes supplied with AutoCAD. It was selected as the default for the layer C-DASH as a response to the LAYER command. To find out what others are available pick **LINETYPE:** from the SETTINGS screen menu.

    Command: **LINETYPE**
    ?/Create/Load/Set: **?** <**ENTER**>
    File to list <ACAD>: <**ENTER**>

This should display the various types as shown in Figure 2.14. Other linetypes can be created, but this is beyond the scope of this book. The method of making new linetypes is described in Appendix B of The AutoCAD Reference Manual. Press **F1** to get back to the graphics screen.

Linetypes defined in file C:\ACAD\ACAD.lin:

Name

DASHED	— — — — — — — — — — — — — —
HIDDEN	- -
CENTER	—— - —— - —— - —— - —— - —— - ——
CENTRE	—— - —— - —— - —— - —— - —— - ——
PHANTOM	—— - - —— - - —— - - —— - - —— - - ——
DOT	....
DASHDOT	— · — · — · — · — · — · — · — · —
BORDER	— —·— —·— —·— —·— —·— —·
DIVIDE	— · · — · · — · · — · · — · · —

?/Create/Load/Set:

Figure 2.14 Standard linetypes

Currently, your drawing has two linetypes loaded, CONTINUOUS and DASHED. The former is always present and the latter was loaded using the LAYER command and Ltype. Other linetypes can be loaded as required by defining layers similarly to C-DASH. Alternatively they can be loaded into the current drawing by picking LINETYPE.

    ?/Create/Load/Set: **L** <**ENTER**>
    Linetype(s) to load: **CENTER,DOT** <**ENTER**>
    File to search <ACAD>: <**ENTER**>
    Linetype CENTER loaded.
    Linetype DOT loaded.
    ?/Create/Load/Set: <**ENTER**>

Either the American or English spelling of CENTER for the linetype is allowed. The only reason one might require to load multiple linetypes would be if you wanted more than one type on a layer. AutoCAD allows you to do this by the "Set" option when all new entities will have the newly set linetype. For example, the following commands would be used to draw a centre-line through the last rectangle without changing layer.

Command: **LINETYPE** <**ENTER**>
?/Create/Load/Set: **S** <**ENTER**>
New entity linetype (or ?) <BYLAYER>: **CENTER** <**ENTER**>
?/Create/Load/Set: <**ENTER**>
Command: **LINE** <**ENTER**> From point: **33,35** <**ENTER**>   (Y)
To point: **62,35** <**ENTER**>   (Z)
To point: <**ENTER**>
Command: **LINETYPE** <**ENTER**>
?/Create/Load/Set: S <**ENTER**>
New entity linetype (or ?) <CENTER>: **BYLAYER** <**ENTER**>
?/Create/Load/Set: <**ENTER**>

The second execution of LINETYPE was to reset all linetypes to whatever the individual default settings of the layers. Thus new lines will now be drawn on C-DASH as DASHED and lines on layer DOODLE will be CONTINUOUS. The LTSCALE value affects all linetypes and doesn't need to be reset.

While this facility gives flexibility to your drafting, it must be used sparingly and with caution. Since different types of line usually convey different types of information it makes sense to collect them onto individual layers. If at all possible use only one linetype per layer.

Similarly lines can be set to have colours other than their layer's default by using the COLOUR command. The AutoCAD Reference Manual gives a stern warning against mixing colours and linetypes on a layer stating that you may get undesirable results.

Saving the drawing

While working in AutoCAD you can periodically save the drawing and any changes you have made to it. To save EXPRESS1 type **SAVE** <**ENTER**> or pick it from the bottom of the root screen menu.

Command: **SAVE** File name <EXPRESS1>: <**ENTER**>

This writes a copy of the drawing to a file called "EXPRESS1.BAK". The ".BAK" stands for backup. You can save another copy with another filename.

Command: **SAVE** File name <EXPRESS1>: **EXPBAKUP** <**ENTER**>

This second SAVE writes a copy to a file called "EXPBAKUP.DWG". If you use any filename other than the one offered as the default a .DWG is used as the extension. You should use SAVE approximately every 15 to 20 minutes during a drawing session. Each time SAVE is used with the default filename the .BAK file is updated. Always do a SAVE before attempting difficult or large tasks (eg copying a large layout) or before attempting something new. Some commands are categorised in this book as potentially dangerous (HATCH, HIDE etc) and a SAVE should be done before executing them.

Finishing up

Before you leave EXPRESS1 as a completed drawing, you can put your name to it. Change to the TEXT1 layer and let's have a preview of the TEXT command. You can insert your own name in place of "M.Y. Name".

    Command: **LAYER <ENTER>**
    ?/Make/Set/New/ON/OFF/Colour/Ltype/Freeze/Thaw: **T <ENTER>**
    Layer name(s) to Thaw: **TEXT1 <ENTER>**

Remember, layer TEXT1 was frozen earlier. Before making it the current layer it must be thawed. You cannot "Set" a frozen layer.

    ?/Make/Set/New/ON/OFF/Colour/Ltype/Freeze/Thaw: **S <ENTER>**
    New current layer <0>: **TEXT1 <ENTER>**
    ?/Make/Set/New/ON/OFF/Colour/Ltype/Freeze/Thaw: **<ENTER>**
    Command: **TEXT <ENTER>**
    Start point or Align/Centre/Fit/Middle/Right/Style: **40,10 <ENTER>**
    Height <0.20>: **2 <ENTER>**
    Rotation angle <0>: **<ENTER>**
    Text: **M.Y. Name <ENTER>**
    Command: **TEXT <ENTER>**
    Start point or Align/Centre/Fit/Middle/Right/Style: **40,6 <ENTER>**
    Height 2.00: **<ENTER>**
    Rotation angle <0>: **<ENTER>**
    Text: **EXPRESS1 <ENTER>**
    Height 2.00: **<ENTER>**
    Rotation angle <0>: **<ENTER>**
    Text: **EXPRESS1 <ENTER>**

There are two ways of finishing an editing session. Now to make a final safe copy of the drawing and exit from the drawing editor use the **END** command which may be found in the UTILITY sub-menu. If you don't want to save any of the changes then you can use the QUIT command, also in the UTILITY sub-menu. As you want to save your work use **END.**

> Command: **END** <**ENTER**>

This will make a copy of the drawing in its current form to the file called "EXPRESS1.DWG" and return you to AutoCAD's main menu (Figure 2.2). Keep a safe copy of this drawing file as it will be useful for the exercise in Chapter 4.

If you did not want to keep the new drawing (or changes to an old one) you can leave the editor by using the QUIT command. The format for quitting the drawing without saving the changes is as follows. You won't be able to try this right now as AutoCAD's main menu is on display.

> Command: QUIT <ENTER>
> Really want to discard all changes to drawing? YES <ENTER>

This provides a quick exit from AutoCAD's editor and is useful if you don't want to keep the drawing. If the drawing already exists then it is left in its original form. QUIT is suitable when you have only been scanning through a drawing and haven't made any alterations. Because of the serious nature of QUIT's usage you are asked to confirm your intentions to discard all the changes. This protects against picking QUIT by mistake from the menu. If you reply by typing NO <ENTER> then the QUIT will be cancelled and the "Command:" prompt will appear.

Using END or QUIT brings you back to the main menu. Select option 0 to leave AutoCAD and return to DOS.

> Enter selection: **0** <**ENTER**>

This completes your first non-stop journey on the AutoCAD Express. In subsequent chapters it will be assumed that <**ENTER**> is pressed at the end of each command line or that the commands are picked from menus.

A note on file security

Many things can go wrong with computers and disks and occasionally with AutoCAD itself. The words "FATAL ERROR" have an ominous ring and it is very annoying when such an event occurs. The only sane way to approach the inevitable is to prepare well, so that when it happens the consequences are minimised. Don't be depressed by all this doom and gloom. With adequate preparation the impact of a computer crash is cushioned.

As mentioned above, it is good practice to have more than one copy of your work. AutoCAD provides facilities for this in two ways. Firstly, if you are going to edit an existing drawing file and select option 2 from the main menu, then AutoCAD automatically makes a copy of the drawing. If the original was called "EXPRESS1.DWG" then the backup copy is called "EXPRESS1 .BAK". This is certainly a very useful security measure but in itself is not foolproof. You should use DOS to make further copies onto other disks or onto a tape streamer. With all important computer files it is recommended to have at least two copies on your working disk, and one safe copy on another disk which should be kept in a safe place. Regular backing up of files is *essential*.

Summary

This chapter has introduced many of AutoCAD's facilities and its methodology. In this way the chapter provides the basis for understanding the way all the commands work.

You should now be able to:

Load the AutoCAD program.
Create a new drawing file.
Pick commands from screen menus.
Get back to the root menu by picking "AutoCAD".
Explore the pull-down menus.
Set up suitable AutoCAD drawing limits.
Create drawing layers and assign linetypes and colours to them.
Draw lines and squares.
Undo and continue lines.
Alter the linetype scale.
Add some text.
Save a drawing file every 15 minutes.
Quit a drawing without saving.
End a drawing, saving all changes.
Exit from AutoCAD.

Chapter 3 CURSOR AND DISPLAY CONTROL

General

Drawing with a mouse or tablet cursor is analogous to drawing freehand with a pencil. In engineering drawing we rely on a host of drawing aids and equipment. T-squares, rulers, setsquares and compass are but a few of the tools necessary to control the positions and sizes of drawn objects. Similarly we need electronic protractors and digital dividers when using AutoCAD. This chapter covers some of the useful cursor control facilities within AutoCAD. Using these facilities will make your drawings into exact graphical representations. You will learn how to set up construction lines. These will then be used to reference drawing items to the key construction points for making a replica of Paris's Eiffel Tower. The tower will be completed in Chapter 5.

For this chapter you will need a new drawing file, called EXPRESS2 with limits of (0,0) to (65,45) and four layers. Start up AutoCAD and enter selection 1 at the main menu.

Main Menu

Enter selection: **1**

Enter NAME of drawing: **EXPRESS2**

Set up the drawing environment using LIMITS and LAYER.

Command: **LIMITS**
ON/OFF/<Lower left corner> <0.00,0.00>: **<ENTER>**
Upper right corner <12.00,9.00>: **65,45**
Command: **LIMITS**
ON/OFF/<Lower left corner> <0.00,0.00>: **ON**
Command: **ZOOM**
All/Centre/Dynamic/Extents/Left/Previous/Window/ <Scale(X)>:**A**
Command: **LAYER**
?/Make/Set/New/ON/OFF/Colour/Ltype/Freeze/Thaw: **N**
New layer name(s): **CLINE,CONST,DOODLE,EIFFEL,1TEXT**

Now define some linetypes for the construction layer and the centre-lines.

> ?/Make/Set/New/ON/OFF/Colour/Ltype/Freeze/Thaw: **L**
> Linetype (or ?) <CONTINUOUS>: **CENTER**
> Layer name(s) for linetype CENTER <0>: **CLINE**
> ?/Make/Set/New/ON/OFF/Colour/Ltype/Freeze/Thaw: **C**
> Color: **RED**
> Layer name(s) for colour 1 (red) <0>: **CONST**
> ?/Make/Set/New/ON/OFF/Colour/Ltype/Freeze/Thaw: **S**
> New current layer <0>: **1TEXT**
> ?/Make/Set/New/ON/OFF/Colour/Ltype/Freeze/Thaw: <**ENTER**>

You can chose an appropriate scale for the dashed and centre-lines.

> Command: **LTSCALE**
> New scale factor <1.0>: **2.5**

Finally, make sure that the drawing units are decimal (see Chapter 2).

Cursor location

If you move the cursor around the drawing area using the mouse, the co-ordinates on the status line change to give the current location. If the values do not change, try pressing the pick button on the mouse. This will give the coordinate of that point. To switch on the continuous read-out of coordinates press ^D (press the CTRL key and while doing so press the D key). This should cause the command prompt line to display

> Command:<coords on>

Pressing ^D a second time will toggle this facility off. It is recommended that the dynamic coordinate display is switched on. The F6 key also does this.

Rulers, grids and snapping

AutoCAD gives two facilities which help you to get your general bearings within the drawing, and a third which helps to pin-point locations exactly. AXIS provides graduations along the bottom of the drawing screen and up the right hand side while GRID causes an array of equally spaced dots to apppear (Figure 3.1). These are analogous to placing a sheet of graph paper as a guide beneath the tracing sheet on a drawing board. They are not part of the drawing and do not appear on plots.

The SNAP command is one of AutoCAD's most powerful (and time saving) facilities. By turning SNAP on you can restrict the movements of the cursor to discrete steps. The cursor jumps from one snap point to the next missing out all the points in between. This is particularly useful if you are drawing an item whose smallest dimension is 5 units. You could set SNAP to a value of 5. This makes point picking with the mouse a lot easier and eliminates the need to type the coordinates when exact locations are required.

The drawing, EXPRESS2, will be created with a SNAP value of 2.5. The GRID will be set to 5 units and the AXIS to 10. This gives a nice relationship between the three settings. Every second snap point will also be a grid point and every fourth will coincide with the axis ticks. The three commands can be found by picking **SETTINGS** from the root menu. Pick **next** to get SNAP.

> Command: **SNAP**
> Snap spacing or ON/OFF/Aspect/Rotate/Style <1.00>: **2.5**

The word "SNAP" should appear on the status line to indicate that it is active. Now pick **LAST** and then **previous** from the screen menu and then **GRID** followed by **AXIS**.

> Command: **GRID**
> Grid spacing or ON/OFF/Aspect/Snap/Style <1.00>: **2X**
> Command: **AXIS**
> Tick spacing or ON/OFF/Aspect/Snap/Style <1.00> **4X**

The "2X" and "4X" signify that the spacing is 2 and 4 multiplied by the SNAP spacing. You could also have responded by giving the actual grid and axis spacings as "5" and "10". As you move the cursor around the drawing screen it should now move in steps taking two hops to get from one grid point to the next.

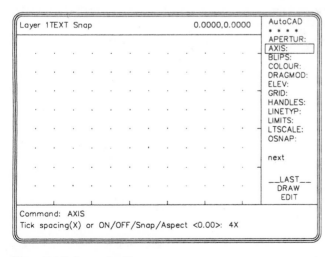

Figure 3.1 Rulers and grid

When using these features try to chose sensible spacings. If the spacing is small the redraw speed will slow down, as AutoCAD has to re-display all the dots and ticks. If the spacing is too small you will get a message "Grid too dense to display" or "Axis ticks too close to display", or maybe both. If this happens just re-issue the comand and set new spacings.

It doesn't matter which layer you are on when activating AXIS, GRID or SNAP. They act as an overlay on the whole drawing. They can be switched on and off as many times as required and can be used independently of each other. The GRID and AXIS will not appear on your print out or plot.

Coordinate notation

You have already used the X,Y coordinate notation. In the last chapter the X was seen to signify horizontal distance from the origin and Y vertical distance. A point on the drawing can be located by keying in a pair of numbers separated by a comma. For example, the coordinates "4,3" belong to a point 4 units to the right and 3 units above the origin. The origin has the coordinates "0,0". Mathematics books call this the Cartesian coordinate system after the French philosopher and mathematician, Descartes. AutoCAD calls it the X-Y WORLD system (WORLD meaning that the values are in relation to the drawing origin).

Sometimes it is more convenient to work in distances relative to one's current location. For example, when giving directions to a stranger in town your instructions might be "Follow this road for half a kilometre and turn right. The Computer Training Firm's offices are a further 350m on the left." This is a lot more meaningful than giving the location in terms of a map grid reference. Similarly, you can tell AutoCAD to draw a line giving directions relative to the cursor location. The notation used in AutoCAD to signify *relative* coordinates is to put "@" in front of the X,Y pair of values. For example to draw margins for EXPRESS2 try the following:

> Command: **LINE**
> From point: **2.5,2.5**
> To point: **@60,0**   (A)
> To point: **@0,40**   (B)
> To point: **@−60,0**   (C)
>   (D)
> To point: **close**

The point A must be in absolute X-Y WORLD coordinates since it is the first point to be input to the drawing. The second point, B, is given as 60 units to the right of A and at the same height. C is 40 units directly above B and so on. Relative coordinates always use the immediately preceeding cursor location as a temporary origin (Figure 3.2).

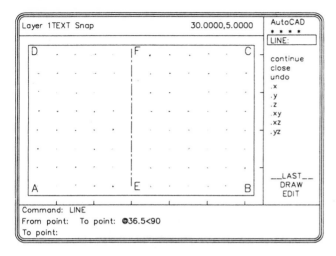

Figure 3.2 Margins and centre-line

If you know the length of a line and the angle it makes with the horizontal then it can be easier to use *relative polar* coordinates. To draw a vertical centre-line from point E (30,5) which is 36.5 units long you could use

Command: **LAYER**
?/Make/Set/New/ON/OFF/Colour/Ltype/Freeze/Thaw: **S**
New current layer <1TEXT>: **CLINE**
?/Make/Set/New/ON/OFF/Colour/Ltype/Freeze/Thaw: **<ENTER>**
Command: **LINE**
From point: **30,5**   (E)
To point: **@36.5<90**   (F)
To point: **<ENTER>**

The "<" or "less than" character indicates that the next character is an angle. Thus the above line will be drawn at 90 degrees from the horizontal. As positive angles are anti-clockwise the line goes up and not down. Again the "@" means that the location is relative to the previous point (30,5). You can use *absolute polar* coordinates when the angles relate to lines from the origin to the new location. This can be cumbersome and is not generally recommended.

If you want to experiment with relative and absolute coooordinate notation try drawing some objects on the DOODLE layer. On this doodle detour of the AutoCAD Express you can take in some sights on the scenic route. If you wish to press ahead without further practice you can skip forward to the next section entitled "Digital setsquares".

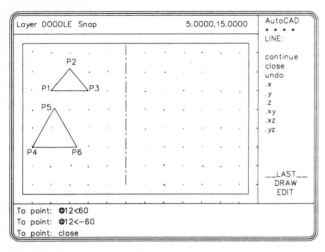

Figure 3.3 The pyramids of Egypt

The pyramids of Egypt can be drawn as triangles:

Command: **LAYER**
?/Make/Set/New/ON/OFF/Colour/Ltype/Freeze/Thaw: **S**
New current layer <CLINE>: **DOODLE**
?/Make/Set/New/ON/OFF/Colour/Ltype/Freeze/Thaw: <**ENTER**>

Command: **LINE**	
From point: **10,30**	(P1)
To point: **@5,6**	(P2)
To point: **@5,−6**	(P3)
To point: **@10<180**	(P1)
To point: <**ENTER**>	
Command: **LINE**	
From point: **5,15**	(P4)
To point: **@12<60**	(P5)
To point: **@12<−60**	(P6)
To point: **close**	

Experiment with other shapes and combinations of the different coordinate notation. Before getting back on the tracks you will need to set the CLINE layer again and freeze the doodles.

Command: **LAYER**
?/Make/Set/New/ON/OFF/Colour/Ltype/Freeze/Thaw: **S**
New current layer <DOODLE>: **CLINE**
?/Make/Set/New/ON/OFF/Colour/Ltype/Freeze/Thaw: **F**
Layer name(s) to freeze: **DOODLE**
?/Make/Set/New/ON/OFF/Colour/Ltype/Freeze/Thaw: <**ENTER**>

Command: **SAVE**
File name <EXPRESS2>: <**ENTER**>

Now is as good a time as any for saving the drawing. Remember the motto "Save early and often".

Digital setsquares

A large part of any drawing consists of horizontal and vertical lines such as the margins and centre-lines above. AutoCAD's ORTHO command allows you to draw these horizontal and vertical lines quickly and with 100% accuracy. When the ORTHO mode is ON then all movements of the cursor are restricted to either the X direction or the Y direction.

The simplest way to switch ORTHO on is to press ˆO (CTRL and the letter O pressed together) or **F8**. You can also turn it on by typing

Command: **ORTHO** ON/OFF: **ON**

Pressing ˆO is easier and pressing it a second time switches back to normal drawing mode. When it is active the word "ORTHO" appears on the status line at the top of the screen and as you switch it on or off the command prompt area will echo your action with "<ORTHO ON>". To examine these effects draw the horizontal construction lines outlined below for EXPRESS2 making sure that ORTHO is ON.

Command: **LAYER**
?/Make/Set/New/ON/OFF/Colour/Ltype/Freeze/Thaw: **S**
New current layer <0>: **CONST**
?/Make/Set/New/ON/OFF/Colour/Ltype/Freeze/Thaw: <**ENTER**>
Command: **LINE**:
From point: **17.5,5**   (G)

Now move the cursor to the right of the centre-line (EF) near to G'. Even though the cursor is not exactly horizontally across from the point G, the line from it is. If you move the cursor back towards G" there is a point when the line suddenly jumps to being vertical. So, wherever you pick the point the line is restricted to the X and Y directions. The governing factor for whether it is vertical or horizontal is the larger magnitude, X or Y, from the first point to the cursor.

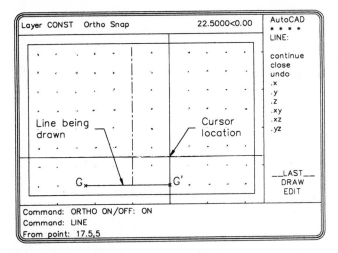

Figure 3.4 ORTHO mode

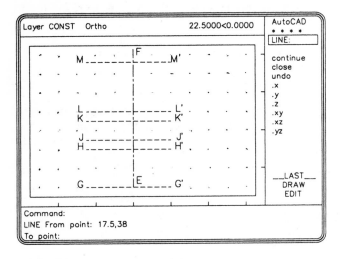

Figure 3.5 Horizontal construction lines

Move the cursor back to G' and pick the end point.

    To point: pick a point to make a horizontal line   (G')
    To point: <ENTER>
    Command: <ENTER>
    LINE From point: **17.5,15**   (H)
    To point: pick a point to make a horizontal line   (H')
    To point: <ENTER>

Do the same for horizontal lines from points J (17.5,17.5), K (17.5,22.5), L (17.5,25) and M (17.5,38). Your drawing should now resemble Figure 3.5 (without the letters). Your construction lines should be solid and red. They are shown as dashed in the figures for clarity.

Now is a good time to save your drawing. You can save it as many times as you like, during a session.

Command: **SAVE** File name <EXPRESS2>: <**ENTER**>

Snapping to objects

The main usefulness of construction lines is that by drawing them you reduce the number of calculations necessary to locate awkward points. The intersection point between a line and a circle is easy to draw but may require clever geometry to calculate. This is not to suggest that the AutoCAD user is not clever. Rather, you just want the fastest and simplest solution!

AutoCAD allows you to snap to key points of previously drawn items. The OSNAP (Object SNAP) menu can be found by picking the "* * * *" from any screen menu or by selecting "**ASSIST**" from the menu bar (ASSIST appears as "TOOLS" on some versions of the menu bar) then pick **OSNAP**. Alternatively, the third button on your mouse (if it has a third button) also causes the TOOLS pull-down menu to appear. This menu gives you facilities to locate the centre or tangent point of a circle or arc, the end point and mid point of a line, the insertion point of text etc.

There are two ways of using OSNAP. Firstly, it can be employed to find a single point by invoking it in response to AutoCAD prompts requesting a point (eg "From point:"). To illustrate this, turn snap off by pressing ^B and draw the

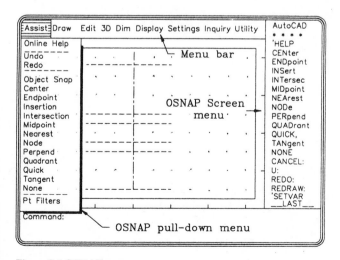

Figure 3.6 OSNAP menu

next line. At the "From point:" prompt pick **ENDpoint** from the OSNAP menu. The prompt changes to "Endpoint of:" and the cursor changes shape to give a little target box. Move the cursor until the you are near point G on the line GG'. Once it is in you sights pick the point.

> Command: **LINE**
> From point: ENDpoint of: pick line near G
> To point: @**17<58**
> To point: <**ENTER**>

To draw a line from the intersection point of the last line and the line JJ' use OSNAP **INTersec** in reply to "From point:" and move the cursor so that point N is within the target box.

> Command: <**ENTER**>
> LINE From point: **Int** of: pick point N
> To point: @**5.5<77**
> To point: <**SPACE BAR**>

Remember, the space bar acts just like the the enter key. Now to draw the vertical line on Figure 3.7 from the point, P, and perpendicular to the line MM', use OSNAP "perp" or "perpend". Use "^B" to toggle the snap mode.

> Command: <**SPACE BAR**>
> LINE From point: **28,25**   (P)
> To point: **PERP** to ^B <Snap off> Pick line MM'
> To point: <**ENTER**>

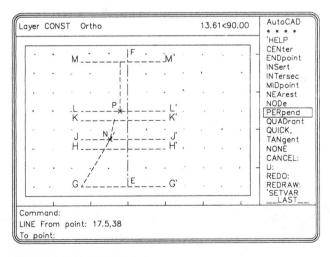

Figure 3.7 Using OSNAP options

This way of using OSNAP gives a single point selection and then returns to normal selection straight away. It can be used only when AutoCAD is expecting you to pick a point.

When you want to connect up a lot of construction points using OSNAP it can become tedious to have to pick, say, INTersec each time. The second way of using OSNAP is to set up a continuous OSNAP mode. This is done by picking **OSNAP:** (note the ":") from the SETTINGS menu or by typing the word **OSNAP.**

> Command: **OSNAP**
> Object snap modes: **INT**

This means that AutoCAD will always snap to the intersection point nearest to the centre of the target box. Now, use this to draw the outline of the tower (Figure 3.8). First change layers.

> Command: **LAYER**
> ?/Make/Set/New/ON/OFF/Colour/Ltype/Freeze/Thaw: **S**
> New current layer <0>: **EIFFEL**
> ?/Make/Set/New/ON/OFF/Colour/Ltype/Freeze/Thaw: **<ENTER>**
> Command: **LINE**
> From point: **22.5,5**   (Q)
> To point: **@−5,0** or pick the point, G   (G)
> To point: **O** <Ortho off> Pick R
> To point: **<ENTER>**
> Command: **<ENTER>**
> LINE From point: Pick S
> To point: Pick R

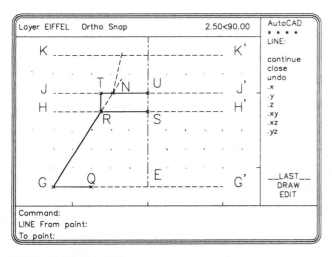

Figure 3.8 OSNAP mode INTersec

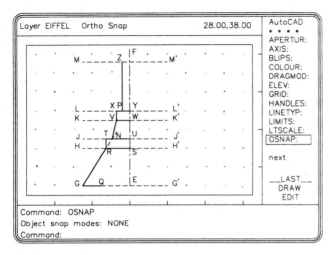

Figure 3.9 Half an Eiffel

Now to draw a line from R perpendicular to the line JJ' select **PERPend** from the OSNAP menu. This overrides INTersec for the next point selection.

> To point: **perp** to: Pick line JJ'   (T)
> To point: Pick U
> To point: <**ENTER**>

This procedure is repeated to draw the remainder of the left hand outline (Figure 3.9).

> Command: **LINE**
> From point: Pick N
> To point: Pick V
> To point: <**ENTER**>
> Command: <**ENTER**>
> LINE From point: Pick W
> To point: Pick V
> To point: **perp** to: Pick line LL'   (X)
> To point: Pick Y
> To point: <**ENTER**>
> Command: <**ENTER**>
> LINE From point: **28,25**   (P)
> To point: Pick intersection point on MM'   (Z)
> To point: <**ENTER**>

Now to turn the OSNAP mode off.

Command: **OSNAP**
Object snap modes: **NONE**

Remember that actually typing the word "OSNAP" or picking "OSNAP:" causes a continuous snapping mode. Always remember to turn the OSNAP mode off when it is not required. Leaving it on by mistake can lead to strange results.

Picking "OSNAP" (without the ":") or "* * * *" displays the menu from which you can select a single point snap mode. After executing the single point snap mode the selection method returns to the previous setting.

If the size of the OSNAP target sight is too small for you to pick things easily then you can increase it with the **APERTURE** command. Execute this and you will be prompted for the "target height" in pixels. Each pixel is the size of a dot on your screen.

Command: **APERTURE**
Object snap target height (1–50 pixels) <old value>: **5**

As you pick points on the screen little blips or crosses appear. The blip gives you some visual feedback about the location of the point and it is easy to see if it is at the correct location. However, the more points you pick the greater the distraction caused by these blips. There is no difference between the apparance of new and old blips. To clear the screen of old blips you must execute the **REDRAW** command. This simply redraws the current display and as the blips are not true parts of the drawing they do not reappear. REDRAW is in the DISPLAY screen menu and also in the DISPLAY pull-down menu.

Command: **REDRAW**

ZOOM and PAN

You have already used the "ZOOM All" command to display the whole drawing area. In this section you will use ZOOM to enlarge the view of the top of the tower being drawn so that greater detail can be added to it. The best way to imagine how zooming works is think of the computer display as the image you would see looking through a camera lens. As you adjust your zoom lens the item you are looking at becomes enlarged while peripheral items are excluded from view. The PAN command is another term from the camera man's vocabulary. It allows you to sweep your "camera lens" over the drawing to look at other parts with the same magnification.

To enlarge the top of the tower pick **DISPLAY** from the root menu and then **ZOOM.** Then pick **Window** from the ZOOM menu. You are asked to give the

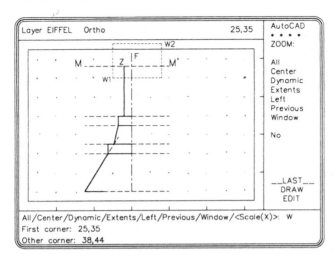

Figure 3.10 Picking a window

two opposite corners of the new window of vision. Pick the points W1 and W2 shown on Figure 3.10.

> Command: **ZOOM**
> All/Centre/Dynamic/Extents/Left/Previous/Window/ <Scale(X)>:**W**
> First corner: **25,35**   (W1)
> Other corner: **38,44**   (W2)

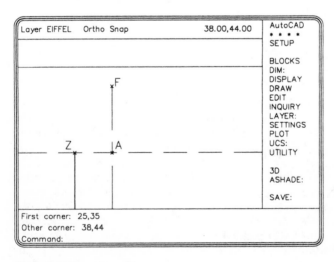

Figure 3.11 The enlarged image

The display should now change to give a close up view of that rectangular window (Figure 3.11). The spacing between the grid points and axis ticks looks larger but the coordinates are just the same. As you move the cursor around the drawing the read-out on the status line will give the coordinates with respect to the drawing origin. Nothing has changed in the drawing, it's just the amount you can see that has altered.

If your display is significantly different from Figure 3.11 then the wrong window must have been chosen. Do a ZOOM All and repeat the ZOOM Window, typing in the coordinates for W1 and W2.

As you are working at a larger scale to draw small items you can change the GRID and SNAP settings.

> Command: **SNAP**
> Snap spacing or ON/OFF/Aspect/Rotate/Style 2.50: **0.5**
> Command: **GRID**
> Grid spacing or ON/OFF/Aspect/Snap/Style 5.00: **2X**
> Command: **AXIS**
> Tick spacing or ON/OFF/Aspect/Snap/Style 0.00: **4X**

Now draw the viewing platform with its roof and aerial (Figure 3.12).

> Command: **LINE**
> From point: **INT** of: Pick A
> To point: **@−2.5,0**   (B)
> To point: **@0,−1**   (C)
> To point: **@2.5,0**   (D)
> To point: **<ENTER>**
> Command: **<ENTER>**
> LINE From point: **INT** of: Pick Z

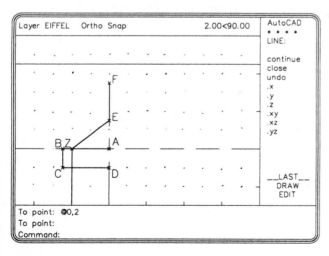

Figure 3.12 Half the viewing platform

You can switch ORTHO off in the middle of the LINE command by pressing ^O and then pick the point E (30,39.5), or you can type the coordinates.

> To point: **30,39.5**   (E)
> To point: **@0,2**   (F)
> To point: **<ENTER>**

Now ZOOM in even closer using window to add some structural detail.

> Command: **ZOOM**
> All/Centre/Dynamic/Extents/Left/Previous/Window/<Scale(X)>:**W**
> First corner: **27,35.5**   (W1)
> Other corner: **30.5,39**   (W2)

The magnification is further increased and using the same SNAP resolution you can draw the vertical line GH and the horizontal line JK, as shown in Figure 3.13.

> Command: **LINE**
> From point: **29,38**   (G)
> To point: **@0,−1**   (H)
> To point: **<ENTER>**
> Command: **<ENTER>**
> LINE From point: **27.5,37.5**   (J)
> To point: **@2.5<0**   (K)
> To point: **<ENTER>**

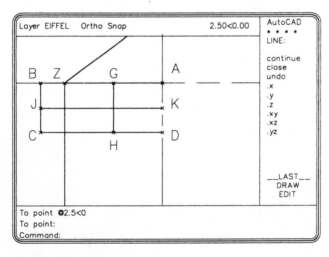

Figure 3.13 Adding some structure

To ZOOM back to the last magnification pick **ZOOM** and then pick **previous** or type:

> Command: **ZOOM**
> All/Centre/Dynamic/Extents/Left/Previous/Window/<Scale(X)>:**P**

AutoCAD stores the settings of up to ten previous zoomed views and so you can step backwards that many times. This facility saves you having to do a **ZOOM All** followed by a new ZOOM Window to get back to an earlier view. Your picture should now resemble Figure 3.12 but with the new lines in place.

Another feature which saves the double task of zooming out and back in is the PAN command. To see something that is currently out of view you can PAN the imaginary camera. For example, to see the middle landing of the Eiffel tower under construction try the following sequence.

> Command: **PAN** Displacement: **2,15**
> Second point: <ENTER>

This moves the drawing two units to the right and 15 units up. If you simply press <ENTER> in reply to the "Second point:" prompt then the first pair of coordinates are taken as a relative displacement. The same movement could have been achieved by entering

> Command: PAN Displacement: 30,37
> Second point: 32,52

The second method gives a vector which controls the movement. The coordinates can also be input by picking points on the screen. However, as the point 33,52 does not appear on the screen in figure 3.14 it has to be typed. Remember, it is only the display that is "moving"; the drawing retains all its original coordinate information.

This middle landing of the tower needs one more line. Draw the line AB using ORTHO and SNAP (Figure 3.14).

> Command: **LINE**
> From point: **30,23.5**   (B)
> To point: **perp** to: pick line AV   (A)
> To point: <ENTER>

To see the lower landing pick **PAN** once more and then pick the points P1 (30,20) and P2 (32,25) and draw the line CD given below.

> Command: PAN Displacement: **30,20**   (P1)
> Second point: **33,27**   (P2)
> Command: **LINE**
> From point: **30,16**   (C)
> To point: **perp** to: pick line RT (Figure 3.9)   (D)
> To point: <ENTER>

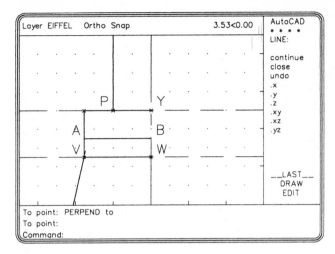

Figure 3.14 Middle landing after PAN

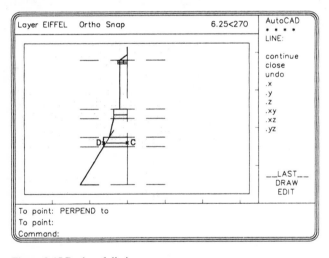

Figure 3.15 Back to full view

Finally,

> Command: **ZOOM**
> All/Centre/Dynamic/Extents/Left/Previous/Window/ <Scale(X)>:**A**

and the display should match Figure 3.15.

The picture may not look like much at the moment, but if you skip ahead a few pages you can see its potential. You will need to use EXPRESS2 again in Chapter 5, so make a safe backup copy.

Command: **SAVE** File name <EXPRESS2>: **TOWER**

Make a copy onto a floppy disk as well. Place a formatted diskette in Drive A: and do another SAVE.

Command: **SAVE** File name <EXPRESS2>: **A:TOWER**

Keyboard toggles and transparent commands

Before ending AutoCAD for this chapter, here are some descriptions of the various switches or toggles that can speed up your drafting. By pressing the CTRL key in combination with other keys, various display control commands can be executed, even in the middle of doing another command. Some of the toggles cause alterations to the current command. Some of the grey keyboard function keys duplicate these, though there can be differences between makes of computer. Here is a list of the main keyboard CTRL combinations.

Table 3.1 Keyboard toggles

^B or F9	Toggles SNAP on and off.
^C	Cancels the current command.
^D or F6	Dynamic/static cursor location read-out on status line.
^G or F7	Toggles the GRID on and off.
^O or F8	Toggles ORTHO on and off.
^Q	Echos all the Command prompts and replies to the printer. ^Q a second time terminates printout.
F1	Flips display between text and graphics mode on single monitor workstations.
ESC	Causes pull down menus to disappear.

A transparent command is one that can be run while another is still being executed. For example, the ORTHO, ^O, command was issued above in the middle of a LINE sequence. This type of transparency of the ORTHO command greatly increases the flexibility with which it can be used. Similarly SNAP and GRID can be used transparently by pressing the CTRL code or function key. The single point usage of OSNAP is another example.

The SNAP, GRID, AXIS and ORTHO settings can also be altered transparently from the pull-down menus of the Advanced User Interface. Pick **Settings** from the menu bar at the top of the screen and then select **Drawing aids** to display the *dialogue box* (Figure 3.16).

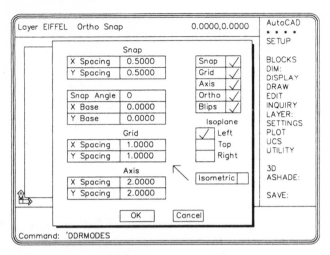

Figure 3.16 Drawing aids dialogue box

The dialogue box can be used by moving the arrow shaped cursor to any of the input rectangles. You know you have entered one of these as it will be highlighted. Pressing the pick button then allows you to change the entry for that box. You then will have to pick the **OK** box to confirm the changes or pick **Cancel.** This dialogue box also allows you to turn off the blips that appear on the drawing screen, though this is not recommended. The Isometric option is described in Chapter 8.

Since AutoCAD version 2.5 more transparent commands have been made available. REDRAW, ZOOM and PAN can run during other commands if they are picked from the DISPLAY pull down menu (Figure 3.16) or if they are prefixed by a ' (eg Command: **'ZOOM** etc..). The 'ZOOM and 'PAN will only work if the change in magnification is less than a factor of about 10. If it is more than 10 then AutoCAD will probably have to REGENerate the drawing to maintain sufficient screen resolution.

HELP!

Another useful feature is the ability to get HELP during a command. There is a general HELP command which can be typed to get information on any command.

> Command: **HELP**
> Command name (RETURN for list): **REDRAW**

The screen display changes to text mode giving information on the REDRAW command. Press **F1** to return to the graphics display. That was the normal way of using HELP. To use it transparently within the LINE command for example you give the response **'HELP** in reply to the "From point:" or "To point:". prompt. This gives the HELP information about that command.

> Command: **LINE**
> From point: **'HELP**

The text screen appears and fills one page. At the end of the page the prompt:

> Press RETURN to resume LINE command.

appears and when all the pages of help have been displayed you are returned to LINE's prompts. At this stage you can continue with the command or **cancel** it.

> From point: ^C

The AutoCAD HELP information is intended as a reference only and not as a learning aid. Its explanations of commands are thorough and so can appear complicated. Use this book for learning new commands and use HELP as a reminder. In this way you will understand the workings of the commands and be relieved of the overhead of having to remember it all. The online help, 'HELP, is also available through the ASSIST (or TOOLS) pull-down menu.

One more command that can be executed transparently is the LAYER. However, not all of the options within LAYER can be used in this way. Pick **SETTINGS** or **Modes** pull-down menu from the menu bar followed by **Modify Layer....** The dialogue box shown will appear in the drawing area (Figure 3.17). By pointing to the various boxes you can change the colour of a layer, its name or set a layer. If you pick the colour box of one of the layers a second dialogue box will be displayed giving the various colour options. You have to

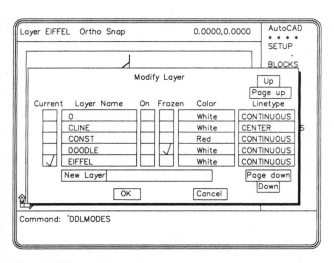

Figure 3.17 Layer dialogue box

pick the **OK** box to confirm each selection or the **Cancel** box to return to the previous screen. Pick the "Frozen" box layer CONST and then pick **OK.** This gives a clearer picture of how the tower is shaping up. Pressing **ESC** removes all the dialogue boxes and pull-down menus.

This can also be used by typing **'DDLMODES** at the comand prompt. As with the 'ZOOM and 'PAN commands the transparent layer changes will not work if the drawing has to be regenerated. Thawing a layer or changing its linetype causes regeneration. AutoCAD will give you a warning message if a regeneration is required and will postpone the changes until the next REGEN is issued.

Finish up for the time being

The final task in this chapter is to END the drawing of the EIFFEL tower and exit AutoCAD for a well deserved break.

> Command: **END**
> Enter selection: **0**

Even though you have used the END command, that is not the end of the EXPRESS2 drawing. END just means to end this editing session. You will return to edit it and add in some fancy iron work in Chapter 5. So don't erase it from your disk! And keep a safe backup copy on another disk. If anyone else is learning AutoCAD from this book, make sure you don't mix up each other's drawings.

Summary

In this chapter you have become an expert LINE drawer. In doing so you have encountered all of AutoCAD's drawing aid facilities in one shape or form. When doing an AutoCAD drawing you need to think in terms of these facilities so that your plan of action makes best use of them and speeds up your drafting. Always start drawings with the key construction lines.

You should now be able to:

Input relative and absolute coordinate locations.
Use polar coordinates for points.
Set up a suitable grid and axis overlay.
Restrict cursor movements to discrete SNAP points.
Restrict cursor movements to ORTHOgonal directions.
Locate the intersection and end points of lines.

ZOOM in to magnify details and ZOOM out to see the whole picture.
PAN across the magnified picture.
Get AutoCAD HELP for individual commands.
Use the drawing aids dialogue box.
Modify a LAYER transparently.

Chapter 4 **DRAWING AND EDITING**

General

The AutoCAD Express takes to the air for this chapter's exercise. The bulk of AutoCAD's drawing entities are introduced along with some simple editing. This express air-service will be by hot air balloon!

As you will be using much the same drawing environment as EXPRESS1-.DWG it can be substituted as the default drawing. AutoCAD normally uses the drawing ACAD.DWG as the default for all new drawings. That is all the settings and any entities on ACAD.DWG are copied into the new drawing.

Before commencing the balloon drawing make sure that you have a copy of your previous drawing EXPRESS1.DWG.

If you don't have a copy of EXPRESS1.DWG handy you could make one up. It should have limits of (0,0) and (65,45) and layers called DOODLE, TEXT1 and C-DASH. Give C-DASH a linetype of DASHED and DOODLE the colour BLUE. Then set an LTSCALE value of 2.5. Now draw some lines. It doesn't matter where or how many but you will have to improvise when erasing them later. Add your name using TEXT at the point (40,10) with a height of 2 units, zero rotation and then END the drawing.

To use an alternative default drawing start up AutoCAD so that the main menu is displayed. Enter selection 1 to create a new drawing and give the name as below.

Main menu

Enter selection: **1**

Enter NAME of drawing: **BALLOON=EXPRESS1**

The "=EXPRESS1" tells AutoCAD to use that drawing as the default and to copy it into the new drawing. The screen should now appear like Figure 4.1 which should be the same as Figure 2.13 (with a change of screen menu).

Use the pull-down menu to modify the layers and add some new ones. Pick **Settings** from the menu bar followed by **Layers** or **Modify Layer**.

Change the colour of the DOODLE layer from blue to white. Pick the colour box containing **5 blue**. A new dialogue box giving the defined colours is dis-

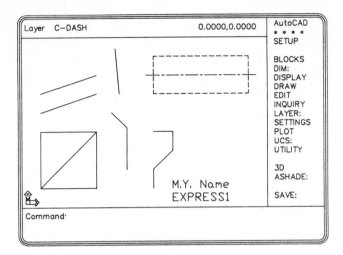

Figure 4.1 BALLOON=EXPRESS1

played. Pick the **WHITE line** box and then pick **OK**. Make layer 0 the current layer by picking the top box in the "Current" column. To create new layers move the cursor to the long "New Layer" box and press the pick button. Enter the new name **DIMS** followed by <**ENTER**> or pick the **OK** box. Repeat this for the other new layer, **HATCH** and give it the colour **RED**. Use the box marked **DOWN** to scroll down the layer information to display a dialogue box similar to Figure 4.3. Finally, when everything is satisfactory pick the **OK** box to confirm all the changes.

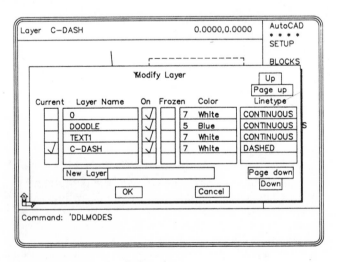

Figure 4.2 Dialogue box before changes

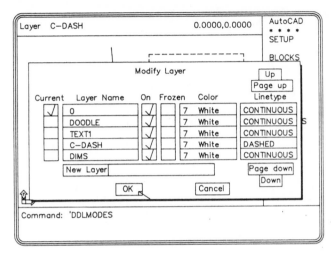

Figure 4.3 Dialogue box after layer changes

Rubbing out and OOPS

When something has been drawn incorrectly or is no longer required on the drawing you can rub it out. This task is a lot easier with AutoCAD than on a conventional drawing board and with AutoCAD's ERASE command you will always get perfect results.

ERASE can be found in the EDIT screen menu. The process is not too difficult and allows you to delete more than one object with one command. The way lines or other objects are selected for erasure is flexible. You can place the cursor on the item to be scratched and press the pick button, move to the next item and pick it and so on. You can select a whole group of entities using a window like in the ZOOM command or you can erase just the last object that was drawn. Indeed, the AutoCAD "Select objects:" procedure can even use a combination of all these methods.

The first part of the exercise is to rub out most of the entities on EXPRESS1 so that you are left with a clean sheet. This will be done in stages to introduce the "Select objects:" procedure. Firstly, you will erase two of the lines by simply picking them (Figure 4.4). After picking **ERASE**, the cursor changes from being two cross-hairs to a little box. This box indicates that you are in the selection mode. Move to the lines and pick the points P1 and P2. If the objects are successfully picked they become dotted or "ghosted" and the message "1 selected, 1 found." is displayed in the prompt area. If you miss the object it won't go dotty and you will get a message such as 1 selected, 0 found.". The ghosting is to highlight which object has been found by AutoCAD. If it is correct carry on and pick P2. If not press ˆC and start again. When you have

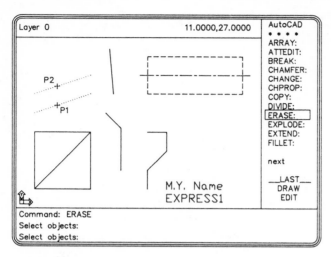

Figure 4.4 Erasing two lines

selected all the objects to be erased just press <**ENTER**> in reply to the "Select objects:" prompt.

    Command: **ERASE**
    Select objects: **11,27** 1 selected, 1 found.   (P1)
    Select objects: **10,32** 1 selected, 1 found.   (P2)
    Select objects: <**ENTER**>
    Command:

When using the window option (Figure 4.5) it is very important to check the number of objects that have been found and which objects have become dotted. Only items that are fully within the window are selected. If any part of an entity is outside the window it will not be erased.

    Command: **ERASE**
    Select objects: **Window**
    First corner: **23,18**   (W1)
    Other corner: **64,43**   (W2)
    8 found.
    Select objects: <**ENTER**>

The two vertical lines that were only partly within the window were not erased.

    Command: **ERASE**
    Select objects: **Crossing**
    First corner: **1,1**   (W3)
    Other corner: **45,20.5**   (W4)

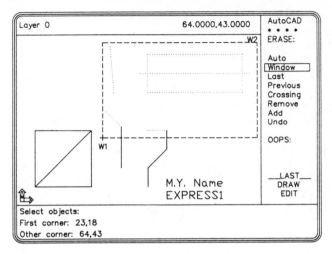

Figure 4.5 Erasing window

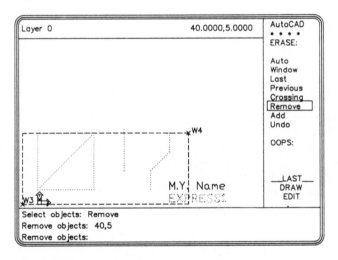

Figure 4.6 Erase crossing

With "Crossing" even the objects that are only partly within the window will be erased (Figure 4.6). To save the text "M.Y. Name" from being deleted you can pick the **Remove** option from the ERASE: screen menu or type it in response to the prompt.

> Select objects: **Remove**
> Remove objects: **40,10**
> Remove objects: **<ENTER>**
> Command:

The name text reverts back to solid line and will not be erased.

The selection process used with the ERASE command is exactly the same for many other commands. Each object that has been ghosted becomes part of a "selection set". The selection set can have more objects added to it or have some removed. The next paragraph describes the selection process in abstract. You can skip this if you wish as the important methods of selection are covered in the example exercises throughout the book.

Other options in the "Select objects" part of the screen menu are Add, SIngle, BOX, AUto, Last and Previous. "Add" is used to change back from removing objects to the "Select objects" prompt. "SI" picks only one object and, with ERASE, immediately rubs it out. "BOX" acts just like window or crossing depending on the order of picking the diagonal points. If the first point picked is to the left of the second point then "box" acts like the "window" option, otherwise it's like "crossing". BOX is not highly recommended. Picking "Auto" after using "window" allows you to specify multiple windows. "Last" selects the most recently drawn object. The "Previous" option picks up the most recently defined selection set. This is described later.

OOPS! I didn't mean to rub that out

If unexpected items disappear from the display, first try a **REDRAW** and then pick the **OOPS:** command.

If one item overlaps another and one of them is erased it looks like all the overlapped section has been deleted. Executing a **REDRAW** corrects this display error. If the missing item doesn't reappear then it probably has been deleted. Pick **OOPS:** from the ERASE menu or type "OOPS". This restores everything that was deleted by the most recent ERASE command execution.

For the more serious blunders you can step back in time by using the UNDO command. With UNDO you tell AutoCAD how many steps or command executions to go back. For example, the commands given below could be used to undo the last three operations.

Command: **UNDO**
Auto/Back/Control/End/Group/Mark/<Number>: **3**

HAZARD WARNING!

This is a dangerous command as it can undo everything that you have done in the current editing session. If you then discover that you have undone too many commands the situation can be retrieved by executing a **REDO** immediately.

Command: **REDO**

Note that this command is more versatile than the "undo" which is on the LINE sub-menu. When the command is written on the screen menu in lower case it means that it can be used within the LINE command. When it is written in upper case it is the general command and cannot be executed transparently.

One of the best features of UNDO is creating marks. Before trying out some complicated manoeuvre you can set a mark. If things don't work out as planned you can use UNDO followed by Back to get back to the drawing as it was when you made the mark.

> Command: **UNDO**
> Auto/Back/Control/End/Group/Mark/<Number>: **M**
> Do a series of AutoCAD commands.
>
> Command: **UNDO**
> Auto/Back/Control/End/Group/Mark/<Number>: **B**

Creating circles, arcs and ellipses

Circles

As you need a clean drawing with just your name on it, be sure to re-ERASE anything that you have restored when trying out OOPS.

> Command: **CIRCLE**
> 3P/2P/TTR/<Center point>: **20,30**
> Diameter/<Radius>: **10**
> Command: **<ENTER>**
> CIRCLE 3P/2P/TTR/<Center point>: @

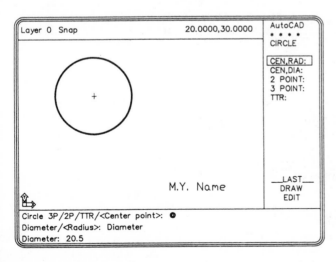

Figure 4.7 Concentric circles

This is equivalent to @0,0 from the last point, ie the centre of the first circle.

> Diameter/<Radius>: **Diameter**
> Diameter: **20.5**
> Command:

This gives two concentric circles (Figure 4.7). On some displays it might be difficult to distinguish between the two circles. Use ZOOM to check that they are really there.

The two point circle is identified by picking the ends of one of its diameters. The three point circle allows some nice geometric constructions. The TTR allows you to draw a circle tangential to two objects and with an input radius.

Many ways to draw an ARC

If you pick **ARC** from the DRAW menu you get a long list of arc creating options. At first this is a bit daunting with all the similar looking abbreviations. In the menu the letter "S" stands for the start point, "C" is the centre and "E" in the start, centre and end points, in that order.

The other letters are "A" for the angle subtended by the arc, "L" meaning the length of the arc, "R" the radius and "D" the diameter. You don't have to remember all these variations as the "S,C,E:" or "3 POINT" options will satisfy most needs. You can also override the expected prompts as and when the need arises.

To draw a cloud for the sky beside the balloon, you will need six arcs. The first arc will be a semi-circle. Since the angle within a semi-circle is 180 degrees the "S,E,A:" option is an appropriate choice. If you had to alter your units in Chapter 2 you will have discovered that angles are measured positive in the anti-clockwise (or counter-clockwise) direction. This means that the start and end points should always be picked so that the arc joining them will go anti-clockwise.

> Command: **ARC** Center/<Start point>: **55,33**   (A1)
> End point: **47,33**   (A2)
> Angle/Direction/Radius/<Center point>: A Included angle: **180**

The second arc can be drawn using **S,E,R**, the start, end and a radius of 3.

> Command: **ARC** Center/<Start point>: **48,34**   (B1)
> End point: **@5<225**   (B2)
> Angle/Direction/Radius/<Center point>: R Radius: **3**

Do the next two arcs with the start, centre and end approach, **S,C,E**.

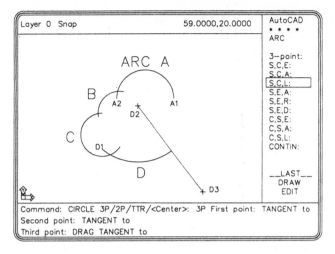

Figure 4.8 Dragging the arc

Command: **ARC** Center/<Start point>: **45,31**	(C1)
Center/End/<Second point>: C Center: **45,28**	(C2)
Angle/Length of chord/<End point>: DRAG **@5<326**	(C3)
Command: **ARC** Center/<Start point>: **45,26**	(D1)
Center/End/<Second point>: C Center: **50,32**	(D2)
Angle/Length of chord/<End point>: DRAG **@15<307**	(D3)

The angles used for the end points look a bit strange, but they are the result of dragging the arc until it looked right. The actual end points are not on the points C3 and D3, but are on the intersection between the arc whose radius is calculated from the start and centre points and the line from the centre to the points C3 and D3. Figure 4.8 shows this procedure for arc D.

The remaining two curves to finish off the cloud can be drawn with three-point arcs.

Command: **ARC** Center/<Start point>: **52,26**
Center/End/<Second point>: **57,25**
End point: DRAG **59,32**
Command: **ARC** Center/<Start point>: **59,30**
Center/End/<Second point>: **60,35**
End point: DRAG **54,34**

Rectangles and ellipses

Older versions of AutoCAD used to have a RECTANG: command as part of the line menu. However, the poor RECTANG: has been replaced by a more general command called PLINE or PolyLINE. You could of course make rectangles by drawing four connected LINEs, but this would be an assembly rather than a single entity. Thus to erase the rectangle formed with LINEs you would have to pick all four sides in the selection of objects. The difference with PolyLINEs is that all the segments are considered as part of one entity. PLINE can be used all the ways that LINE is used and a few more besides. Firstly, you can use it in place of LINE to draw the rectangle for the balloon's basket (Figure 4.9). PLINE: can be found by picking the **DRAW** option from the screen menu.

Command: **PLINE**
From point: **15,10**   (A)
Current line-width is 0.0000
Arc/Close/Halfwidth/Length/Undo/Width/<Endpoint of line>: @**10<0**   (B)
Arc/Close/Halfwidth/Length/Undo/Width/<Endpoint of line>: @**5<90**   (C)
Arc/Close/Halfwidth/Length/Undo/Width/<Endpoint of line>: @**10<180**   (D)
Arc/Close/Halfwidth/Length/Undo/Width/<Endpoint of line>: **Close**

That worked just like the LINE command except that the "To point:" was replaced by the long list of options. You will come across those options later in this chapter. The other difference is that the PLINE rectangle is one single entity. If you try to **ERASE** it just pick one point on the rectangle and the whole thing will be selected. Use ^C to avoid rubbing it out or **OOPS** to bring it back.

To draw the ellipses on the smaller circle of the balloon pick the **DRAW** screen menu and then **ELLIPSE**:. You will be prompted to give the two end points of one of the axes and one end of the other axis. In this example you will use OSNAP quadrant to locate the top and bottom of the inner circle for the major axis. The quadrant points of a circle correspond to the 0, 90, 180 and 270 degree points.

Command: **ELLIPSE**
<Axis endpoint 1>/Center: **QUADRANT** of pick point E   (20,40)
Axis endpoint 2: **QUADRANT** of pick point F   (20,20)
<Other axis distance>/Rotation: **12,30**   (G)

Repeat this procedure for two more ellipses to complete the balloon (see Figure 4.10 below).

Command: **ELLIPSE**
<Axis endpoint 1>/Center: **QUADRANT** of pick point E   (20,40)
Axis endpoint 2: **QUADRANT** of pick point F   (20,20)
<Other axis distance>/Rotation: **15,30**
Command: <**ENTER**>
ELLIPSE
<Axis endpoint 1/Center: **QUADRANT** of pick point E   (20,40)
Axis endpoint 2: **QUADRANT** of pick point F   (20,20)
<Other axis distance>/Rotation: **18,30**

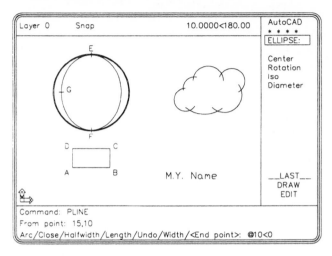

Figure 4.9 Basket and ellipse

To connect up the basket to the balloon, some cables must be provided. Use SNAP to locate the end points on the basket and OSNAP TANGENT on the ellipses.

    Command: **LINE** From point: **15,15**
    To point: **TANGENT** To **10,30**   (inner circle)
    To point: **<ENTER>**
    Command: **<ENTER>**
    LINE From point: **17,15**
    To point: **TANGENT** To **13,26**   (first ellipse)
    To point: **<ENTER>**
    Command: **<ENTER>**
    LINE From point: **19,15**
    To point: **TANGENT** To **16,25**   (second ellipse)
    To point: **<ENTER>**

And for the cables on the right hand side:

    Command: **<ENTER>**
    LINE From point: **21,15**
    To point: **TANGENT** To **24,25**   (second ellipse)
    To point: **<ENTER>**
    Command: **<ENTER>**
    LINE From point: **23,15**
    To point: **TANGENT** To **27,26**   (first ellipse)
    To point: **<ENTER>**
    Command: **<ENTER>**
    LINE From point: **25,15**
    To point: **TANGENT** To **30,30**   (inner circle)
    To point: **<ENTER>**

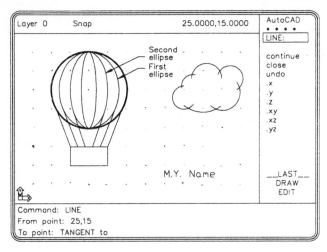

Figure 4.10 More ellipses and cables

Adding text

Textual annotations are an important part of any engineering drawing. The annotations may include information about the objects on the drawing or about the drawing itself. AutoCAD allows you to insert text on a drawing giving you full control over how this should be done and how the text should look.

Already in the drawing EXPRESS1 you have added your name using the TEXT command. In that example you picked the start point of the text and its height and rotation. To repeat a similar operation switch to the TEXT1 layer and try the following:

> Command: **LAYER**
> ?/Make/Set/New/ON/OFF/Colour/Ltype/Freeze/Thaw: **S**
> New current layer <0>: **TEXT1**
> ?/Make/Set/New/ON/OFF/Colour/Ltype/Freeze/Thaw: <**ENTER**>
> Command: **TEXT**
> Start point or Align/Centre/Fit/Middle/Right/Style: **45,40**
> Height <2.00>: **2.5**
> Rotation angle <0>: <**ENTER**>
> Text: **Sky high** <**ENTER**>
> Command:

This gives left justified text, ie the first letter is lined up with the start point.

The most common mistake people make when entering text is not paying attention to the prompt line. As most text is inserted with an angle of 0 degrees it is easy to forget that you have to re-input the angle every time. This type of error is more likely to crop up if you are inputting a lot of text and paying more attention to the difficult operation of typing than to the screen.

Of the other options for inserting text, "Center" is the next most useful. It can be used to centre the characters on a point. This is particularly good for making up posters and signs. Remember, to make the most impact with text it must look good. The default type of lettering available is called the TXT font which is fast and memory efficient but doesn't do much for artistic impression. AutoCAD provides a number of different text fonts ranging from the simplicity of SIMPLEX to the extremely complicated and flamboyant GOTHIC (Release 9 and later).

AutoCAD has a rather confusing arrangement of text fonts and styles. You cannot use the fonts by themselves but must define a text style based on the font. You can create a new text style by picking **STYLE:** from the **TEXT** screen menu. AutoCAD prompts you for a name for the new style and then to define some default parameters. The sequence below defines two new styles which will be used shortly. The rules for naming the style are the same as for layer names.

        Command: **STYLE** Text style name (or ?) <STANDARD>:
          BALLOON-GOTH
        New style.
        Font file <txt>: **GOTHICE**   (note the spelling)
        Height <0.0000>: <**ENTER**>
        Width factor <1.00>: <**ENTER**>
        Obliquing angle <0>: <**ENTER**>
        Backwards? <N>: <**ENTER**>
        Upside-down? <N>: <**ENTER**>
        Vertical? <N>: <**ENTER**>
        BALLOON-GOTH is now the current text style.

Accept all the defaults after defining the font to be used. If the font file is not on your disk you will be prompted for another font name.

        Command: <**ENTER**>
        STYLE Text style name (or ?) <BALLOON-GOTH>:
          B-SIMPLEX
        New style.
        Font file <txt>: **SIMPLEX**
        Height <0.0000>: <**ENTER**>
        Width factor <1.00>: <**ENTER**>
        Obliquing angle <0>: <**ENTER**>
        Backwards? <N>: <**ENTER**>
        Upside-down? <N>: <**ENTER**>
        Vertical? <N>: <**ENTER**>
        B-SIMPLEX is now the current text style.
        Command:

All new text will now be drawn in the new style. The height of 0.0000 specified for the default simply means that the default will vary. An obliquing angle could be used to form an *italic* style and backwards text produces mirror writing.

Use centred text to position a message in the balloon's basket.

> Command: **TEXT**
> Start point or Aligned/Center/Fit/Middle/Right/Style: **C**

You must use the abbreviated form for the option. If you type "center", AutoCAD will assume you want to use OSNAP and the centre of an arc or circle.

> Center point: **20,12**   (middle of basket)
> Height <2.5>: **1.8**
> Rotation angle <0>: **<ENTER>**
> Text: **Fly Me <ENTER>**

You can change the text to BALLOON-GOTH by typing "S" as the reply to the "Start point. . . ." prompt. This will only work for styles that have been defined in the drawing. Erase the "M.Y. Name" text on the drawing and replace it with fancy gothic lettering.

> Command: **ERASE**
> Select objects: **40,10**   (M.Y. Name)
> Select objects: **<ENTER>**
> Command: **TEXT**
> Start point or Aligned/Center/Fit/Middle/Right/Style: **S**
> Style name (or ?) <B−SIMPLEX>: **BALLOON-GOTH**
> Start point or Aligned/Center/Fit/Middle/Right/Style: **40,7**
> Height <2.5>: **1.8**
> Rotation angle <0>: **<ENTER>**
> Text: **M.Y. Name <ENTER>**

Now if you hit ENTER in response to the "Command:" prompt and again in response to "Start point. . . ." AutoCAD will allow you to enter another line of text and position it immediately below the last line.

> Command: **<ENTER>**
> Start point or Aligned/Center/Fit/Middle/Right/Style: **<ENTER>**
> Text: **Air Express <ENTER>**
> Command:

This procedure makes it easy to enter multiple lines of text. AutoCAD automatically calculates the line spacing and uses all the responses given to the prompts at the first line. You can input multiple lines of centred or right justified text.

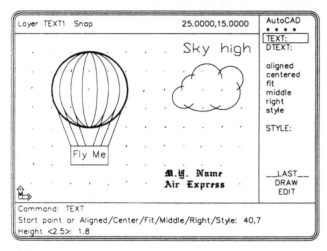

Figure 4.11 Adding text with style

Inserting text using the "Middle" option is similar to centred but text is balanced about the point horizontally and vertically. With "C" the text is balanced horizontally. With "Aligned" text you give the start and end points and AutoCAD calculates the height so that your text just fits. The rotation angle in defined by the two end points. "Fit" is similar to aligned but you can specify a text height and AutoCAD calculates the text width. The final option, "Right", allows you to input the end point, height and rotation of the text and AutoCAD works out the start point.

On serious drawings it is important to keep control of the text heights that are used. Too many different heights spoil the appearance of the drawing. Furthermore, it is vital that all text be legible on the final plot or print out. Thus, the text heights should be chosen carefully and with a view to the final legibility.

On large drawings the time taken to regenerate all the text can be considerable. While editing, you can speed things up by using the simple fonts, TXT and SIMPLEX, and changing to the fancy ones at the end. You can also put all the text on suitable layers and freeze them until the end. The disadvantage of the latter approach is that while the text is invisible you may draw something on top of it. An alternative approach is to turn on the QTEXT or quick text mode. When QTEXT is on, all the text is displayed as rectangles (Figure 4.12). With this you at least know where the text is. **QTEXT:** is on the SETTINGS screen menu.

> Command: **QTEXT** ON/OFF <OFF>: **ON**
> Command: **REGEN**

Turn QTEXT back OFF and change to the DOODLE layer for the next section.

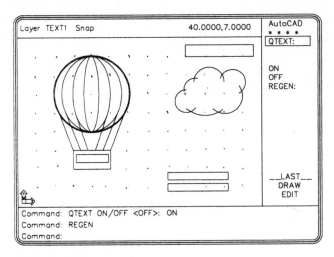

Figure 4.12 Quick text mode

Command: **QTEXT** ON/OFF <OFF>: **OFF**
Command: **REGEN**
Command: **LAYER**
?/Make/Set/New/ON/OFF/Colour/Ltype/Freeze/Thaw: **S**
New current layer <0>: **DOODLE**
?/Make/Set/New/ON/OFF/Colour/Ltype/Freeze/Thaw: **<ENTER>**

Wide lines

Up to this point we haven't been too concerned with the width of the lines we were drawing. In fact everything we have drawn has had a notional line width of zero. AutoCAD uses zero width to mean that no matter how much you magnify the line it always appears the same width. Similarly, it doesn't matter how far you zoom out from an object the width doesn't change.

There are many times when you might want to draw a line with a specified width: printed circuit board drawings, for example. In this section you will cover the methods of assigning widths and using them in the balloon drawing artwork. The same commands and methods can be used in any type of drawing where wide lines are required.

WARNING! Assigning width is mildly dangerous for plotted output

Assigning non-zero widths should only be used where the width serves a particular purpose. If you have a drawing convention that, say, all outlines are to be drawn in 0.5mm line width then it might be better to assign a particular colour to the layer containing the outlines. Then, at plot time, you can specify that the outline colour will be drawn using a 0.5mm pen. If you assign a width on the AutoCAD drawing itself and plot the drawing at a scale of 1:10 the width will be plotted at the reduced width.

In early versions of AutoCAD the only method of drawing wide lines was to use the TRACE command. This works similarly to the LINE command but without the close, continue or undo facilities. To draw a frame for the balloon drawing (Figure 4.13) use **TRACE** with a width of 0.5 units. Make sure ORTHO is on and SNAP is set to 1 and that the current layer is DOODLE.

<pre>
Command: TRACE
Trace width <0.0000>: 0.5
From point: 35,1   (A)
To point: 64,1   (B)
To point: 64,44   (C)
</pre>

Nothing appears on the screen until the third point is picked because AutoCAD must work out the mitre detail at the second point. This mitre depends on the angle between the first and second lines.

<pre>
To point: 1,44   (D)
To point: 1,1   (E)
To point: 35,1   (A)
To point: <ENTER>
</pre>

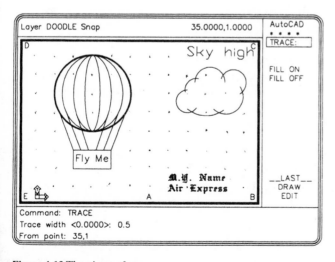

Figure 4.13 The picture frame

The reason for starting and finishing at (35,1) is to ensure that all the corners are correctly mitred. If you start and end on a corner point then that corner will have a gap in it. The trick with using TRACE for closed polygons is to have the first and last line segments in the same direction.

If your TRACE is drawn in outline only, then you should turn the FILL ON from the TRACE screen menu and REGENerate the drawing.

```
Command: FILL
ON/OFF <current>: ON
Command: REGEN
```

Filling in wide lines and solid objects can slow down AutoCAD's responses. Turning FILL off will speed up the REDRAW and REGEN commands.

The second way of generating wide lines is to use the PLINE command. With polylines it is possible to assign a constant width or a varying width to the line. You can also draw wide arcs with PLINE. In the following sequence of operations you will add some mountain scenery to the picture (Figure 4.14). The first PLINE will have a series of segments with two different constant widths. The second will have varying widths, while the third will combine varying width with arcs. The listing of the commands and prompts looks long, but most of the work is done by AutoCAD. If you pick any wrong points or get the widths mixed up, use the "Undo" option to step backwards along the polyline.

```
Command: PLINE
From point: 29,4                                                          (F
Current line-width is 0.0000
Arc/Close/Halfwidth/Length/Undo/Width/<Endpoint of line>: W
Starting width 0.0000: 0.1
Ending width <0.1000>: <ENTER>
Arc/Close/Halfwidth/Length/Undo/Width/<Endpoint of line>: @6,10    ((
Arc/Close/Halfwidth/Length/Undo/Width/<Endpoint of line>: @4,-2    (F
Arc/Close/Halfwidth/Length/Undo/Width/<Endpoint of line>: @4,5     (
```

Now change the width to 0.75 units.

```
Arc/Close/Halfwidth/Length/Undo/Width/<Endpoint of
   line>: W
Starting width <0.1000>: 0.75
Ending width <0.7500>: <ENTER>
Arc/Close/Halfwidth/Length/Undo/Width/<Endpoint of line>: @4,-5   ('
Arc/Close/Halfwidth/Length/Undo/Width/<Endpoint of line>: @8<60   (
```

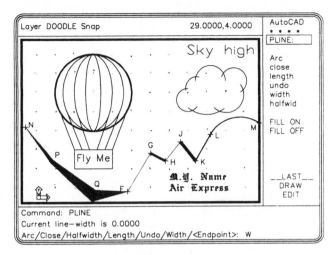

Figure 4.14 Varying PLINE's wid

Now change over to drawing an arc.

> Arc/Close/Halfwidth/Length/Undo/Width/<Endpoint of line>: **ARC**
> Angle/CEnter/CLose/Direction/Halfwidth/Line/Radius/
>   Second pt/Undo/Width/<Endpoint of arc>: @**13,3**   (M)
> Angle/CEnter/CLose/Direction/Halfwidth/Line/Radius/
>   Second pt/Undo/Width/<Endpoint of arc>: <**ENTER**>

The arcs in a polyline are always drawn tangential to the previous PLINE segment. This ensures a smooth transition between the straight lines and the curve.

The mountains on the other side of the balloon will be made up of varying width polylines.

> Command: **PLINE**
> From point: **2,21**   (N)
> Current line-width is 0.7500
> Arc/Close/Halfwidth/Length/Undo/Width/<Endpoint of line>: **H**
> Starting half-width <0.3750>: **0**
> Ending half-width <0.0000>: **0.5**
> Arc/Close/Halfwidth/Length/Undo/Width/<Endpoint of line>: **9.12**   (P)
> Arc/Close/Halfwidth/Length/Undo/Width/<Endpoint of line>: **H**
> Starting half-width <0.5000>: <**ENTER**>
> Ending half-width <0.5000>: **1.5**
> Arc/Close/Halfwidth/Length/Undo/Width/<Endpoint of line>: **20,3** (Q)

And now to reduce the half-width back to zero and connect up with the first PLINE.

    Arc/Close/Halfwidth/Length/Undo/Width/<Endpoint of line>: **H**
    Starting half-width <1.5000>: **<ENTER>**
    Ending half-width <1.5000>: **0**
    Arc/Close/Halfwidth/Length/Undo/Width/<Endpoint of line>: **29,4**   (F)
    Arc/Close/Halfwidth/Length/Undo/Width/<Endpoint of line>: **<ENTER>**

The final polyline will be used to draw the silhouetted bird in flight (Figure 4.15). Every self respecting sky should have one. This is achieved by starting out with a straight line segment with a half-width going from zero to 0.2. This is the blended with an arc whose half-width increases from 0.2 to 0.4 followed by a short line segment. The reverse procedure gives the other wing. As this is an intricate manoeuvre it is prudent to ZOOM in.

    Command: **ZOOM**
    All/Center/Dynamic/Extents/Left/Previous/Window/<Scale(X)>: **W**
    First corner: **29,16**
    Other corner: **42,24**
    Command: **PLINE**   (A)
    From point: **30,18**
    Current line-width is 0.0000

Set up half-width.

    Arc/Close/Halfwidth/Length/Undo/Width/<Endpoint of line>: **H**
    Starting half-width <0.0000>: **<ENTER>**
    Ending half-width <0.0000>: **0.2**
    Arc/Close/Halfwidth/Length/Undo/Width/<Endpoint of line>: **@2,1**   (B)
    Arc/Close/Halfwidth/Length/Undo/Width/<Endpoint of line>: **H**
    Starting half-width <0.2000>: **<ENTER>**
    Ending half-width <0.2000>: **0.4**

Change over to drawing arcs.

    Arc/Close/Halfwidth/Length/Undo/Width/<Endpoint of line>: **ARC**
    Angle/CEnter/CLose/Direction/Halfwidth/Line/Radius/
      Second pt/Undo/Width/<Endpoint of arc>: **@2,0**   (C

Change back to straight lines.

> Angle/CEnter/CLose/Direction/Halfwidth/Line/Radius/
>   Second pt/Undo/Width/<Endpoint of arc>: **Line**
> Arc/Close/Halfwidth/Length/Undo/Width/<Endpoint of line>: **L**
> Length of line: **1.4** (D)
> Arc/Close/Halfwidth/Length/Undo/Width/<Endpoint of line>: **@1.25,0.63** (E)

And draw the second half of the bird.

> Arc/Close/Halfwidth/Length/Undo/Width/<Endpoint of line>: **H**
> Starting half-width <0.4000>: **<ENTER>**
> Ending half-width <0.4000>: **0.2**
> Arc/Close/Halfwidth/Length/Undo/Width/<Endpoint of line>: **ARC**
> Angle/CEnter/CLose/Direction/Halfwidth/Line/Radius/
>   Second pt/Undo/Width/<Endpoint of arc>: **@2,0** (F)
> Angle/CEnter/CLose/Direction/Halfwidth/Line/Radius/
>   Second pt/Undo/Width/<Endpoint of arc>: **Line**
> Arc/Close/Halfwidth/Length/Undo/Width/<Endpoint of line>: **H**
> Starting half-width <0.2000>: **<ENTER>**
> Ending half-width <0.2000>: **0**
> Arc/Close/Halfwidth/Length/Undo/Width/<Endpoint of line>: **L**
> Length of line: (G)
> Arc/Close/Halfwidth/Length/Undo/Width/<Endpoint of line>: **<ENTER>**

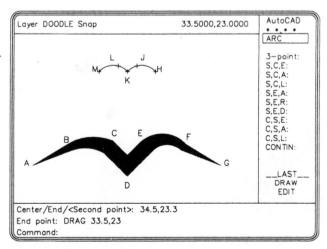

Figure 4.15 Silhouetted birds

The second bird in the distance is just two normal three-point ARCs.

Command: **ARC** Center/<Start point>: **36.5,23**	(H)
Center/End/<Second point>: **35.5,23.3**	(J)
End point: DRAG **35,23**	(K)
Command: **ARC**	
Center/<Start point>: @	(K)
Center/End/<Second point>: **34.5,23.3**	(L)
End point: DRAG **33.5,23**	(M)
Command: **ZOOM**	
All/Center/Dynamic/Extents/Left/Previous/Window/<Scale(X)>: **ALL**	

Solid objects

AutoCAD's SOLID command is used to create filled polygons. Its usage is a little tricky. Here you will draw a little house on the hillside (Figure 4.16). This is made up of a solid triangle on top of a rectangle. Before drawing the object, ZOOM in for greater detail.

Command: **ZOOM**
All/Center/Dynamic/Extents/Left/Previous/Window/<Scale(X)>: **W**
First corner: **0,0**
Other corner: **26,16**

To draw the triangular roof is not too difficult. Pick **SOLID:** from the second part of the DRAW menu and then pick the three points.

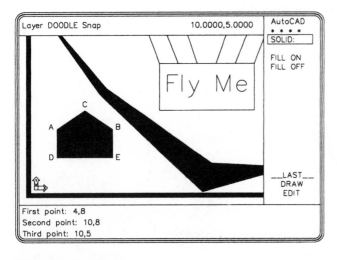

Figure 4.16 A solid house

Command: **SOLID** First point: **4,8**   (A)
Second point: **10,8**   (B)
Third point: **7,10**   (C)
Fourth point: <**ENTER**>
Third point: <**ENTER**>

Since there is no fourth point you simply hit <ENTER> or the space bar. The extra "Third point:" is to allow you to draw another solid using the last two points as the first and second. Pressing <ENTER> a second time exits from the solid command. For triangles the order of picking the points is not important. However, the order is crucial for four-sided objects. To draw the rest of the house pick the points in the order given below.

Command: **SOLID** First point: **4,8**   (A)
Second point: **10,8**   (B)
Third point: **4,5**   (D)
Fourth point **10,5**   (E)
Third point: <**ENTER**>
Command:

If you put in the points in the wrong order you will get a bow-tie effect instead of a rectangle. You could have drawn the whole house and roof in one SOLID command sequence by picking the points in the order DEABC and then pressing <ENTER> twice. However, the chances of success are increased if you simplify the object and draw each triangle and rectangle separately.

Many users have difficulty with the SOLID command. If you do, then do not despair, for PLINE can do everything that SOLID can do.

Here's one final solid object, a filled circle. The amusingly named DONUT (can also be spelt "DOUGHNUT") is in fact a little program based on the PLINE Arc. It can be found on the DRAW screen menu. As the name suggests you can use it to draw fat circles. If the inside diameter of the doughnut is zero then you have a filled circle. To draw the sun in Figure 4.17 you will first have to ZOOM All and change the colour to yellow.

Command: **ZOOM**
All/Center/Dynamic/Extents/Left/Previous/Window/<Scale(X)>: **All**
Command: **COLOUR**
New entity color <BYLAYER>: **YELLOW**

Draw the sun.

Command: **DOUGHNUT**
Inside diameter <0.5000>: **0**
Outside diameter <1.0000>: **6**
Center of doughnut: **37,40**
Center of doughnut: <**ENTER**>
Command: **COLOUR**
New entity color <2 (yellow)>: **BYLAYER**

This means that the colours of new entities will be the same as their layer's default colour. This was set up using the LAYER command.

Shading with patterns

Many types of architectural and engineering drawings use standard hatching patterns to indicate such things as cross sections and material type. In Chapter 2 you have already seen some of the patterns available in AutoCAD's library (Figures 2.6 and 2.7). For many purposes a simple pattern of diagonal lines is sufficient.

For HATCH to work correctly the area to shaded should be within a closed boundary. Furthermore, the entities, lines, arcs etc, making up the perimeter must intersect at their end points. If they don't, or if there are any protruding ends, the results may be incorrect with some strange shading.

It is always a good policy to make a small test box for hatching so that the effectiveness of the pattern scale can be assessed before hatching a larger area.

```
Command: LAYER
?/Make/Set/New/ON/OFF/Colour/Ltype/Freeze/Thaw: S
New current layer <0>: HATCH
?/Make/Set/New/ON/OFF/Colour/Ltype/Freeze/Thaw: <ENTER>
Command: LINE
From point: 34,9
To point: @5,0
To point: @0,-5
To point: @-5,0
To point: Close
```

HAZARD WARNING!

The HATCH command is dangerous. Always save your drawing before executing this command.

```
Command: SAVE
File name <BALLOON>: <ENTER>
Command: HATCH
Pattern (? or name/U,style): U
Angle for crosshatch <0>: 45
Spacing between lines <1.0000>: <ENTER>
Double hatch area? <N>: Y
```

Once the pattern has been defined the command enters the "Select object:" routine. When all the objects defining the boundary have been selected correctly you press <ENTER> to execute the shading.

> Select objects: **W**
> First corner: **34,9**
> Other corner: **@5,-5**
> 4 found.
> Select objects. **<ENTER>**

If the pattern seems satisfactory you can proceed to shade in the stripes on the balloon. If the hatching is not as shown in Figure 4.17 then ERASE it and try again. Make sure that you use the correct spacing and that the four sides of the square are selected.

> Command: **HATCH**
> Pattern (? or name/U,style) <U>: **<ENTER>**
> Angle for crosshatch <45>: **<ENTER>**
> Spacing between lines <1.0000>: **<ENTER>**
> Double hatch area? <Y>: **<ENTER>**

To select the stripes use **Window** and include the inner circle and all the ellipses of the balloon.

> Select objects: **W**
> First corner: **10,20**
> Other corner: **30,40**
> 4 found.
> Select objects. **<ENTER>**

The shading shown in Figure 4.17 results because boundaries have been selected within other boundaries. If the area to be hatched contains another selected boundary then AutoCAD can shade it in one of three styles. The Normal style is the default and uses a hierarchy of shading every second area starting at the outermost. This is what happened with the balloon. The second style is called "Outermost" and can be selected by picking "u,o" from the menu. In this only the outermost area is shaded. The last style of hatching, "u,i", "ignores" any interior boundaries and shades in the whole area.

Despite the hazard warning there is little to fear from shading in objects with patterns. Take heed of the warning and follow the advice on saving the drawing. The reason for this caution is that if the pattern scale is small then it will use up a lot of memory. One single hatch command with an inappropriate scale can fill a 30Mb disk! Remember ˆC will stop a rogue hatch in progress.

As with text, the more complicated the pattern the more it will slow down your redraw time. You will save time if you can leave any hatching as late as possible in the drawing. Freeze the layer when the hatching is not required to be displayed.

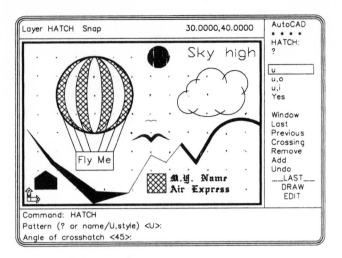

Figure 4.17 The AutoCAD Air Express

Summary

You have encountered AutoCAD's most important drawing commands and entity types in this chapter. You have also used AutoCAD's entity selection procedure. This is common to many commands incuding ERASE and HATCH. Polylines are versatile entities combining liines, arcs, traces and solids. You can speed up REDRAWs by turning FILL off, QTEXT on and freezing the hatch layers.

You should now be able to:

ERASE unwanted entities.
Restore items deleted in error.
Draw a circles, arcs and ellipses.
Insert multiple lines of text.
Insert centred lines of text.
Define text styles using different fonts.
Draw closed TRACEs.
Draw polylines with constant and varying widths.
Merge polylines with arcs.
Create SOLID triangles, rectangles, circles and doughnuts.
Select a simple hatch pattern and perform a test shading.
Shade in multiple objects.
Speed up REDRAWs.

Chapter 5 **CONSTRUCTIVE EDITING**

General

The term constructive editing is used to describe those commands which either replicate existing entities or alter their characteristics. This chapter begins with some of the commands that alter the objects and then considers some of the ways to duplicate them. This will help to accelerate the repetitive type of work needed to complete the Eiffel tower that was started in Chapter 3.

Start up AutoCAD, enter selection 1 at the main menu and give EXPRESS2 as the default drawing name.

Main menu

Enter selection: **1**

Enter NAME of drawing: **EIFFEL=EXPRESS2**

This copies all of the EXPRESS2.DWG file to EIFFEL.DWG and leaves the old file unchanged. Now set SNAP to 2.5, GRID to 5 and skip to the next section, "Drawing the Arch".

If you haven't got the EXPRESS2.DWG file or another file containing the drawing from Chapter 3, Table 5.1 summarises what you will need.

Drawing the arch

Before engaging in all this editing let's do a bit more preparatory work on the tower. Making sure that EIFFEL is the current layer, start by drawing the arch at the base of the tower. If you type the command you will have to input all the responses in bold but if you pick **C,S,A** (centre, start point and angle) from the

Table 5.1 EXPRESS2.DWG summary

Layer	Status	LINETYPE
0	ON	CONTINUOUS
EIFFEL	ON	CONTINUOUS
CONST	FROZEN	DASHED
CLINE	ON	CENTER
1TEXT	ON	CONTINUOUS

Current layer: EIFFEL

SNAP = 2.5, GRID = 5.0, AXIS = 10.0

The centre-line is drawn from (30,41.5) to (30,5) and is on the CLINE layer. The following lines are all on layer EIFFEL.

Draw lines from (22.5,5) to (17.5,5) to (23.75,15) to (30,15)
From (23.75,15) to (23.75,17.5) to (30,17.5)
From (23.75,16) to (30,16)
From (25.3,17.5) to (26.5,22.5) to (30,22.5)
From (26.5,22.5) to (26.5,25) to (30,25)
From (26.5,23.5) to (30,23.5)
From (30,37) to (27.5,37) to (27.5,38) to (30,38)
From (27.5,37.5) to (30,37.5)
From (28,25) to (28,38) to (30,39.5) to (30,41.5)
From (29,37) to (29,38)

screen menu you will only have to type the numbers. ARC can be found at the top of the DRAW sub-menu.

Command: **ARC** Center/<Start point>: **C** Center: **30,5**   (A)
Start point: **@7.5<90**   (B)
Angle/Length of chord/<End point>: **A** Included angle: DRAG
90
Command: **ARC** Center/<Start point>: **C** Center: **30,5**   (A)
Start point: **@8.5<90**   (C)
Angle/Length of chord/<End point>: **A** Included angle: DRAG
30

Add some text but this time use the Dynamic version of the TEXT command. **DTEXT** is on the DRAW menu and also on the TEXT menu. All the options and responses are the same as with the normal TEXT command. The difference is that with DTEXT the characters appear on the drawing as they are being typed while with the normal command they only appear after you press <ENTER>. This allows you to see when you might need to add a second line.

Command: **DTEXT** Start point or Align/Center/Fit/Middle/Right/
    Style: **7,15**
Height <0.20>: **1.8**
Rotation angle <0>: **<ENTER>**

As you are prompted to input your text a box should appear on the drawing at the insertion point. This box indicates the position of the next character and moves as you type the text. If you make a mistake while typing you can use the backspace key to remove the letters (as long as you haven't pressed <ENTER>).

> Text: **The Trifle** <ENTER>

It is clear from the drawing (Figure 5.1) that to include the full caption a second line of text is needed to avoid overwriting the actual tower. As you hit <ENTER> the DTEXT command automatically moves its box to the next line to allow more text to be input.

> Text: **Tower** <ENTER>
> Text: <**ENTER**>

Finally to end the command press <**ENTER**> without typing any new text. Don't worry that this text has not been put on the 1TEXT layer. This sloppy practice will be corrected later.

A small corner of the drawing will be used as the prep area where the metalwork for the tower will be assembled. **ZOOM** in and draw the structure panels.

> **Command: ZOOM**
> All/Center/Dynamic/Extents/Left/Previous/Window/<Scale(X)>: **W**
> First corner: **2.5,2.5**
> Other corner: **9,6.5**
> Command: **SNAP**
> Snap spacing or ON/OFF/Aspect/Rotate/Style <0.5000>: **0.25**

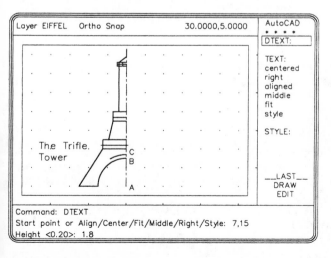

Figure 5.1 The Trifle Tower

The basic structure panel is a cross-braced frame. It is first drawn to fit within a 1 by 1 box so that it can later be scaled to fit the different parts of the tower.

Command: **LINE**	
From point: **3,5**	(A)
To point: **@1,1**	(B)
To point: **@−1,0**	(C)
To point: **@1,−1**	(D)
To point: **<ENTER>**	
Command: **<ENTER>**	(E)
Line From point: **3.5,5**	(F)
To point: **@0,1**	
To point: **<ENTER>**	

Each landing will have a series of mini-arches comprising an arc and two lines each. For the following construction you must pick the commands from the screen menu.

Command: **<ENTER>**	
Line From point: **5,5**	(G)
To point: **@0,0.5**	(H)
To point: **<ENTER>**	

Now move to the ARC menu and pick **CONTIN:**

Command: ARC Center/<Start point>:	
End point: DRAG **@0.75<0**	(J)

This automatically selects the last line end point as the start of the arc and also makes the arc tangential to that line. Now go back to the LINE menu and pick **continue.** The word "Cancel" will appear on the screen but don't worry about it as this is just a safety precaution used by AutoCAD in case you had picked "continue" with an inappropriate command. The LINE command is automatically restarted in the continuation mode.

Command: **LINE** From point: Pick **continue** from menu. *Cancel*	
Command: LINE	
From point:	
Length of line: **0.5**	
To point: **<ENTER>**	(K)

The "LINE continue" option automatically starts on the last line or arc end point. If an arc was drawn more recently than the last line then this new line will also be tangential to the arc. This is a special feature of using "CONTIN:" and "continue".

The final component to be used is the fancy iron scrolling for the large arch at the base. For this you should use a PLINE.

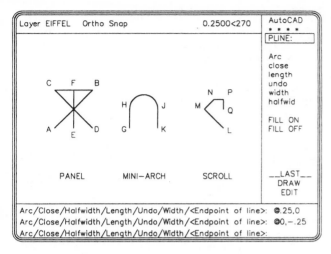

Figure 5.2 Structure panels

Command: **PLINE**   (L)
From point: **7.5,5**
Current line-width is 0.0000
Arc/Close/Halfwidth/Length/Undo/Width/<Endpoint of line>: @**−0.5,0.5** (M)
Arc/Close/Halfwidth/Length/Undo/Width/<Endpoint of line>: @**.25,.25** (N)
Arc/Close/Halfwidth/Length/Undo/Width/<Endpoint of line>: @**.25,0**   (P)
Arc/Close/Halfwidth/Length/Undo/Width/<Endpoint of line>: @**0,−.25** (Q)
Arc/Close/Halfwidth/Length/Undo/Width/<Endpoint of line>: **<ENTER>**

This should give you the three objects shown in Figure 5.2. As usual, the letters
on the diagram are only for reference and will not appear in your drawing.

Editing a polyline with PEDIT

Polylines are probably the most flexible entities in AutoCAD. This means that
they can also be cumbersome to edit. There are so many possibilities for
making changes that it is difficult to describe in a concise manner. In this
section you will encounter the more important facilities of PEDIT.

The PLINE scroll drawn above requires a few small changes. Firstly, it is too small and secondly, it looks too square to be *art nouveau*. To make it a bit bigger an extra point must be inserted and one vertex must be moved in the polyline. Select PEDIT: from the second page of the EDIT menu.

Command: **PEDIT** Select polyline: **7.5,5**   (L)
Close/Join/Width/Edit vertex/Fit curve/Spline curve/Decurve/
    Undo/eXit <X>: **Edit**

Choose the edit vertex option. The prompt line changes and an X appears on the polyline at its first point or vertex.

Next/Previous/Break/Insert/Move/Regen/Straighten/Tangent/
    Width/eXit <N>: **N**   (M)

The **N** selects the next vertex on the polyline and the "X" should now be at point M (7.0,5.5). Now type **Insert** to put in a new point.

Next/Previous/Break/Insert/Move/Regen/Straighten/Tangent/
    Width/eXit <N>: **I**
Enter location of new vertex: **@.25<90**   (R)

The new shape should look like Figure 5.3(b) with the X still at point M. Move the X to vertex, N (7.25,5.75), by typing **Next** twice. Once the X is at the correct vertex the vertex can be moved to its new location (Figure 5.3c).

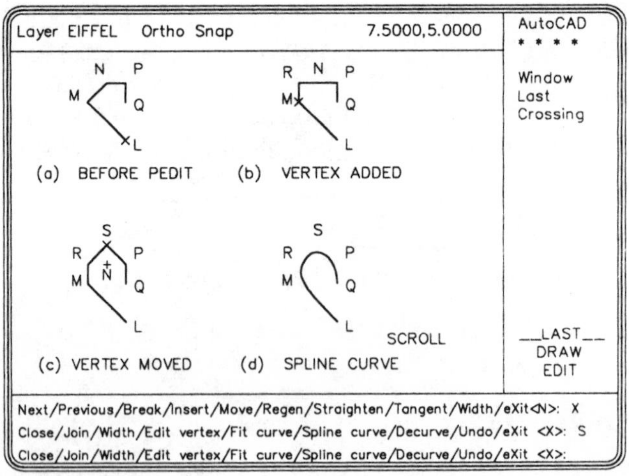

Figure 5.3 PEDIT

Next/Previous/Break/Insert/Move/Regen/Straighten/Tangent/
 Width/eXit <N>: **N**   (R)
Next/Previous/Break/Insert/Move/Regen/Straighten/Tangent/
 Width/eXit <N>: **N**   (N)
Next/Previous/Break/Insert/Move/Regen/Straighten/Tangent/
 Width/eXit <N>: **M**   (S)
Enter new location: @**.25<90**
Next/Previous/Break/Insert/Move/Regen/Straighten/Tangent/
 Width/eXit <N>: **X**
Close/Join/Width/Edit vertex/Fit curve/Spline curve/Decurve/
 Undo/eXit <X>: **S**
Close/Join/Width/Edit vertex/Fit curve/Spline curve/Decurve/
 Undo/eXit <X>: **X**

Selecting the X option exits from the "Edit vertex" routine and returns you to the PEDIT prompt. To make the polyline into a smooth curve select the Spline curve option by typing **S.** This executes a quadratic B-spline curve fitting routine (Release 10 also allows cubic B-splines). This type of curve gives an extremely smooth shape fitted to the vertex points of the orginal polyline. The curve won't actually pass through the vertices but will be drawn nearby. The technique is named after the mathematician, Bezier, who invented it. Bezier is regarded by many as the father of computer graphics and surface modelling. You can select the quadratic or cubic splines by setting the AutoCAD system variable "SPLINETYPE" to 5 or 6 respectively. The quadratic version resembles the original polyline shape more closely, while the cubic gives more "appealing" curves.

Command: **SETVAR**
Variable name or ?: **SPLINETYPE**
New value for SPLINETYPE <5>: **6**

Early versions of AutoCAD gave only the "Fit curve" option for smoothing polylines. This just changes all the line segments into arc segments. The arcs all pass through the original vertices. It is faster but visually inferior to the spline.
 Other options for editing polylines include making it into a closed polyline, joining two polylines together and changing the width. You can also "Decurve" a spline or fitted curve.
 The scroll work should now resemble the curlicue shown in Figure 5.3(d).

Moving objects

All AutoCAD entities can be edited to alter their position in the drawing. This gives great flexibility when making a drawing as you don't have to worry about getting everything to fit exactly. As the drawing progresses conflicts can be resolved by moving the objects to give a clearer picture.

In the above example you made use of ZOOM and "window" to draw the panels in close up. Now you can zoom out for a better view and move the panels into position, starting with the mini-arch. Pick **MOVE** from the second page of the EDIT menu. AutoCAD enters the "Select objects:" mode and you can make a window around the mini-arch. When all the selections have been made you will be asked how far you want to move it.

> Command: **ZOOM**
> All/Center/Dynamic/Extents/Left/Previous/Window/<Scale(X)>: **W**
> First corner: **2.5,2.5**
> Other corner: **35,27.5**

You can use ZOOM W for windows larger than the current display but you will have to input the coordinates at the keyboard.

> Command: **MOVE**
> Select objects: **Window**
> First corner: **5,5**
> Other corner: **@1,1**
> 3 found.

If the correct three objects, one arc and two lines have been selected press <**ENTER**> to end the selection procedure.

> Select objects: <**ENTER**>
> Base point or displacement: **5,5**

This is the point from which the object is to be moved. You are then prompted for the new location.

> Second point of displacement: **24,15**

The mini-arch is then moved to the first landing (Figure 5.4).

The base point and second point do not have to be at the old and new locations. All that is important is the relative displacement between the two points. For example, the above movement would also have been achieved if the points (0,0) and (19,10) were input.

> Base point or displacement: 0,0
> Second point of displacement: 19,10

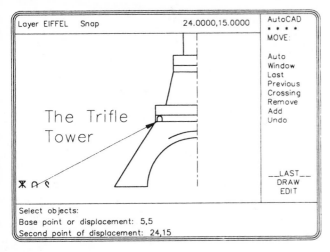

```
┌─────────────────────────────────────────────────────────┐
│ Layer EIFFEL  Snap              24.0000,15.0000 │ AutoCAD │
│                                                 │ • • • • │
│                                                 │ MOVE:   │
│                                                 │         │
│                                                 │ Auto    │
│                                                 │ Window  │
│                                                 │ Last    │
│                                                 │ Previous│
│            The  Trifle                          │ Crossing│
│                                                 │ Remove  │
│            Tower                                │ Add     │
│                                                 │ Undo    │
│                                                 │         │
│                                                 │ __LAST__│
│  X ⋏ ⸦                                          │  DRAW   │
│                                                 │  EDIT   │
├─────────────────────────────────────────────────────────┤
│ Select objects:                                           │
│ Base point or displacement: 5,5                           │
│ Second point of displacement: 24,15                       │
└─────────────────────────────────────────────────────────┘
```

Figure 5.4 Moving the mini-arch

A third way of achieving the same result is to input the relative displacement at the first prompt and just press <ENTER> at the second.

    Base point or displacement: 19,10
    Second point of displacement: <ENTER>

Rotating objects

Before moving the scroll work to the main arch it must be put into the correct orientation. The scroll will be used to fill the area between the shorter and longer arcs. As the shorter one has an included angle of 30 degrees the scroll has to be rotated by that angle (Figure 5.5). To see the operation clearly, zoom in closely.

    Command: **ZOOM**
    All/Center/Dynamic/Extents/Left/Previous/Window/<Scale(X)>:**W**
    First corner: **5,3**
    Other corner: **11.5,7.5**

The ROTATE command is also on the second page of the EDIT menu. The selection procedure is standard and when all the objects have been found you are asked for the centre of rotation and the angle.

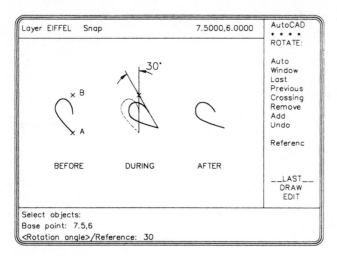

Figure 5.5. Rotating the polyline

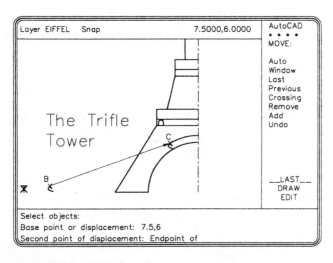

Figure 5.6 The scroll in the arch

Command: **ROTATE**
Select objects: **7.5,5**   (Pick the polyline at A.)
1 selected, 1 found.
Select objects: **<ENTER>**
Base point: **7.5,6**   (B)
<Rotation angle>/Reference: **30**

The scroll has been rotated 30 degrees anti-clockwise about the point (7,6). Now do a "ZOOM Previous" and move the polyline to the end of the shorter arc. The point (7,6) will be used as an imaginary handle by which the curve will be moved (Figure 5.6).

Command: **ZOOM**
All/Center/Dynamic/Extents/Left/Previous/Window/<Scale(X)>: **P**
Command: **Move**
Select objects: Pick scroll. 1 selected, 1 found.
Select objects: <**ENTER**>
Base point or displacement: **7.5,6**   (B)
Second point of displacement: **endpoint** of Pick ARC at point C.

Copying

The basic structure panel is still on the ground awaiting erection. Instead of simply moving it over you can copy it to each tier of the structure (Figure 5.7). The COPY command operates a bit like MOVE. You first select the objects to copy and then provide a displacement showing where you want them copied to. Unlike MOVE the original objects are left untouched and duplicates appear in the new positions.

In this particular operation you will make multiple copies of the panel, an extra feature of COPY. The first copy will be made to point E at the base, the second to point F and the third to the upper tier at G. The base point for all three copies will be the lower left corner of the panel, D (3,5).

Command: **COPY**
Select objects : **Window**
First corner: **3,5**   (D)
Other corner: **@1,1**
4 found.

This surrounds the panel and finds its four lines.

Select objects: <**ENTER**>
<Base point or displacement/Multiple: **Multiple** Base point: **3,5**   (D)
Second point of displacement: **17.5,5**   (E)

The panel should now appear at the point E and the prompt asks for "Second point.." for the next copy. This uses the original base point.

Second point of displacement: **INTERSEC** of Pick point F.

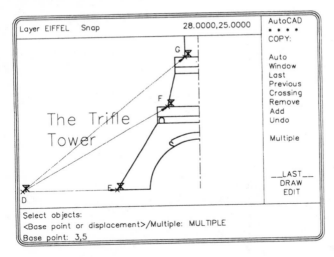

Figure 5.7 Multiple copies

The third copy is made to point G (28,25)

> Second point of displacement: **28,25**   (G)
> Second point of displacement: **<ENTER>**

When all the desired copies have been made press <ENTER> without giving any "Second point..".

The COPY command can also be used to make single copies. To do this give the coordinates of the "Base point or displacement" instead of typing "Multiple". It will then work as above but will ask you for a single "Second point..." before returning to the "Command:" prompt.

To draw the "inside leg" of the tower (Figure 5.8) you can copy the inclined lines. Copy the line EH to a point 3.3333 units to the right and the leg of the middle tier 2.5 to the right.

> Command: **COPY**
> Select objects: Pick line EH. 1 selected, 1 found.
> Select objects: **<ENTER>**
> <Base point or displacement>/Multiple: **3.3333,0**
> Second point of displacement: **<ENTER>**
> Command: **<ENTER>**
> COPY
> Select objects: Pick inclined line near F. 1 selected, 1 found.
> Select objects: **<ENTER>**
> <Base point or displacement>/Multiple: **2.5,0**
> Second point of displacement: **<ENTER>**

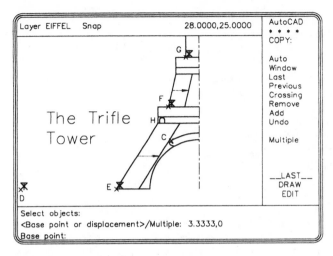

Figure 5.8 The inside leg

Altering objects' characteristics

All the basic pieces of the tower are now in place. Something must be done to correct their sizes to make them all fit. The panels are too small and there is a gap between the short arc at C and the inner part of the leg. Also the original panel is still at the point (3,5).

The first bit of tidying up is to sort out the use of layers. The text was put on the EIFFEL layer but ideally it should have been on 1TEXT. Also there was a small spelling error in the name of the tower! Can one command rescue the situation?

The CHANGE command is one of AutoCAD's most powerful editing tools. Many of the other commands described in this section are just convenient subsets of CHANGE. With CHANGE you can alter the end points of lines, the colour and linetypes of entities, make extensive alterations to text and move things from layer to layer.

To illustrate this pick **CHANGE:** from the EDIT menu. The prompt areas asks you to select objects in the usual manner. To correct the spelling error pick the "The Trifle" and press **<ENTER>**.

> Command: **CHANGE**
> Select objects: **7.5,15** 1 selected, one found.
> Select objects: **<ENTER>**

You are then prompted for the Properties or the Change point. If you input a new point it will be used to move the text from the base point, (7.5,15). Just press <**ENTER**> to leave the text where it is and let AutoCAD move on to the next prompt which in this instance is also asking for a new insertion point for the text. With changing text you get two shots at moving it!

> Properties/<Change point>: <**ENTER**>
> Enter text insertion point: <**ENTER**>
> Text style: STANDARD
> New style or RETURN for no change: <**ENTER**>
> New height <1.8>: <**ENTER**>
> New rotation angle <0>: <**ENTER**>
> New text <The Trifle>: **The Eiffel**

The only thing that required changing was the text itself, so all the prompted defaults were accepted except the last one. The old text is then replaced by the new (Figure 5.9). Using CHANGE to correct typing errors in drawing text is much faster than erasing and re-typing. As you can see from the prompts this command also allows you to edit all the other text settings. More information on editing text entities is given in Chapter 12.

Now, to move the two lines of text onto layer 1TEXT you can use CHANGE once more. This time select a window around both lines of text.

> Command: **CHANGE**
> Select objects: **Window**
> First corner: **6,10**
> Other corner: **23,19**
> 2 found.
> Select objects: <**ENTER**>

At the next prompt reply with "P" for properties and select LAYER.

> Properties/<Change point>: **P**
> Change what property (Color/Elev/LAyer/LType/Thickness)?
>   **LAYER**
> New Layer <EIFFEL>: **1TEXT**
> Change what property (Color/Elev/LAyer/LType/Thickness)?
>   <**ENTER**>

You are then prompted for another property to change. Press <**ENTER**> and the two lines of text are erased from layer EIFFEL and re-drawn on 1TEXT.

If the drawing does not contain the layer 1TEXT you will get an error message "Cannot find layer 1TEXT". If this happens use ^C to cancel and then create a new layer before returning to this example.

Rather than erasing the panel of the structure that is still at the point (3,5) you can move it to the CONST layer. As that layer is presently frozen, this change will cause the panel to become invisible. If you want to check that it still exists you can thaw the CONST layer.

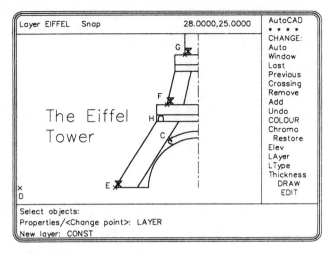

Figure 5.9 Changing text and layers

> Command: **CHANGE**
> Select objects: **Window**
> First corner: **3,5**
> Other corner: **@1,1**
> 4 found.
> Select objects: **<ENTER>**
> Properties/<Change point>: **LAYER**
> New layer: **CONST**

In the CHANGE operation you can pre-empt the "Change what property?" prompt by typing the name of the property in reply to "Change point". Of the other properties that you might wish to change "Elevation" and ""Thickness" are covered in the section on 3D in Chapter 8. The colour and linetype changes allow you to reset those properties, or to set them to their layers' defaults (ie BYLAYER).

In AutoCAD Release 10 the command CHPROP has been introduced. This works exactly like CHANGE but doesn't give the "Change point" option. For example to do the previous operation you would type:

> Command: CHPROP
> Select objects: Window
> First corner: 3,5
> Other corner: @1,1
> 4 found.
> Select objects: <ENTER>
> Change what property (Color/LAyer/LType/Thickness)? LAYER
> New layer: CONST

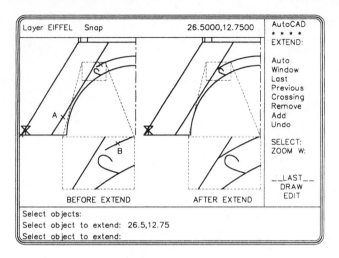

Figure 5.10 Extending the arch

The Change point facility allows the user to make clever geometrical edits to entities. It is of great use to those involved in digitising drawings from paper originals. Inaccuracies in the digitising process mean that some lines that should meet at a point either don't meet or do so at the wrong point. The AutoCAD user can use CHANGE, EXTEND or TRIM, to force the lines to meet.

In EIFFEL there is a gap between the inner part of the tower's leg and the shorter of the two arcs in the arch. The EXTEND command can be used to change the arc's end point so that it meets the line exactly (Figure 5.10). Having picked **EXTEND** from the EDIT menu you then must give AutoCAD the boundary edges to which you want to extend the entity. In this case pick the inner line.

    Command: **EXTEND**
    Select boundary edge(s)...
    Select objects: **22,7**   (A)

You will then be prompted for a second edge. In this example, only one edge is required. AutoCAD then asks for the objects to be extended. Pick the shorter arc and the curve is projected to meet the line.

    Select objects: **<ENTER>**
    Select object to extend: **26.5,12.75**   (B)
    Select object to extend: **<ENTER>**

You can extend more than one item so AutoCAD prompts for more. Pressing **<ENTER>** without making another selection exits back to the "Command:" prompt.

While EXTEND is used to project to a new intersection point the TRIM command is used for objects that are already crossing. TRIM works similarly to EXTEND; the boundary edges are selected first and then the objects to trim.

Enlarging objects

In order to fit, each of the tower leg structure panels must be enlarged. The top panel, near the point G must be increased by a factor of 2, the middle panel near F by a factor of 2.5 and the bottom one by 3.3333. The SCALE command allows you to increase the dimensions of an object (Figure 5.11). Its operation is similar to that of ROTATE. You select the objects to SCALE and give a base point about which the objects will move when enlarging. Finally, you specify the magnification factor. The factor must be positive and not equal to zero. Giving a factor less than 1 reduces the size of the object while values greater than 1 increase it. The the X and Y dimensions are changed by the same amount.

Using an initial panel size that fitted within a 1 by 1 box makes the calculation of the appropriate scale factors straightforward. To enlarge the panel at point G pick **SCALE** from the EDIT menu. Then select the panel using **window,** give point G as the base point and finish up by giving the scale factor of **2.**

> Command: **SCALE**
> Select objects: **Window**
> First corner: **28,25**   (G)
> Other corner: **@1,1**
> 4 found.
> Select objects: **<ENTER>**
> Base point: **28,25**
> <Scale factor>/Reference: **2**

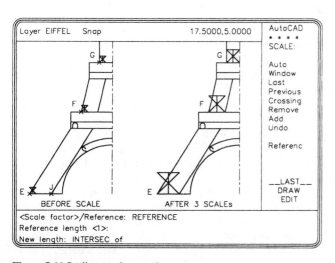

Figure 5.11 Scaling up the panels

Now scale the panel at F.

> Command: <**ENTER**>
> SCALE
> Select objects: **Window**
> First corner: **25,17**   (near F)
> Other corner: **27,19**
> 4 found.
> Select objects: <**ENTER**>
> Base point: **INTERSEC** of Pick point F.
> <Scale factor>/Reference: **2.5**

And finally to scale the bottom panel. This time use the intersection points at E and J to specify the scale factor.

> Command: <**ENTER**>
> SCALE
> Select objects: **Window**
> First corner: **17.5,5**   (E)
> Other corner: **@1,1**
> 4 found.
> Select objects: <**ENTER**>
> Base point: **17.5,5**   (E)
> ale factor/Reference: **Referenc**
> Reference length <1>: <**ENTER**>
> New length: **INTERSEC** of Pick point J.

The reference length is the length of the original object. It can be picked by giving two points on the object. In this case the length of 1 is correct.

Stretching objects into shape

The two lower panels are now the required size but they are the wrong shape for the inclined legs. To fit they must be changed to become skew with the angle of the respective leg. Concentrating on the bottom panel first, zoom in for a closer view. To make it skew, the top of the panel must be moved sideways while the bottom stays put. That is, all the line end points in the top half will be shifted to the right by the distance from S1 to S2. The STRETCH command, like EXTEND has the ability to act on one end of an entity while leaving the other end untouched.

STRETCH is easiest to operate if it is picked from the EDIT menu's second page. When you pick **STRETCH** you will be given the message that you must select the objects using a window and the Crossing option is automatically chosen. The "Crossing" option picks up all objects totally or partially within the window. This window has to contain all the end points to be shifted.

Command: **STRETCH**
Select objects to stretch by window...
Select objects: C	(Crossing)
First corner: **17,7.5**	(W1)
Other corner: **21.5,9**	(W2)
5 found.	

Even the inclined leg becomes ghosted because it crossed through the window. As only the end points that were actually within the window are stretched, the leg will be okay. However, if you are in doubt as to whether an object might be undesirably stretched you can **Remove** it from the selection set. For practice remove the leg.

Select objects: **Remove**	
Remove objects: **21.5,11.5**	(Point R1 on leg)
Remove objects: **<ENTER>**	

When the selection/de-selection has been completed you are prompted for the point to stretch from and the new destination.

Base point: **INTERSEC** of Pick point S1.
New point: **INTERSEC** of Pick point S2.

The panel should now fit snugly into the inclined leg (Figure 5.12).
  Repeat this procedure to make the panel at point F fit its leg. Remember that only the end points that are within the window are stretched.

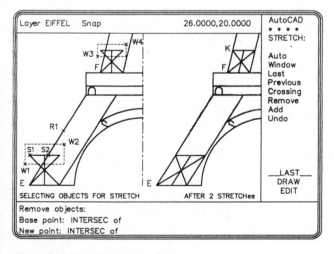

Figure 5.12 Stretching some points

```
Command: STRETCH
Select objects to stretch by window…
Select objects: C                                    (Crossing)
First corner: 25,19.5                                (W3)
Other corner: 28,20.5                                (W4)
5 found.
```

If you don't use the "Crossing option" you will get the message "1 found" and you will have to add the unghosted lines of the panel.

```
Select objects: <ENTER>
Base point: INTERSEC of 25,20     (Point near the top left corner)
New point: INTERSEC of 26,20      (Point near intersection with leg)
```

The COPY command has already been used to make multiple copies of the original structure panel. It will now be used to duplicate the panel on the middle tier near point F. The other tiers require multiple copies of their panels. As these copies are in regular patterns, AutoCAD's ARRAY command will be used. This allows objects to be copied in rows and columns and circular arrays. The scroll work will first be mirrored to complete the heart shape and copied in a circular array along the arch.

To copy the panel at D use **COPY Window** to select and use **OSNAP INTERSEC** at points **F**, near (25.25,17.5), and **K**, near (26,20), to give the displacement.

```
Command: COPY
Select obects: Window
First corner: 25,17
Other corner: 28.5,20.5
4 found.
Select objects: <ENTER>
<Base point or displacement>/Multiple: INTERSEC of Pick point F.
Second point of displacement: INTERSEC of Pick point K.
```

Mirror image

Mirroring objects allows the user to take advantage of symmetries in the object being drawn. For example, only half of the tower is being drawn since it is symmetrical about the centre-line. At the end of the chapter it will be mirrored to complete the picture.

To illustrate the MIRROR command the scroll in the arch will be reflected in a line at an angle of 120 degrees (remember that is was previously rotated by 30 degrees from the vertical and 30+90=120). Before mirroring zoom in for a better view. Pick **MIRROR** from the "next" page of the EDIT menu and select the scroll polyline. For the mirror line give the intersection point of the polyline and the lower arc as the first point and a relative displacement with an angle of 120 degrees for the second.

Command: **ZOOM**
All/Center/Dynamic/Extents/Left/Previous/Window/<Scale(X)>: **W**
First corner: **22.5,10**
Other corner: **29,14.5**
Command: **MIRROR**
Select objects: Pick point on scroll.
1 found.
Select objects: **<ENTER>**
First point on mirror line: **INTERSEC** of Pick point M1.
Second point: **@10<120**

The length of the mirror line doesn't matter.

Delete old objects? <N> **<ENTER>**

You do not wish to delete the original, so press **<ENTER>** and the heart is complete (Figure 5.13). At the end do a **ZOOM Previous** to get back to the last display magnification.

Command: **ZOOM**
All/Center/Dynamic/Extents/Left/Previous/Window/<Scale(X)>: **P**

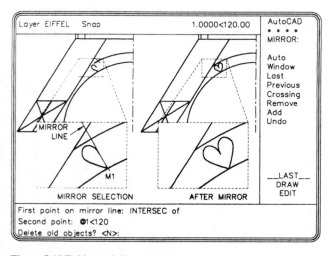

Figure 5.13 Taking polylines to heart

Multiple copies using ARRAY

In the tower drawing there are two simple patterns to be copied. Firstly, the mini-arches at the first landing will be copied to give two rows and six columns. Then the panels in the top section will be copied to give six rows and one column. Two slightly more difficult operations are involved to copy the hearts along the arch and the panels along the lower leg.

Rectangular arrays

With the ARRAY command you select the original objects to be arrayed. Then you specify whether they are to be copied in a rectangular grid or circular pattern and finally you give the dimensions of the pattern's repeated unit.

To make the rows of mini-arches in Figure 5.14, pick **ARRAY** from the EDIT menu and select the two lines and the arc of the original.

> Command: **ARRAY**
> Select objects: **24.75,15.25** 1 selected, 1 found.   (A1 on right line)
> Select objects: **24.375,15.875** 1 selected, 1 found.   (A2 on arc)
> Select objects: **24,15.1** 1 selected, 1 found.   (A3 on left line)
> Select objects: <**ENTER**>
> Rectangular or Polar array (R/P): **R**

This selects the rectangular grid pattern. You are now prompted for the number of rows and columns.

> Number of rows (---) <1>: **2**
> Number of columns ($\stackrel{|||}{|||}$) <1>: **6**

The "(---)" is to remind you that the rows are always horizontal and the "($\stackrel{|||}{|||}$)" is for the vertical columns. Now input the distance between the rows and the columns.

> Unit cell or distance between rows (---): **1**
> Distance between columns ($\stackrel{|||}{|||}$): **1**

The mini-arch should be repeated to give a total of 12 arches. Note that the distance between the rows and columns is the length between a point on the original object and the corresponding point on its immediate neighbour. Inputting positive distances causes the duplicates to appear to the right and above the original. To make them appear on the left give a negative distance between columns. Similarly a negative distance between the rows causes the new objects to be drawn below the original.

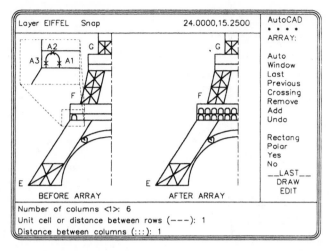

Figure 5.14 Rectangular array

To ARRAY the panel in the top part of the structure try the following:

Command: **ARRAY**
Select objects: **Window**
First corner: **28,25**   (G)
Other corner: **@2,2**
4 found.
Select objects: **<ENTER>**
Rectangular or Polar array (R/P): **R**
Number of rows (---) <1>: **6**
Number of columns (‖‖) <1>: **<ENTER>**
Unit cell or distance between rows: **2**

This should fill up the top of the structure with a total of 5 copies plus the original panel.

Circular arrays

The circular or polar array option is used to copy objects around some central focus point. For example, the spokes on a bicycle wheel could be drawn by copying one line in a circular pattern centred on one of the end points. In the EIFFEL tower drawing, the heart shapes will be copied along the arch. This can be done by using a polar array centred on the point A (at the arc centre) and repeating the object through 30 degrees.

Zoom in for more detail. Pick **ARRAY,** select the two halves of the heart shaped scroll and then opt for the **Polar** array.

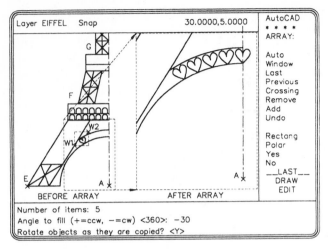

Figure 5.15 Polar array

```
Command: ZOOM
All/Center/Dynamic/Extents/Left/Previous/Window/<Scale(X)>: W
First corner: 17,4
Other corner: 32,15
Command: ARRAY
Select objects: Window
First corner: 25,11                                                          (W1)
Other corner: 27,13                                                          (W2)
2 found.
Select objects: <ENTER>
Rectangular or Polar array (R/P): P
```

You are now prompted for the centre point of the array, the number of items to be in the array (copies plus the original) and the number of degrees to fill.

```
Center point of array: 30,5                                                  (A)
Number of items: 5
Angle to fill (+=ccw, −=cw) <360>: −30
Rotate objects as they are copied? <Y> <ENTER>
```

The minus sign indicates a clockwise angle (as shown in the parentheses). A positive angle would cause the copies to appear anti-clockwise of the orginal. The final prompt asks you if the objects are to be copied in their current orientation or if they are to be rotated. In this case they should be rotated.

If you respond to "Rectangular or Polar array (R/P):" with "C" you will get a circular array. The results are much the same as for the polar array but the prompts are slightly different.

Non-orthogonal rectangular arrays

In rectangular arrays above, the rows were vertically above each other. Similarly the columns are separated by horizontal distances. This is because the ARRAY directions are always parallel and perpendicular to the SNAP angle. The default snap angle is zero. Using **SNAP** you can rotate the snap angle to 58 degrees (the angle of the lower leg). Then the ARRAY command can be used to copy the panel along the leg.

>
> Command: **SNAP**
> Snap spacing or ON/OFF/Aspect/Rotate/Style <0.5000>: **Rotate**
> Base point <0.0000,0.0000> **17.5,5**   (E)
> Rotation angle <0.00>: **58**

As you select a new snap angle the cursor cross-hairs, grid and axes all rotate by 58 degrees. Note that the drawing coordinates have not changed. It's just the snap locations that have altered. You can use ARRAY to copy along the 58 degree leg. This array has one row and three columns as the leg direction is the effective horizontal. The distance between the columns can be found by OS-NAPping to points E and N (Figure 5.16).

>
> Command: **ARRAY**
> Select objects: **Window**
> First corner: **17.5,5**   (E)
> Other corner: **23,9**
> 5 found.

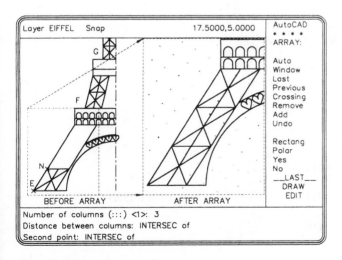

Figure 5.16 Rotated rectangular array

The horizontal line at the bottom of the leg may be selected. If so remove it.

> Select objects: **Remove**
> Remove objects: **20,5**   (point on horizontal line)
> Remove objects: <**ENTER**>
> Rectangular or Polar array (R/P): **R**
> Number of rows (---) <1>: **1**
> Number of columns (|||) <1>: **3**
> Distance between columns: **INTERSEC** of Pick point E.
> Second point: **INTERSEC** of Pick point N.

Now reset the SNAP angle back to zero.

> Command: **SNAP**
> Snap spacing or ON/OFF/Aspect/Rotate/Style <0.5000>: **Rotate**
> Base point <17.5000,5.0000> <**ENTER**>
> Rotation angle <58.00>: **0**
> Command: **Zoom**
> All/Center/Dynamic/Extents/Left/Previous/Window/<Scale(X)>:**A**

Finishing up

The tower is now near completion. All that remains is to copy the mini-arches to the second level and to mirror everything about the centre-line. As this particular operation involves a lot of entities it will be fairly computationally intensive.

> Command: **COPY**
> Select obects: **Window**
> First corner: **24,15**
> Other corner: **26.75,17**
> 18 found.
> Select objects: <**ENTER**>
> <Base point or displacement>/Multiple: **24,15**
> Second point of displacement: **27,22.5**

Before executing any big copying operation you should save the drawing.

> Command: **SAVE**
> File name <EIFFEL>: <**ENTER**>

Now you can mirror the left half of the tower including the text.

> Command: **MIRROR**
> Select objects: **Window**
> First corner: **5,5**
> Other corner: **30,40**
> 132 found.

Only the centre-line and the aerial on the roof should remain solid. If the actual number of objects found on your drawing is much greater than 132 it means that you probably have copied some items onto themselves. Appendix B gives some tips on how to locate and delete such unwanted duplicates.

    Select objects: <**ENTER**>
    First point on mirror line: **30,5**   (A)
    Second point: @**35<90**
    Delete old objects? <N> <**ENTER**>

Again the length of the mirror line doesn't matter, just its location and direction.

Did the text become inverted? AutoCAD supports two modes of mirroring text. The normal mode is for it to be inverted like everything else. Many times this can yield silly results. The second mode which prevents all text from becoming reversed is invoked by setting an AutoCAD system variable. The variable is called MIRRTEXT and when its value is set to zero the mirrored text will not be inverted.

To try this out you need to use the AutoCAD SETVAR (set variables) command.

    Command: **SETVAR**
    Variable name or ?: **MIRRTEXT**
    New value for MIRRTEXT <1>: **0**

If you type "?" at the variable name prompt you will get a full list of all the variables. You don't have to worry about these. All the important ones are introduced in this book.

Now ERASE the inverted text and repeat the MIRROR command for the original text only.

    Command: **ERASE**
    Select objects: **50,15** 1 selected, 1 found.   (top line of text)
    Select objects: **50,12** 1 selected, 1 found.   (bottom line of text)
    Select objects: <**ENTER**>
    Command: **MIRROR**
    Select objects: **10,15** 1 selected, 1 found.   (top line of text)
    Select objects: **10,12** 1 selected, 1 found.   (bottom line of text)
    Select objects: <**ENTER**>
    First point on mirror line: **30,5**
    Second point: @**1<90**
    Delete old objects? <N> <**ENTER**>

Finally, freeze all the layers save EIFFEL.

    Command: **LAYER**
    ?/Make/Set/New/ON/OFF/Color/Ltype/Freeze/Thaw: **Freeze**
    Layer name(s) to Freeze: *

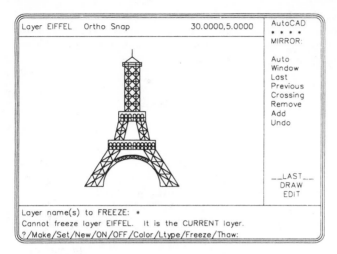

```
Layer EIFFEL    Ortho Snap              30.0000,5.0000   │ AutoCAD
                                                         │ * * * *
                                                         │ MIRROR:
                                                         │
                                                         │ Auto
                                                         │ Window
                                                         │ Last
                                                         │ Previous
                                                         │ Crossing
                                                         │ Remove
                                                         │ Add
                                                         │ Undo
                                                         │
                                                         │
                                                         │
                                                         │ __LAST__
                                                         │ DRAW
                                                         │ EDIT
────────────────────────────────────────────────────────
Layer name(s) to FREEZE: *
Cannot freeze layer EIFFEL.  It is the CURRENT layer.
?/Make/Set/New/ON/OFF/Color/Ltype/Freeze/Thaw:
```

Figure 5.17 The completed Eiffel tower

The asterisk is AutoCAD's wildcard and means all the layers in this case. However, the current layer cannot be frozen and AutoCAD gives the message:

> Cannot freeze layer EIFFEL. It is the CURRENT layer.
> ?/Make/Set/New/ON/OFF/Color/Ltype/Freeze/Thaw: **<ENTER>**

Everything but the actual tower should become invisible as shown in Figure 5.17. Note that the two sets of text also disappear. This is because the MIRROR command preserves the layer of the entity. So even though you were working with EIFFEL as the current layer you could copy things on other layers. Furthermore the copied items are always put on the same layer as their original.

> Command: **END**

Summary

In this chapter you have been introduced to most of AutoCAD's editing commands. Some new aspects of other commands have also been covered.

You should now be able to:

Edit polylines and create smooth curves.
Move, rotate and copy objects within a layer.

Make multiple copies of objects in regular patterns.
Alter text.
Move things from one layer to another.
Change the proportions of objects.
Use the MIRROR command.
Set the MIRRTEXT variable.

Chapter 6 **SUPER-ENTITIES**

General

A number of entities can be grouped together to form a single new super-entity. In a way polylines are super-entities since they cause a number of lines and arcs to be grouped together. AutoCAD provides a more general way of linking objects together to form *blocks*. Blocks are mini-drawings that can be called up or inserted into a drawing at any location and as many times as desired. By compounding entities to form frequently used shapes or symbols AutoCAD can avoid unnecessary duplication of drafting. Blocks can be made globally available to drawings allowing AutoCAD users to build up libraries of complicated shapes which can be easily incorporated into any new drawing. Indeed, the true benefits of AutoCAD only become apparent when you have such libraries set up. Large assembly drawing can be quickly created by inserting the standard details from your library.

Blocks are more than just a stored shape. They can also contain non- drawing information such as a part number or a cost for the item. This extra information can be accessed to provide a bill of materials which could significantly improve the accuracy and speed of your estimates for the job.

The exercise in this chapter uses the fitted kitchen industry to illustrate how to create and use blocks. This will also cover adding text information to blocks and extracting this information. While making up some suitable objects for AutoCAD Express Kitchens Ltd you will encounter a couple of new editing commands, FILLET and OFFSET. The chapter finishes off with a look at some of AutoCAD's inquiry commands which give information about the drawing and also about the computer.

Making a block

To start with you should begin a new drawing, calling it KITCHEN. The operating unit for the drawings in this chapter is the millimetre and so the limits must be set for an upper right corner of (6500,4500). The layers should be set up as given in Table 6.1. When this is done and the snap, grid and axis are set you can begin on the first block. This is to be the symbol for a door and comprises some lines and an arc.

Table 6.1 Layer setting for drawing KITCHEN

Layer Name	State	Colour	Linetype
0	On	7 (white)	CONTINUOUS
FITTINGS	On	7 (white)	CONTINUOUS
CONST	On	2 (yellow)	DASHED

Current layer: 0

```
Command: LIMITS
ON/OFF/<Lower left corner> <0.0000,0.0000>: <ENTER>
Upper right corner <12.0000,9.0000>: 6500,4500
Command: <ENTER>
LIMITS
ON/OFF/<Lower left corner> <0.0000,0.0000>: ON
Command: ZOOM
All/Center/Dynamic/Extents/Left/Previous/Window/<Scale(X)>: All
```

Now set the snap value to 100 with the grid at 200 and axes at 500.

```
Command: SNAP
Snap spacing or ON/OFF/Aspect/Rotate/Style <1.0000>: 100
Command: GRID
Grid spacing(X) or ON/OFF/Snap/Aspect <0.0000>: 2X
Command: AXIS
Tick spacing(X) or ON/OFF/Snap/Aspect <0.0000>: 5X
```

A standard size door in a dwelling house has an opening approximately 800mm wide. Allowing for the frame, the door itself will make an arc with a radius of 750mm (Figure 6.1).

```
Command: LINE
From point: 1000,1000                                          (A)
To point: @25,0                                               (B)
To point: @0,750                                              (C)
To point: <ENTER>
Command: ARC
Center/<Start point>: @          (This selects the last point, C.)
Center/End/<Second point>: C              (The centre point, B.)
Center: 1025,1000            (The intersection of the two lines.)
Angle/Length of chord/<End point>: Angle
Included angle: -90
```

The negative angle is required since the positive direction for angles is anti-clockwise.

> Command: **LINE**
> From point: **1800,1000**   (D)
> To point: **@-25,0**   (E)
> To point: **<ENTER>**

This is a door which is hinged on its left hand side. The arc indicates the area swept by the door as it is opened. The assembly is now ready for BLOCKing (Figure 6.1). Pick **BLOCKS** from the root menu and then pick **BLOCK:**. The colon after a menu item means that it is an executable command. You will then be prompted for a name for the block, an insertion base point and after that you select the objects to be included in the block. The insertion base point is the reference point on the object by which it will be located. It is in effect the origin point for the block.

> Command: **BLOCK**
> Block name (or ?): **DOOR**

The rules for naming bocks are the same as for naming LAYERS: up to 31 characters long containing letters, numbers and the characters "$", "-" and "__". No spaces are allowed in the block name.

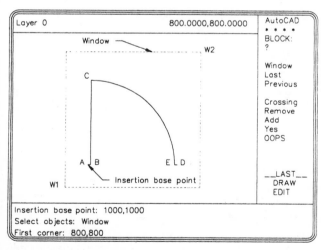

Figure 6.1 Blocking the door

Insertion base point: **1000,1000**   (The left hand end of the door, A.)
Select objects: **Window**
First corner: **800,800**   (W1)
Other corner: **2000,2000**   (W2)
4 found.

The four objects, three lines and an arc should become ghosted indicating that
they have been selected. End the selection procedure.

Select objects: **<ENTER>**

All four objects should now disappear from the screen, leaving only the blips
marking the window corners. To check that it is still part of the drawing,
execute the BLOCK command once more and reply to the block name prompt
with a "?". This will give a list of all the blocks in the current drawing. If you
wish to restore the objects that have disappeared use the
OOPS command.

Command: **<ENTER>**
BLOCK Block name (or ?): **?**

The screen flips to text mode giving the information:

Defined blocks.

DOOR

1 user blocks, 0 unnamed blocks.

Block information.

Press the **F1** key to restore the graphics screen. Any block that is listed can be
INSERTed in the drawing as described in the next section.

Inserting blocks

To draw the block pick **LAST** on the BLOCK: menu and then pick **INSERT:**.
This is almost the reverse of the blocking procedure. You are asked for a block
name to insert and where to place its insertion base point. There is considerable
flexibility with inserting blocks. You can position it anywhere. You can alter its
scale in either the X or Y direction and also change its orientation.

Command: **INSERT**
Block name (or ?): **DOOR**

If the DRAGMODE is on you should now be able to drag the image of the door around the drawing. If the door doesn't appear as you move the cursor then type **DRAG** followed by pressing **<ENTER>** in response to the insertion point prompt. You can then position the door either by picking a point or by typing the coordinates.

> Insertion point: **DRAG <ENTER> 2000,2000**

As soon as you input the insertion point the command prompts you for a scale factor to be applied in the X direction. The door may seem to disappear at this stage or it may be magnified on the screen. This is because AutoCAD is using the position of the cursor to calculate the scale factor. If the cursor is moved from (2000,2000) to (2100,2000) the scale factor is being taken as 100. In most cases it is safest to input the scale factor by keying in the number. The default scale factor is 1 which will draw the block at the same size as when it was defined. Press **<ENTER>** to accept the default.

> X scale factor <1>/Corner/XYZ: **<ENTER>**
> Y scale factor (default=X): **<ENTER>**

A different Y scale can be used to elongate or squash the object. The default situation is to use the same scale factor for both X and Y. Finally, you are asked for a rotation angle. A non-zero angle will cause the door to be rotated about its insertion point. You can also use the cursor to drag the door into the desired orientation. For this example press **<ENTER>** for zero rotation.

> Rotation angle <0>: **<ENTER>**

The door should now appear in a position similar to "Xscale 1, Yscale=1, angle=0" in Figure 6.2. If it didn't, try the command again but this time type all the responses fully. If you use the keyboard arrows to position the cursor then pressing **<ENTER>** picks the cursor location and not the default value.

To insert a door with the hinge on the right hand side use an X scale of −1 and Y scale of +1.

> Command: **<ENTER>**
> INSERT Block name (or ?) <DOOR>: **<ENTER>**

The last block name to be inserted is offered as the default.

> Insertion point: **DRAG <ENTER> 4000,2000**
> X scale factor <1>/Corner/XYZ: **−1**
> Y scale factor (default=X): **1**
> Rotation angle <0>: **<ENTER>**

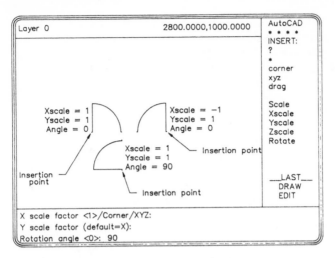

Figure 6.2 Inserting doors

Finally, to insert a door at right angles to the other two use a rotation angle of 90 degrees (positive = anti-clockwise).

> Command: **<ENTER>**
> INSERT Block name (or ?) <DOOR>: **<ENTER>**
> Insertion point: **2800,1000**
> X scale factor <1>/Corner/XYZ: **<ENTER>**
> Y scale factor (default=X): **<ENTER>**
> Rotation angle <0>: **90**

Global blocks

As mentioned above, blocks can be considered as mini-drawings. The converse is also true. Drawings themselves can be considered as large blocks. Indeed a whole drawing can be inserted into the current drawing using INSERT in the normal way. Instead of giving a block name you give the drawing file name (and the DOS path if it is in another DOS directory but without the ".DWG" extension). The insertion base point will be normally be the origin but can be set to any point. Thus, all drawings are also blocks. As they are available to be inserted in any other drawing I call this type of block the "global block".

Blocks created in the same way as the DOOR above are only available within the drawing in which they were defined. They can be converted into global blocks, available to all drawings by using the **WBLOCK** command. This makes a copy of the block to a standard AutoCAD drawing file. WBLOCKs retain their layer, colour and linetype settings. To write the DOOR block to a drawing file called WDOOR.DWG use the following command sequence.

> Command: **WBLOCK**
> File name: **WDOOR**
> Block name: **DOOR**

The block is copied to WDOOR.DWG. The original is still intact in the current drawing. Only layers that are actually used in the block are retained in WDOOR. In this case all the entities were drawn on layer 0. Normally when a WBLOCK or BLOCK is inserted it will be put on layer names defined by the drawing or BLOCK. Thus if a block was originally created on the FITTINGS layer it will always be inserted on that layer. If the receiving drawing doesn't already have a layer called FITTINGS one will be created automatically. The one exception to this is a block created on layer 0. Such blocks will always be inserted onto the receiving drawing's current layer.

Inserting a global block is much the same process as that described above. Use the INSERT command and give the WBLOCK name, ie "WDOOR", as the block name and proceed as before. You don't include the ".DWG" extension in the block name. As long as there is no block called "WDOOR" already in the drawing AutoCAD will search the current DOS directory for the drawing "WDOOR.DWG".

As a corollary to WBLOCK insertion, any AutoCAD drawing file can be INSERTed in another drawing. You simply give the drawing name at the "Block name:" prompt and carry on as usual. The insertion base point will be the origin of the external drawing unless a different base point has been specially specified. When creating a drawing to be used later as a block you can set a suitable base point with the BASE command. For example, to set the point (100,100) as the insertion base point of a drawing you would use the following command sequence:

> Command: **BASE** Base point <0.0000,0.0000>: **100,100**

To set the base point back to the origin use the command once more.

> Command: **BASE** Base point <100.0000,100.0000>: **0,0**

Making a library of useful symbols

The main items in a small modern fitted kitchen are the sink or basin, the cooker, refrigerator or fridge-freezer, washing machine, dishwasher, storage units and worktops. There are of course many more items that could be included but those mentioned will suffice to illustrate the different block definition methods and also some new editing commands.

Before starting on the rest of the symbols, delete all the doors that you inserted above and change to the FITTINGS layer.

> Command: **ERASE**
> Select objects: **Window**
> First corner: **0,0**
> Other corner: **6500,4500**
> 3 found.
> Select objects: **<ENTER>**
> Command: **LAYER**
> ?/Make/Set/New/ON/OFF/Color/Ltype/Freeze/Thaw: **S**
> New current layer <0>: **FITTINGS**
> ?/Make/Set/New/ON/OFF/Color/Ltype/Freeze/Thaw: **<ENTER>**

Note that in the selection, 3 objects were found. Each block is considered by AutoCAD as a single object.

The kitchen sink

To draw the double drainer sink use the LINE command. A rectangular ARRAY can be used to draw the drainers. The curved corners of the basin are formed by filleting the rectangle. You might find it useful to zoom in using a window from (800,800) to approximately (2800,2200).

> Command: LINE
> From point: **1000,1000**   (A)
> To point: @**1500,0**   (B)
> To point: @**0,600**   (C)
> To point: @**−1500,0**   (D)
> To point: **CLOSE**

The basin is another rectangle.

> Command: **<ENTER>**
> LINE From point: **1500,1100**   (E)
> To point: @**500,0**   (F)
> To point: @**0,400**   (G)
> To point: @**-500,0**   (H)
> To point: **CLOSE**

And the drainer is made up of parallel lines.

> Command: **<ENTER>**
> LINE From point: **1100,1100**   (J)
> To point: @**300,0**   (K)
> To point: **<ENTER>**

The sink is taking shape and should look like Figure 6.3(a). The rest of the drainer can be made by using a 5 row by 2 column array as shown in Figure 6.3(b).

Command: **ARRAY**
Select objects: **LAST**

This picks up the last line JK.

Select objects: <**ENTER**>
Rectangular or Polar array (R/P): **R**
Number of rows (---) <1>: 5
Number of columns (¦¦¦) <1>: 2
Unit cell or distance between rows (---): **100**
Distance between columns (¦¦¦): **1000**

Now to round off the corners on the basin use the FILLET command. With this command you can replace the sharp intersections between lines and other entities with a circular arc with a given radius. The arc will be drawn so as to be tangential to both intersecting objects. **FILLET** can be picked from the EDIT menu.

Command: **FILLET**
Polyline/Radius/<Select two objects>: **RADIUS**
Enter fillet radius <0.0000>: **50**

This sets the radius for the fillet arcs. You only have to set the radius once and it will remain at that value until it is changed by another **FILLET** command. To

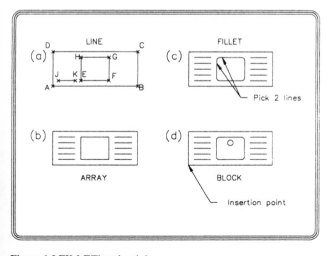

Figure 6.3 FILLETing the sink

operate on the lines pick FILLET once more or press <**ENTER**>. When picking the intersecting lines with the mouse try to pick points near the intersection (see Figure 6.3c).

> Command: **FILLET**
> Polyline/Radius/<Select two objects>: Pick line HE near point E
>   and then pick EF near E.

Now repeat this for the other three corners (points F, G and H). Finally, add the drainage hole using a circle.

> Command: **CIRCLE**
> 3P/2P/TTR/<Center point>: **1750,1400**
> Diameter/<Radius>: **50**

This completes the double drainer sink. All that remains is to make it into a block. Use the lower left corner as the insertion base point. When everything has been successfully exit from the "select objects" procedure by pressing <**ENTER**> once more.

> Command: **BLOCK**
> Block name (or ?): **SINK**
> Insertion base point: **1000,1000**
> Select objects: **Window**
> First corner: **1000,1000**
> Other corner: @**1500,600**
> 23 found.
> Select objects: <**ENTER**>

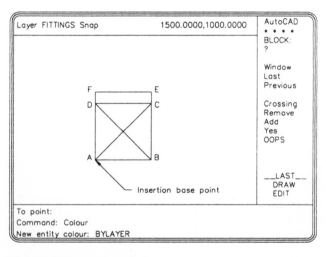

Figure 6.4 Fridge-freezer block

Coloured blocks

As blocks are inserted onto the layer names that they were created on, they will take up the colour of that layer. This means that if you change the colour of layer FITTINGS to blue and insert the SINK block it will be drawn blue. In many instances symbols or blocks have meaningful colours which we would like to keep constant, irrespective of the colour setting of the layer. In this section a fridge-freezer block (Figure 6.4) will be defined to have a constant blue colour and a cooker block will be partly defined as red in the following section.

The colour of an AutoCAD entity can be defined by its layer or may be specially set using the COLOUR command. Set the entity colour to blue and draw the fridge block.

Command: **COLOUR**	
New entity color: **BLUE**	
Command: **LINE**	
From point: **1000,1000**	(A)
To point: **@500,0**	(B)
To point: **@0,500**	(C)
To point: **@−500,0**	(D)
To point: **@0,−500**	(A)
To point: **@500,500**	(C)
To point: **@0,100**	(E)
To point: **@−500,0**	(F)
To point: **@0,−100**	(D)
To point: **@500,−500**	(B)
To point: **<ENTER>**	
Command: **COLOUR**	
New entity color: **BYLAYER**	

This completes the fridge-freezer in blue. Always reset the colour back to "BYLAYER" when finished with the special colour. This means that new entities will be drawn in the default colour assigned to the layer.

Now to group the entities into a block.

Command: **BLOCK**
Block name (or ?): **FFREEZER**
Insertion base point: **1000,1000**
Select objects: **Window**
First corner: **1000,1000**
Other corner: **@500,600**
9 found.
Select objects: **<ENTER>**

Editing a block

To draw the cooker use the normal colour for the outline and red circles for the cooking elements. The array command can be used to copy the elements. For convenience you can edit the fridge-freezer block. To do this you will have to insert the block and break it down into its constituent entities. The EXPLODE command does just that.

> Command: **INSERT**
> Block name (or ?) <DOOR>: **FFREEZER**
> Insertion point: **1000,1000**
> X scale factor <1>/Corner/XYZ: <**ENTER**>
> Y scale factor (default=X): <**ENTER**>
> Rotation angle <0>: <**ENTER**>
> Command: **EXPLODE**
> Select block reference, polyline, or dimension: **LAST**

EXPLODE only works on blocks that have equal X and Y scale factors. It can be used to break up polylines as well.

Now use the change command to set the colours to "bylayer" and then erase the diagonal lines.

> Command: **CHANGE**
> Select objects: **Window**
> First corner: **1000,1000**
> Other corner: **@500,600**
> 9 found.

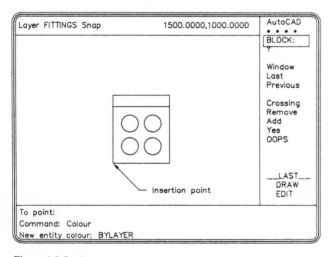

Figure 6.5 Cooker block

Select objects: <**ENTER**>
Properties/<Change point>: **P**
Change what property (Color/Elev/LAyer/LType/Thickness)? **C**
New colour <5 (blue)>: **BYLAYER**
Change what property (Color/Elev/LAyer/LType/Thickness)?
   <**ENTER**>
Command: **ERASE**
Select objects: **1100,1100**
1 selected, 1 found.
Select objects: **1400,1100**
1 selected, 1 found.
Select objects: <**ENTER**>

Now set the colour red and draw the cooking rings.

Command: **COLOUR**
New entity color <BYLAYER>: **RED**
Command: **CIRCLE**
3P/2P/TTR/<Center point>: 1150,1150
Diameter/<Radius>: **75**
Command: **ARRAY**
Select objects: **LAST**
Select objects: <**ENTER**>
Rectangular or Polar array (R/P): **R**
Number of rows (---) <1>: **2**
Number of columns (¦¦¦) <1>: **2**
Unit cell or distance between rows (---): **200**
Distance between columns (¦¦¦): **200**

This should now look like the picture in Figure 6.5. The only way to edit part of
a block is to decompose it completely into the original entities. One way of
achieving this is to EXPLODE it as above. A similar effect results by prefixing
the block name with an asterisk when inserting it.
For example:

Command: INSERT
Block name (or ?) <DOOR>: *FFREEZER
Insertion point: 1000,1000
Scale factor <1>: <ENTER>
Rotation angle <0>: <ENTER>

This gives the same result as the INSERT and EXPLODE used above. This
method can only be used when actualy inserting a block. EXPLODE can be
used on a block at any time after it has been inserted.

Now to block the cooker.

    Command: **BLOCK**
    Block name (or ?): **COOKER**
    Insertion base point: **1000,1000**
    Select objects: **Window**
    First corner: @
    Other corner: @**500,600**
    11 found.
    Select objects: <**ENTER**>
    Command: **COLOUR**
    New entity color <1 (red)>: **BYLAYER**

One must be careful when defining special colours for blocks or parts of blocks. As blocks can be nested within other blocks it can become difficult to keep track of the colours. The best policy is to keep the colouring of blocks as simple as possible and to use special colour settings sparingly.

There is one other colour setting that has not been discussed so far. For blocks that are made up of entities on different layers, the BYBLOCK colour option can be used. This forces all the entities making up the block to have the same colour (whatever colour the block is set to). This is irrespective of the colour settings of the individual layer and is the converse of having a multi-colour block on one layer.

Finally, all of the rules given above for the COLOUR command can be equally applied to the LINETYP command. LINETYP can be used to override the Ltype settings on individual layers. It works in exactly the same way as COLOUR.

Assigning text information to blocks

One of the strongest reasons for using blocks on AutoCAD drawings is that extra non-graphic information can be assigned to the blocks. Furthermore, the attribute information attached to a block can be varied each time the block is inserted. All this information can be gathered together and written to an external file which can then be transferred to a bill of materials program to extract quantities and cost estimates.

In this section a simple attribute will be defined for an electrical appliance block. This will identify what type of appliance has been inserted. Attributes will also be defined for cupboard units and worktop finishes.

Defining an attribute

An attribute is treated by AutoCAD like any other drawing entity. Once it has been defined it can be included with other entities to form a block. To create the electrical appliance block, first draw its outline.

Command: **LINE**
From point: **1000,1000**
To point: **@600,0**
To point: **@0,500**
To point: **@−600,0**
To point: **close**

Now include hot and cold inlet pipes and the waste outlet point at the back of the box.

Command: **LINE**
From point: **1100,1500**
To point: **@0,100**
To point: **<ENTER>**
Command: **<ENTER>**
LINE From point: **1200,1500**
To point: **@0,100**
To point: **<ENTER>**
Command: **<ENTER>**
LINE From point: **1200,1500**
To point: **@0,100**
To point: **<ENTER>**

Now to define the attribute pick **BLOCKS** from the root menu and then pick **ATTDEF:**.

Command: **ATTDEF**
Attribute modes -- Invisible:N Constant:N Verify:N Preset:N
Enter (ICVP) to change, RETURN when done: **V**

This allows you to reset the verify mode. This means that when the block is inserted you will be asked to verify that the value of the attribute is correct. All the other modes are okay for this block. It will not be invisible, constant, or preset but will be verified.

Attribute modes – Invisible:N Constant:N Verify:Y Preset:N
Enter (ICVP) to change, RETURN when done: **<ENTER>**
Attribute tag: **APPLIANCE__TYPE**

The attribute tag is the name for that attribute and will be used by AutoCAD to identify it. Any characters can be used for the tag except blank spaces.

Attribute prompt: **Enter appliance type**
Default attribute value: **W.M.**

The prompt is the message that will be displayed when the block is being inserted. It should be clear so that others using your library of blocks can understand what is required of them. The default value will be offered in

AutoCAD's usual way. The "W.M." stands for washing machine; the alternative will be "D.W." for dishwasher. You can use more descriptive attribute values if you wish. The command then asks for the start point of the attribute text in a similar fashion to the TEXT command. Position it centrally in the appliance box and use a large text height to make it visible.

> Start point or Align/Center/Fit/Middle/Right/Style: **C**
> Center point: **1300,1100**
> Height <0.20>: **140**
> Rotation angle <0>: **<ENTER>**

The text "APPLIANCE__TYPE" should be written across the box. This will be replaced by the actual attribute value when the block has been created and inserted. To create the block with the attribute, pick LAST from the ATTDEF menu and then pick **BLOCK:**. Select the objects for inclusion using a window big enough to surround the attribute as well.

> Command: **BLOCK**
> Block name (or ?): **APPLIANCE**
> Insertion base point: **1000,1000**
> Select objects: **Window**
> First corner: **300,700**
> Other corner: **2400,1900**
> 8 found.
> Select objects: **<ENTER>**

Now to check that it works insert it at (1000,1000). If you are confronted with the Attribute Dialogue Box, similar to the one shown in Figure 6.14, just pick the **OK** box to proceed. To disable the dialogue box reset the system variable, ATTDIA, to 0 using the SETVAR command.

> Command: **INSERT**
> Block name (or ?) <FFREEZER>: **APPLIANCE**
> Insertion point: **1000,1000**
> X scale factor <1>/Corner/XYZ: **<ENTER>**
> Y scale factor (default=X): **<ENTER>**
> Rotation angle <0>: **<ENTER>**
> Enter attribute values
> Enter appliance type <W.M.>: **<ENTER>**
> Verify attribute values
> Enter appliance type <W.M.>: **<ENTER>**

The block should now be inserted with the "W.M." written in it. Try inserting it again but give "D.W." as the attribute value. You should get something like Figure 6.6. Using attributes in this way saves having to define different blocks for each type of large electrical appliance.

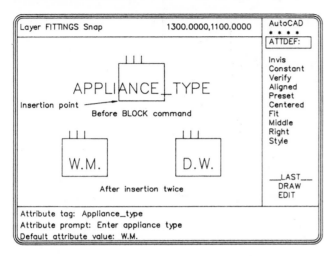

Figure 6.6 Electrical appliance blocks with attributes

The attributes of a block can be invisible. This is useful when the text is not relevant to the actual picture or if it would crowd the drawing too much. In the following sequence you will define a block for the cupboard units with an invisible attribute giving information on the number of doors on the unit. As blocks can have more than one attribute you can also include an attribute for the type of finish the customer requires on the unit.

The standard unit size is 500mm wide by 600mm deep. Two units can be joined to form a double, etc. Draw the unit using a polyline this time and use a thicker line to indicate the side with the door. Be sure to **ERASE** all the copies of the APPLIANCE block you have just inserted.

Command: **PLINE**
From point: **1000,1000**
Current line-width is 0.0000
Arc/Close/Halfwidth/Length/Undo/Width/<Endpoint of line>:
    @600<90
Arc/Close/Halfwidth/Length/Undo/Width/<Endpoint of line>:
    @500,0
Arc/Close/Halfwidth/Length/Undo/Width/<Endpoint of line>:
    @0,−600
Arc/Close/Halfwidth/Length/Undo/Width/<Endpoint of line>:
    Width
Starting width <0.0000>: **25**
Ending width <25.0000>: **<ENTER>**
Arc/Close/Halfwidth/Length/Undo/Width/<Endpoint of line>:
    CLOSE

Now define the first attribute for the number of doors in the unit.

> Command: **ATTDEF**
> Attribute modes – Invisible:N Constant:N Verify:Y Preset:N
> Enter (ICVP) to change, RETURN when done: **I**

This will make the attribute invisible. The verify setting is the same as the last block.

> Attribute modes – Invisible:Y Constant:N Verify:Y Preset:N
> Enter (ICVP) to change, RETURN when done: **<ENTER>**
> Attribute tag: **DOORS**
> Attribute prompt: **Enter the number of doors in unit (1,2 or 3)**
> Default attribute value: **1**
> Start point or Align/Center/Fit/Middle/Right/Style: **C**
> Center point: **1250,1400**
> Height <0.20>: **140**
> Rotation angle <0>: **<ENTER>**

Now repeat this for the surface finish attribute.

> Command: **ATTDEF**
> Attribute modes – Invisible:Y Constant:N Verify:Y Preset:N
> Enter (ICVP) to change, RETURN when done: **<ENTER>**
> Attribute tag: **FINISH**
> Attribute prompt: **Enter the type of surface finish**
> Default attribute value: **OAK**
> Start point or Align/Center/Fit/Middle/Right/Style: **C**
> Center point: **1250,1100**
> Height <0.20>: **140**
> Rotation angle <0>: **<ENTER>**

You are ready to make the block now.

> Command: **BLOCK**
> Block name (or ?): **CUPBOARD**
> Insertion base point: **1000,1000**
> Select objects: **Window**
> First corner: **300,300**
> Other corner: **1900,1900**
> 3 found.
> Select objects: **<ENTER>**

When you insert this block later you will be prompted for the two attributes. The order will be the reverse of the definition, ie you will be prompted for the surface finish first. The block will be drawn with both attributes invisible

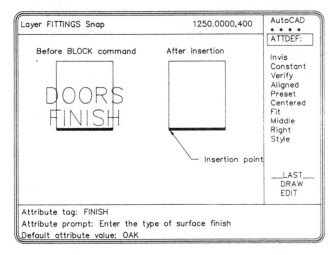

Figure 6.7 The cupboard with two attributes

(Figure 6.7). You can experiment with inserting this block or wait for the next part of the exercise in which all the blocks will be used to assemble the AutoCAD Express Fitted Kitchen. Be sure to **ERASE** everything before proceeding.

To get a listing of all the blocks in the drawing you can use the "?" option with either the BLOCK or INSERT commands. The display will flip to text mode and give the names.

> Command: **BLOCK**
> Block name (or ?): **?**

> Defined blocks.
> DOOR
> SINK
> FFREEZER
> COOKER
> APPLIANCE
> CUPBOARD
>
> 6 user blocks, 0 unnamed blocks.
>
> Block listing.

To return to the graphics screen press the **F1** key.

Drawing the kitchen

Before inserting all the blocks, let's do the outline of the kitchen. It's only a small kitchen with a simple shape. This should be done on layer 0.

> Command: **LAYER**
> ?/Make/Set/New/ON/OFF/Color/Ltype/Freeze/Thaw: **S**
> New current layer <FITTINGS>: **0**
> ?/Make/Set/New/ON/OFF/Color/Ltype/Freeze/Thaw:
>   **<ENTER>**
> Command: **PLINE**
> From point: 1000,1000   (
> Current line-width is 25.0000
> Arc/Close/Halfwidth/Length/Undo/Width/<Endpoint of line>: **Width**
> Starting width <0.0000>: **10**
> Ending width <10.0000>: **<ENTER>**
> Arc/Close/Halfwidth/Length/Undo/Width/<Endpoint of line>: **@3300,0**   (
> Arc/Close/Halfwidth/Length/Undo/Width/<Endpoint of line>: **@0,3100**   (
> Arc/Close/Halfwidth/Length/Undo/Width/<Endpoint of line>: **@−3300,0** (
> Arc/Close/Halfwidth/Length/Undo/Width/<Endpoint of line>: **CLOSE**

Now to draw the outside edge of the wall you can use AutoCAD's OFFSET command. This can be used to draw objects which are the same as the original but offset by a given amount. For example, it can be used to draw parallel lines. The offset command causes offset circles to be concentric with the original and has a similar effect on closed polylines (Figure 6.8). Pick **OFFSET:** from the second page of the EDIT menu. You will then be asked for an offest distance, which will be the thickness of the wall. Then you must select the object to offset by picking it or giving a point on it. Finally you must choose on which side of the original to place the offset.

> Command: **OFFSET**
> Offset distance or Through <Through> **100**
> Select object to offset: **1000,1000**   (A)
> Side to offset: **900,1000**   (E)

This picks a point on the outside of the original rectangle. AutoCAD then asks for another object to offset. Press **<ENTER>** to exit the command.

> Select object to offset: **<ENTER>**

Note that you cannot use window, crossing or last to select the object to offset despite the appearance of the "last" on the screen menu.

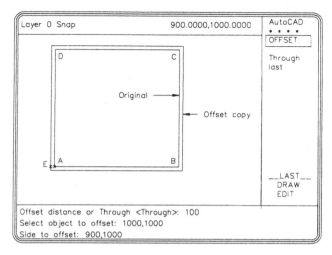

Figure 6.8 Offsetting a closed polyline

Now that the walls are up we must break through some door openings. This introduces another AutoCAD editing command, BREAK.

Command: **ZOOM**
All/Center/Dynamic/Extents/Left/Previous/Window/<Scale(X)>: **W**
First corner: **500,500**
Other corner: **3000,2400**
Command: **BREAK**
Select object: **1000,1200**   (F)
Enter second point (or F for first point): **@0,800**   (G)

This breaks an 800mm opening from point F to G (Figure 6.9). The first point had the dual purpose of selecting the object and indicating the start of the break. Sometimes it is not convenient to select the object at the actual break point. In such a case you would use the "F" reply at the second prompt above. For example, to break the outside polyline use the following sequence:

Command: **<ENTER>**
BREAK Select object: **900,1600**
Enter second point (or F for first point): **F**
Enter first point: **900,2000**   (H)
Enter second point: **@0,−800**   (J)

This achieves a similar result and allows you extra flexibility in selecting the object. This can be particularly useful when two objects intersect at the desired break point. AutoCAD may select the wrong object if you pick the intersection point. BREAK can also be used on lines, circles and arcs.

The final stage in making the opening is to draw the two short polylines.

```
Command: PLINE
From point: 900,1200                                               (J)
Current line-width is 10.0000
Arc/Close/Halfwidth/Length/Undo/Width/<Endpoint of line>:
   @100,0                                                         (F)
Arc/Close/Halfwidth/Length/Undo/Width/<Endpoint of line>:
   <ENTER>
Command: <ENTER>
PLINE
From point: 900,2000                                               (H)
Arc/Close/Halfwidth/Length/Undo/Width/<Endpoint of line>:
   @100,0                                                         (G)
Arc/Close/Halfwidth/Length/Undo/Width/<Endpoint of line>:
   <ENTER>
```

ZOOM to the opposite corner and insert another door opening and a window. Break the door from (4400,2700) to (4400,3500) and draw the window from (1600,4150) to (3600,4150). Repeat the breaks for the inside polyline and then join up all the loose ends (Figure 6.10).

```
Command: ZOOM
All/Center/Dynamic/Extents/Left/Previous/Window/<Scale(X)>: W
First corner: 1500,2000
Other corner: 4600,4400
Command: BREAK
Select object: 4400,2700                                          (K)
Enter second point (or F for first point): @0,800                 (L)
Command: <ENTER>
BREAK Select object: 4300,2700                                    (M)
Enter second point (or F for first point): @0,800                 (N)
```

To join up the loose ends draw four more polylines.

```
Command: PLINE
From point: 4300,2700                                              (M)
Current line-width is 10.0000
Arc/Close/Halfwidth/Length/Undo/Width/<Endpoint of line>:
   @100,0                                                         (K)
Arc/Close/Halfwidth/Length/Undo/Width/<Endpoint of line>:
   <ENTER>
Command: <ENTER>
PLINE
From point: 4300,3500                                              (N)
Current line-width is 10.0000
```

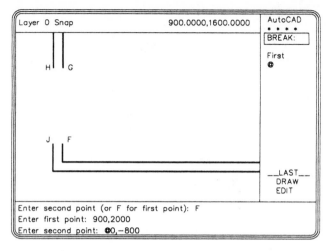

Figure 6.9 Breaking a polyline

Arc/Close/Halfwidth/Length/Undo/Width/<Endpoint of line>:
    @**100,0**   (L)
Arc/Close/Halfwidth/Length/Undo/Width/<Endpoint of line>:
    <ENTER>
Command: **<ENTER>**
PLINE
From point: **1600,4100**   (P)
Current line-width is 10.0000
Arc/Close/Halfwidth/Length/Undo/Width/<Endpoint of line>:
    @**0,100**   (Q)
Arc/Close/Halfwidth/Length/Undo/Width/<Endpoint of line>:
    <ENTER>
Command: **<ENTER>**
PLINE
From point: **3600,4100**   (R)
Current line-width is 10.0000
Arc/Close/Halfwidth/Length/Undo/Width/<Endpoint of line>:
    @**0,100**   (S)
Arc/Close/Halfwidth/Length/Undo/Width/<Endpoint of line>:
    <ENTER>

Now draw the window as a horizontal line.

Command: **LINE**
From point: **1600,4150**   (Mid pt of line PQ.)
To point: @**2000,0**   (Mid pt of line RS.)
To point: **<ENTER>**
Command: **ZOOM**
All/Center/Dynamic/Extents/Left/Previous/Window/<Scale(X)>: **ALL**

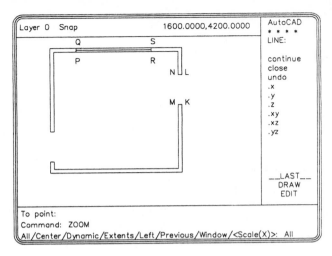

Figure 6.10 The empty kitchen

Assembling the fitted kitchen

Assembling the fittings and fixtures of the kitchen is now just a matter of inserting all the blocks in their correct locations. If the customer wants things moved around then that's no problem with AutoCAD. You don't have to change layers when inserting as each block automatically goes to its layer of origin (in this case the FITTINGS layer).

Insert the sink first with a view out the window.

> Command: **INSERT**
> Block name (or ?) <CUPBOARD>: **SINK**
> Insertion point: 1600,3500
> X scale factor <1>/Corner/XYZ: <**ENTER**>
> Y scale factor (default=X): <**ENTER**>
> Rotation angle <0>: <**ENTER**>

Now put the washing machine and dishwasher beside the sink (Figure 6.11).

> Command: **INSERT**
> Block name (or ?) <SINK>: **APPLIANCE**
> Insertion point: **3100,3500**
> X scale factor <1>/Corner/XYZ: <**ENTER**>
> Y scale factor (default=X): <**ENTER**>
> Rotation angle <0>: <**ENTER**>
> Enter appliance type <W.M.>: <**ENTER**>
> Verify attribute values
> Enter appliance type <W.M.>: <**ENTER**>

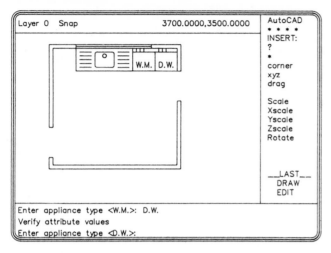

Figure 6.11 Appliances in position

Command: **INSERT**
Block name (or ?) <APPLIANCE>: <**ENTER**>
Insertion point: **3700,3500**
X scale factor <1>/Corner/XYZ: <**ENTER**>
Y scale factor (default=X): <**ENTER**>
Rotation angle <0>: <**ENTER**>
Enter appliance type <W.M.>: **D.W.**
Verify attribute values
Enter appliance type <D.W.>: <**ENTER**>

The rest of the block information is given in tabular form. Use the INSERT command and the appropriate responses taken from Table 6.2. Figure 6.12 shows the fitted kitchen.

Table 6.2 Block insertion parameters

Block name	Insertion point	X scale	Y scale	Rotation	Attribute values
FFREEZER	3700,2600	1	1	-90	
COOKER	1600,2600	1	1	90	
CUPBOARD	1600,3100	2	1	90	PINE, 1
CUBBOARD	1600,2100	1	1	90	PINE, 1
CUPBOARD	3700,2100	2.2	1	-90	PINE, 2
CUPBOARD	3700,1600	3	1	180	PINE, 3
DOOR	950,2000	1	1	-90	
DOOR	4350,2700	-1	1	90	

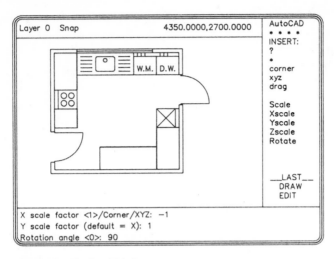

```
Layer 0   Snap                    4350.0000,2700.0000    AutoCAD
                                                         • • • •
                                                         INSERT:
                                                         ?
                                                         *
                                                         corner
                                                         xyz
                                                         drag

                                                         Scale
                                                         Xscale
                                                         Yscale
                                                         Zscale
                                                         Rotate



                                                         __LAST__
                                                         DRAW
                                                         EDIT

X scale factor <1>/Corner/XYZ: −1
Y scale factor (default = X): 1
Rotation angle <0>: 90
```

Figure 6.12 The fitted kitchen

Editing attributes

The first thing to do now is to check that all the attributes on the drawing are in fact correct. To make the invisible attributes appear on the drawing pick **DISP-LAY** from the root menu and then pick **ATTDISP**. This command allows you to alter the display setting for all the attributes in the drawing. The normal display mode is that only attributes defined as visible are shown. Setting ATTDISP to ON causes all attributes to become visible irrespective of their definition. ATTDISP OFF would cause all to become invisible.

> Command: **ATTDISP**
> Normal/ON/OFF <Normal>: **ON**

From Figure 6.13 the cupboard in the lower right hand corner has 2 doors. Since it is in the corner, one of these doors will be blocked by the other cupboard. To save the customer unnecessary expense only one door should be provided. Thus the attribute must be edited. The easiest way to do this is to use the pull-down menus and the ATTEDIT dialogue box.

Pick **EDIT** from the menu bar at the top of the screen. Then pick the **Attedit** or **Edit** attribute option. This causes the DDATTE command to be executed and you are prompted to select the block to edit.

> Command: DDATTE
> Select block: **3700,1900**

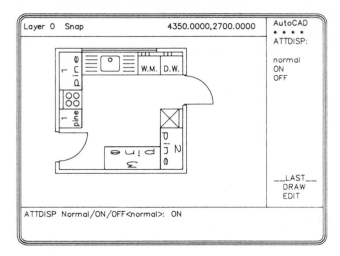

Figure 6.13 ATTDISP set ON

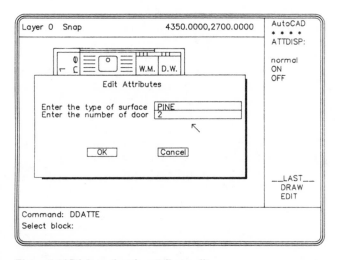

Figure 6.14 Dialogue box for attribute edits

The dialogue box shown in Figure 6.14 should then appear. This gives the two attribute values and their prompts. To change the 2 doors to 1 move the arrow cursor until the rectangle containing the 2 goes into reverse video. When this happens key in **1** and pick the **OK** box at the right of the rectangle. To execute this change pick the **OK** box at the bottom of the dialogue screen. When the dialogue box disappears the "2" in the block will be changed to "1".

To set the attribute display back to normal use ATTDISP once more.

Command: **ATTDISP**
Normal/ON/OFF <ON>: **Normal**

This dialogue box can also be used during block insertion if the AutoCAD system variable, ATTDIA is set to 1. A value of zero disables it. It is usually quicker to insert blocks without the dialogue box. Use the SETVAR command to control this variable.

A simple bill of materials

Information about all blocks that have attributes can be extracted from the drawing and output to a text file. The text file could then be incorporated in a report, a spreadsheet or a bill of quantities. There are three ways to extract this information, using AutoCAD's DXF format, a CDF file or an SDF. The easiest way is to use a template file to control which attributes are required for output to either an SDF or a CDF file.

A CDF file (Comma Delimited File) is an ASCII text file where the block's information fields are separated by commas. In an SDF they are separated by spaces while the DXF file uses AutoCAD's drawing exchange protocol. This latter is of use to program developers but is rather cumbersome.

In order to use the SDF or CDF method you first have to define a template file. This has to be an ASCII file created with a text editor. The file name must have the extension ".TXT. The file given below is suitable for use on the KITCHEN drawing. The comments in brackets should not be included in the actual KITCHEXT.TXT file. The first item on each line is a key-word indicating what is to be extracted, the second gives the format for writing that information to the CDF or SDF file. If the information is a number then the second field should start with "N"; if it is text then "C" should be used. The first three digits after the "C" or "N" indicate how many spaces are to be reserved for that field. The second three indicate how many digits are required after the decimal point. Thus "N007001" would output a number such as "1234.5" but not "1234.56". Always leave one space for a possible minus sign. Make sure that there are no blank lines in the template file.

When you are in the drawing editor with the KITCHEN drawing you can generate the bill of materials using the ATTEXT command.

Command: **ATTEXT**
CDF, SDF or DXF Attribute extract (or Entities)? <C>: S
Template file <>: **KITCHEXT**
Extract file name <KITCHEN>: <**ENTER**>
6 records extracted.

BL:NAME	C010000	(Block name with up to 10 characters)
FINISH	C007000	(Finish attribute with up to 7 characters)
APPLIANCE_TYPE	C007000	(Appl. type attribute with up to 7 characters)
DOORS	N006000	(No. of doors attribute up to 6 digit integer)
BL:XSCALE	N007001	(X scale factor, number with 1 digit after ".")
BL:YSCALE	N007001	(Y scale factor, number with 1 digit after ".")

KITCHEXT.TXT

Now to see the result use the external command TYPE.

Command: **TYPE**
File to list: **KITCHEN.TXT**

APPLIANCE	W.M.	0	1.0	1.0
APPLIANCE	D.W.	0	1.0	1.0
CUPBOARD pine		1	1.0	1.0
CUPBOARD pine		1	2.0	1.0
CUPBOARD pine		1	2.2	1.0
CUPBOARD pine		3	3.0	1.0

KITCHEN.TXT

Only blocks that contain the attributes included in the template file are extracted. The DOOR, SINK COOKER and FFREEZER block don't appear as they have none of the attributes. You can include more information fields, if desired, to extract the insertion points and other data. See the AutoCAD Reference Manual for the full list of key-words. The SDF file is suitable for use with a FORTRAN and some database programs while the CDF format works with BASIC.

Hints on using blocks

Blocks should be used for commonly used shapes and symbols. You can build up a library of symbols in the form of WBLOCKS. This is more efficient than using a default drawing that contains many block definitions.

Try to develop a consistent method for naming your blocks and store the WBLOCKS in a separate DOS directory. For example you might create a sub-directory of \ACAD called "\ACAD\SYMBOLS" and include that path in the WBLOCK file name. The more symbols you have the more effort you will have to devote to managing this storage.

Blocks forming part of a symbols library should always contain some attribute definitions. This will enable information about them to be extracted for bill of material purposes.

If a complicated object (containing more than 20 entities) appears more than once in a drawing then BLOCK it and INSERT it as required. This is more efficient than simply copying all the entities, as AutoCAD stores the shape of the block only once. The only other items of information required are the relevant insertion points. This saves memory and disk space.

Avoid using nested blocks if possible. By nested, one means that one block can contain others. This can lead to difficulties if you want to make changes to the block definition at a later date.

AutoCAD's inquiry commands

A number of other information extraction commands are available in the INQUIRY screen menu. These allow you to get the area enclosed by a polyline (AREA command), the distance between two points (DIST command) or the coordinates of a particular point (ID). LIST allows you to find out all the information about any entities. DBLIST gives the same information about *all* the entities in the drawing. As DBLIST can take a long time to scroll through the whole database, it can be interrupted by pressing "^C".

The STATUS command gives a listing of the current drawing status and also the amount of memory available in the computer and on the disk. This is useful for keeping tabs on your hardware and the current AutoCAD default settings. The TIME command tells you the time, according to your computer's internal clock. It also displays the total time spent editing the current drawing. This can be helpful for anybody who has to keep time sheets for various projects.

Summary

This chapter has introduced the fundamentals of AutoCAD block creation. Blocks are a useful feature for storing standard symbols. They can be exported from the original drawing and so be made available to other drawings. Some more editing features have been used to create the blocks. Finally, the information extraction facility has been demonstrated.

You should now be able to:

Create blocks and global blocks.
List the names of blocks in a drawing.
Assign text information to blocks and edit it.
Round off corners with the FILLET command.
Offset objects and break gaps in entities.
Alter the entity colour.
Interrogate the drawing database.

Chapter 7 ADVANCED DRAWING AND DIMENSIONING

General

Most of AutoCAD's drawing commands have been covered by now. In this chapter you will discover the reason for creating AutoCAD drawings at full scale. The various dimensioning and measuring commands all calculate their distances in the drawing units. To demonstrate the more important automatic dimensioning facilities you will draw a relatively simple object, a mechanical engineer's gland! In doing this a few more new commands will be introduced. Then the dimensions will be added.

Drawing a gland

Start a new AutoCAD drawing and give it the name "GLAND". Set the LIMITS from (0,0) to (65,45) and make sure that decimal units are being used with 4 places after the decimal point. You will need the layers given in Table 7.1

To begin the drawing put the centre-lines of the circles at convenient locations. Use ^O to turn on the ORTHO mode. If the lines don't appear with dashes change the LTSCALE value.

```
Command: LINE
From point: 13,20                                              (a)
To point: @44,0                                                (b)
To point: <ENTER>
Command: <ENTER>
LINE From point: 35,11                                         (c)
To point: @0,18                                                (d)
To point: <ENTER>
```

Table 7.1 Layer settings for drawing GLAND

Layer name	State	Colour	Linetype
0	On	7 (white)	CONTINUOUS
GLAND	On	7 (white)	CONTINUOUS
CLINE	On	7 (white)	CENTER
DASH	On	7 (white)	DASHED
DIMENSIONS	On	7 (white)	CONTINUOUS
POLYGON	On	7 (white)	CONTINUOUS

Current layer: CLINE

POINT and DIVIDE

These are the major axes for the gland's cylinder (Figure 7.5). The line ab is 44cm long and the distance from the centre of the gland to the bolt holes on either side is 11cm. Thus the quarter points of ab can be used to position the holes. To find the quarter points use the DIVIDE command from the EDIT menu. This can be used to divide a line, arc or polyline into any number of equal segments. Rather than actually break the line into different entities the DIVIDE command inserts AutoCAD POINTs at the relevant intervals (Figure 7.1).

POINTs are drawing entities. Their main use is for marking special locations for object snapping. Object snap "node" jumps to the nearest point entity. These normally appear on the drawing as dots. To create a point entity pick **POINT:** from the second page of the DRAW screen menu. You then give it a location and a dot is drawn. Dots have no dimension and are difficult to see, particularly if the grid is on. AutoCAD gives a number of options for the display of points depending on the setting of a system variable called PDMODE. If PDMODE is zero then dots are drawn, if it is 1 nothing is drawn, 2 gives a cross like a blip, 3 an x and 4 causes a small vertical tick to appear. Pick "Points example:" to see the different point styles. Then pick "remove example:" to get back to the drawing. (You will have to pick the lines with the "example:".) For visibility PDMODE=3, producing x shaped points, is desirable. This can be set by picking **Pdmode:** from the POINT screen menu and giving the new value as **3**. Another setting that affects the visibility of points is the PDSIZE value. This can also be picked from the POINT menu. The default PDSIZE is zero which produces a point size which is a percentage of the screen display. This means that no matter how much you zoom in it will always look the same size. Negative values of PDSIZE also work on a percentage basis, eg -4 implies 4% of the screen size. Non-zero sizes can be specified but are not normally necessary.

> Command: SETVAR Variable name or ? <>: PDMODE
> New value for PDMODE <0>: **3**

Picking Pdmode: from the menu actually runs a little program involving the SETVAR command to change the variable setting. Once Pdmode: is picked from the menu you only have to type the response giving the new value.

Now to divide the line ab into four pick **DIVIDE:** from the EDIT menu. You are then asked for the object to divide. Pick a point on the line ab and give the number of segments as 4.

> Command: **DIVIDE**
> Select object to divide: **16,20**   (Point on ab)
> <Number of segments>/Block: **4**

The "Block" option allows you to insert a named block at the dividing locations instead of points. The points should now appear along the line as shown in Figure 7.1. Another feature of this command is that all the points are put in the "previous" selection set and can be deleted by picking "ERASE" followed by "Previous".

AutoCAD's MEASURE command is very similar to DIVIDE but it puts the point markers at multiples of a specified distance from the end point of the entity. Thus you could use MEASURE to do the same as the above by giving the distance to measure out as 11 units.

> Command: MEASURE
> Select object to measure: 16,20   (Point on ab)
> <Segment length>/Block: 11

This will include as many markers as will fit on the line. In this instance four will be drawn at 11, 22, 33 and 44 units from the point a. It is important to pick the

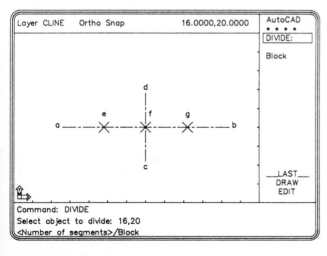

Figure 7.1 Dividing line

line to be measured near to the end you want the measurement to start, particularly if the line length is not a whole multiple of the segment length.

You can now set the OSNAP mode to node to snap the circle centres to the dividing points. Change to layer GLAND and draw circles at the points e, f and g (Figure 7.2). Use diameters of 16, 14, 8, 4 and 2 as given below. Pick CEN,DIA: from the CIRCLE menu.

> Command: **OSNAP**
> Object snap modes: **node**
> Command: **LAYER**
> ?/Make/Set/New/ON/OFF/Color/Ltype/Freeze/Thaw: **S**
> New current layer <CLINE>: **GLAND**
> ?/Make/Set/New/ON/OFF/Color/Ltype/Freeze/Thaw: <**ENTER**>

Three large circles picking **CEN,DIA:**.

> Command: **CIRCLE** 3P/2P/TTR/<Center point>: (Pick point at f)
> Diameter/<Radius>: **D** Diameter: **16**
> Command: **CIRCLE** 3P/2P/TTR/<Center point>: (Pick point at f)
> Diameter/<Radius>: **D** Diameter: **14**
> Command: **CIRCLE** 3P/2P/TTR/<Center point>: (Pick point at f)
> Diameter/<Radius>: **D** Diameter: **8**

Two small circles.

> Command: **CIRCLE** 3P/2P/TTR/<Center point>: (Pick point at e)
> Diameter/<Radius>: **D** Diameter: **4**
> Command: **CIRCLE** 3P/2P/TTR/<Center point>: (Pick point at e)
> Diameter/<Radius>: D Diameter: **2**

You will place the objects at g later using a mirroring operation. Now erase the three dividing points and turn off the OSNAP mode.

> Command: **ERASE**
> Select objects: **Previous**
> 3 found.
> Select objects: <**ENTER**>
> Command: **OSNAP**
> Object snap modes: **NONE**

If the points are not deleted and you get the message "No previous selection set" it is probably because you have used a command that required you to "Select objects:". If you do such a command after the DIVIDE and before the erase then the selection set will be altered. In that case you will have to delete the points individually.

You can build up a selection set of objects for use with the "previous" option in ERASE and other commands. This is done with the SELECT command. The format is just like ERASE but without anything being deleted.

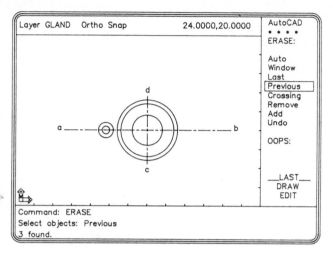

Figure 7.2 Gland circles

Command: **SELECT**
Select objects: Pick objects or use Window, Crossing etc.
Select objects: <**ENTER**>

To draw the flange for the gland, zoom in on the four circles and draw two lines tangential to both of the outer circles (Figure 7.3). Use **ZOOM Center** to position the centre of the large circles at the middle of the screen. A magnification factor of **3** should be suitable.

Command: **ZOOM**
All/Center/Dynamic/Extents/Left/Previous/Window/<Scale(X)>: **C**
Center point: **35,20**
Magnification or Height <65.0000>: **3X**

Be sure to type the "X" after the "3". This ensures that the circles will be magnified. Responding with just a number is used to specify the height of the zoomed area. If the circles look a bit crude you can smooth them by regenerating the drawing. To draw the lines use **OSNAP** mode **TANgent**, and since you will be using **INTERSEC** shortly it can be included in the command.

Command: **REGEN**
Command: **OSNAP**
Object snap modes: **TANGENT,INTERSEC**

This selection of two modes means that AutoCAD will look for either a tangent point or an intersection point every time a point is picked.

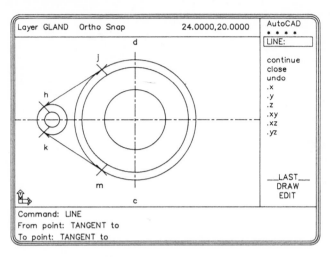

Figure 7.3 Tangential lines

Command: **LINE**
From point: (Pick the small outer circle near point h)
To point: (Pick the largest circle near point j)
To point: <**ENTER**>

Note that the OSNAP mode overrides the ORTHO mode. Also note that the line did not appear until the second point was picked. This was because AutoCAD had to calculate the tangent point on the first circle and this was dependent on the second point of the line. Now repeat this process for points k and m.

Command: <**ENTER**>
LINE From point: (Pick the small outer circle near point k)
To point: (Pick the largest circle near point m)
To point: <**ENTER**>

Trimming entities

The two outer circles must now be trimmed back to their intersection points with the tangents (Figure 7.4). The **TRIM** command works like EXTEND and can be found on the second part of the EDIT menu. You are first prompted for the boundary lines or arcs, etc, to define the trimming edges. Then you specify the entities to trim.

Command: **TRIM**
Select cutting edge(s) . . .
Select objects: (Pick the line hj near its mid point)
Select objects: (Pick the line km near its mid point)

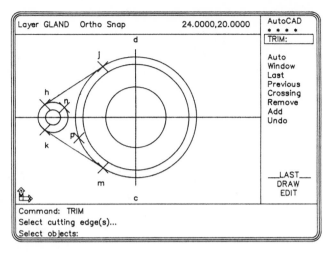

Figure 7.4 Trimming the flange

The two lines should now appear ghosted. If anything else has been selected by mistake type Remove and pick the unwanted objects. When the selection of the boundaries is completed press <**ENTER**> to proceed with trimming the circles.

> Select objects: <ENTER>
> Select objects to trim: (Pick the small outer circle near n)
> Select objects to trim: (Pick the largest circle near p)
> Select objects to trim: <ENTER>

Before going any further you must reset the **OSNAP** mode to **None**. It is easy to forget about the object snap mode and that could lead to undesirable results when picking points later.

> Command: **OSNAP**
> Object snap modes: **NONE**

Now to complete this view you can mirror the half-flange about the centre-line, cd.

> Command: **MIRROR**
> Select objects: **Window**
> First corner: **21,12**
> Other corner: **37,29**
> 4 found.
> Select objects: <ENTER>
> First point of mirror line: **35,11**   (c)
> Second point: (Pick a point vertically above c using ORTHO)
> Delete old objects? <N>: <ENTER>

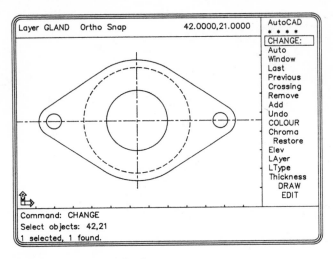

Figure 7.5 Plan view of gland

The large circle can be trimmed on the other side as before.

Command: **TRIM**
Select cutting edge(s) . . .
Select objects: **44,24**
1 found.
Select objects: **44,16**
1 found.
Select objects: <**ENTER**>
Select objects to trim: **43,19**
Select objects to trim: <**ENTER**>
Command:

For the plan view to be complete the 14cm diameter circle should be drawn in dashed linetype (Figure 7.5). To do this change it to the DASH layer.

Command: **CHANGE**
Select objects: **42,21**
1 selected, 1 found.
Select objects: <**ENTER**>
Properties/<Change point>: **LAYER**
New layer: **DASH**

Dimensioning

As the gland has been drawn to full scale, all the correct length information is already stored in the drawing. To extract this information and display it in the conventional way with dimension lines, etc, you will have to enter AutoCAD's "**DIM:**" program. This is a sub-program of AutoCAD which is used to produce all the dimension lines semi-automatically and interactively. All the types of dimensioning normally found on engineering and architectural drawings are catered for, and as with the rest of AutoCAD you have complete control over how it is drawn.

In this section you will add horizontal and vertical dimensions, a diameter and radius and add centre markings for the flange bolt holes. Before actually drawing any dimensions you should change layers and choose some settings for their display. For example, the height of the dimension text has to be selected. Once you enter the "DIM:" environment only the AutoCAD commands related to dimensioning and display can be executed. You can see the current display settings for the dimension lines and text by picking **status** from the screen menu (Figure 7.6). All toggles and object snapping are available but the usual AutoCAD drawing and editing commands are not. If things go wrong, ^C will always cancel the command and return you to the "Dim:" prompt. To execute commands other than dimensioning, you will have to exit from the "Dim:" prompt by typing **EXIT**.

> Command: **LAYER**
> ?/Make/Set/New/ON/OFF/Color/Ltype/Freeze/Thaw: **S**
> New current layer <GLAND>: **DIMENSIONS**
> ?/Make/Set/New/ON/OFF/Color/Ltype/Freeze/Thaw: <**ENTER**>
> Command: **DIM**
> Dim: **STATUS**

This gives two pages of text information on the settings of a total of 36 system variables. To see the second page press <**ENTER**>. This is quite an eyeful of similar looking items. Don't despair as most of these are already set to the correct values. Their meanings will be explained in due course. The most important variables are the ones that control the text size and the arrow size. The default text size is given by the variable DIMTXT which has a value of 3.0000 units (0.1800 units for Release 9). The arrow size is also 3.0000 (0.1800 units in Release 9) units, from the DIMASZ variable. As both of these are much too large for the current drawing they should be changed. Rather than having to change all the size variables for each drawing, AutoCAD provides an overall scale factor, DIMSCALE, which can be used to increase or decrease the sizes by its value. To get a reasonable display set DIMSCALE to 0.4. The variable, DIMASO, should be ON. If yours is off pick **dim vars** followed by **dimaso** and **ON**. This makes the dimension lines associative and allows them to be edited more easily. Furthermore, if one of the extension lines of an

DIMSCALE	1.0000	Overall scale factor
DIMASZ	3.0000	Arrow size
DIMCEN	−3.0000	Center mark size
DIMEXO	2.5000	Extension line origin offset
DIMDLI	10.0000	Dimension line increment for continuation
DIMEXE	2.5000	Extension above dimension line
DIMTP	0.0000	Plus tolerance
DIMTM	0.0000	Minus tolerance
DIMTXT	3.0000	Text height
DIMTSZ	0.0000	Tick size
DIMRND	0.0000	Rounding value
DIMDLE	0.0000	Dimension line extension
DIMTOL	Off	Generate dimension tolerances
DIMLIM	Off	Generate dimension limits
DIMTIH	On	Text inside extensions is horizontal
DIMTOH	On	Text outside extensions is horizontal
DIMSE1	Off	Suppress the first extension line
DIMSE2	Off	Suppress the second extension line
DIMTAD	Off	Place text above the dimension line
DIMZIN	0	Zero inches/feet control

– Press RETURN for more –

Figure 7.6 Status of dimension variables

associative dimension is edited by the STRETCH command then the dimension text will automatically change to the new correct length.

If you are in doubt as to what values your dimension variables should have you can set the more important ones as follows:

> Dim: **DIMSCALE**
> Current value <1.0000> New value: **0.4**
> Dim: **DIMTXT**
> Current value <default> New value: **3**
> Dim: **DIMASZ**
> Current value <default> New value: **3**
> Dim: **DIMASO**
> Current value <default> New value: **ON**
> Dim: **DIMTAD**
> Current value <default> New value: **OFF**

This can also be achieved by picking **dim vars** from the DIM: screen menu. The dimscale variable is on the second menu page and so you must pick **next** and then **dimscale** as shown in Figure 7.7. You can get back to the DIM: menu by picking **DIMMENU**.

The commands in the upper half of the DIM: menu are used to create the dimension lines and text. The lower half contains some utilities. The "redraw" is similar to the normal REDRAW command and redisplays the current display. Undo is like the normal version of the command but in Dim: it only undoes the dimension commands. Style can be used to change the dimension

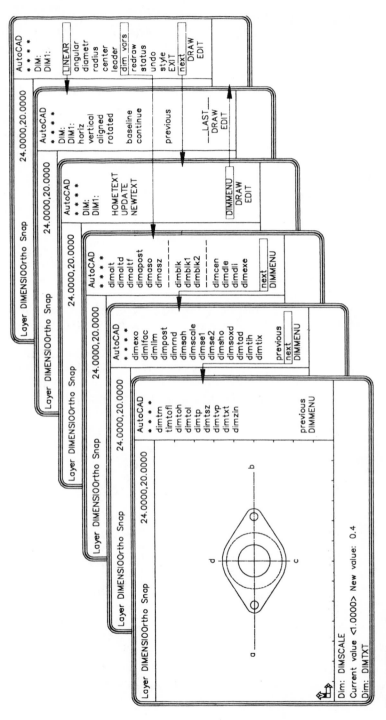

Figure 7.7 Dimension menus

text style. Picking either DRAW or EDIT from the bottom of the menu causes AutoCAD to exit from Dim: and go to the relevant menu. The "next" option gives three editing commands which operate on dimension entities.

To dimension the flange of the gland pick **LINEAR** from the DIM: menu. Then pick **horiz**. You are prompted for the "first extension line origin". Pick the leftmost point of the flange (point a on Figure 7.8). You could use the object snap INTERSEC for this. Pick the furthest right point for the second extension line origin. After selecting the two points to be dimensioned you are asked where you want the actual dimension line to be drawn. Give any point whose y coordinate is 38 units.

> Dim: **horiz**
> First extension line origin or RETURN to select: **22,20**   (a)
> Second extension line origin: **48,20**   (b)
> Dimension line location: **50,38**
> Dimension text <26.0000>: <**ENTER**>

Finally, you are asked for the text to put on the dimension line. AutoCAD calculates the horizontal distance between the two extension line origins and offers that as the default. Four places of decimals are given since that is the current UNITS setting. Pressing <ENTER> accepts the default and the dimension is included as shown in Figure 7.8. You can override the default by simply typing whatever text you wish.

If your dimension is not correct, type undo to erase it and try again. If the text is too large or too small, check the values of DIMSCALE, DIMTXT and DIMASZ. Pick status to do this. Then use DIMVARS as shown previously.

The "horiz" dimensioning command produces the horizontal distance between any two points. The distance is calculated from the X coordinates of

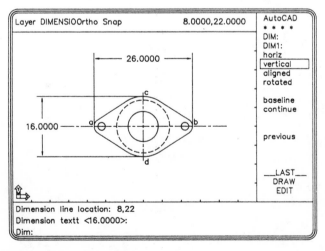

Figure 7.8 Overall dimensions

the two extension line origins. The "vertical" operates in a similar fashion for vertical distances calculated from the Y coordinates. Pick **vertical** from the screen menu and give the quadrant points at c and d as the extension line origins. The dimension line should be located at (8,22).

Dim: **vertical**
First extension line origin or RETURN to select: **quad**
of (Pick point c near 35,28)
Second extension line origin: **quad**
of (Pick point d near 35,12)
Dimension line location: **8,22**
Dimension text <16.0000>: <**ENTER**>

To add the distance between the flange bolt holes and the radius of the smaller flange arc use **horiz** once more followed by **continue** (Figure 7.9). Pick the centres of the two bolt holes as the extension line origins and position the dimension line below the 26.0000, above the gland.

Dim: **horiz**
First extension line origin or RETURN to select: **cen**
of (Pick bolt hole circle at 24,20)
Second extension line origin: **cen**
of (Pick right hand hole at 46,20)
Dimension line location: **45,35**
Dimension text <22.0000>: <**ENTER**>

Now to continue the dimension line to the right for the distance to the end of the flange pick **continue**. Picking this from the menu causes AutoCAD to exit from the Dim: prompt and to re-enter it immediately. This is to allow you to pick continue at the Command: prompt.
    You may see the following sequence on your screen. Ignore it!

Dim: *Cancel*
Command: dim
Dim: CONT

Once AutoCAD has sorted itself out it will prompt you as below.

Second extension line origin: **48,20**   (b)
Dimension text <2.0000>: <**ENTER**>

This should give the new horizontal dimension lines shown in Figure 7.9. The "2.0000" is too long to fit between the extension lines so AutoCAD automatically places it outside. Continue can also be used for vertical dimensions.
    When dimensioning the dashed circle the text and arrows are also too large to fit within the extension lines. However, there is room for the text by itself. AutoCAD can be forced to put the text inside by setting the variable DIMTIX

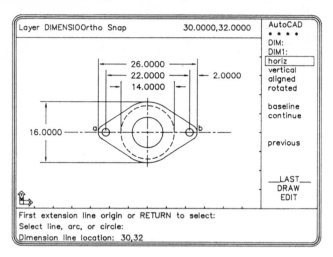

Figure 7.9 More horizontal dimensions

to ON (DIMension Text Inside eXtension line). This is a Release 10 feature and is not available in earlier versions. Pick **dim vars**, then **next** and **dimtix**. Type **ON** as the new value.

> Dim: **dimtix**
> Current value <Off> New value: **ON**

Now to dimension the dashed circle pick **DIMMENU** followed by **LINEAR** and **horiz**. Then rather than giving the extension line origins press **<ENTER>** to select the object and pick the circle.

> Dim: **horiz**
> First extension line origin or RETURN to select: **<ENTER>**
> Select line, arc, or circle: **30,25** (Point on dashed circle)
> Dimension line location: **30,32**
> Dimension text <14.0000>: **<ENTER>**

This should cause the dimension arrows to be drawn outside the extension lines and the text on the inside (Figure 7.9). If you are using AutoCAD Release 9 or earlier you will have to exit from Dim:, explode the dimension and move the text "manually".

It is good practice to switch dimtix off again when it is not required.

> Dim: **dimtix**
> Current value <On> New value: **OFF**

To demonstrate the use of the "radius" and "diameter" commands, the right-hand bolthole and the central circle will now be dimensioned (Figure 7.10).

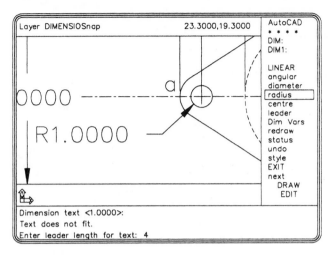

Figure 7.10 Radius and 'ZOOM

Pick **DIMMENU** or **previous** to return to the Dim: menu. Pick or type **radius** and then pick the small circle to the right of the point, a. As the point on the circle that you pick determines where the dimension line will be drawn, you should take some care to pick the circle in its lower left quadrant (near the point 23.3,19.3). If snap and/or ortho are currently on toggle them off using the CTRL key with B and then with O. In the sequence given below a transparent zoom command is used to get a closer look. Accept the default dimension text and as this does not fit inside the circle you will be prompted for a leader length.

> Dim: **Radius**
> Select arc or circle: **'ZOOM**
> >>Center/Dynamic/Left/Previous/Window/<Scale(X)>:
>   **Window**
> >>First corner: **7,10**
> >>Other corner: **29,26**
> Resuming DIM command:
> Select arc or circle: ^**B**<Snap off> ^**O**<Ortho off> (Pick point
>   23.3,19.3)
> Dimension text <1.0000>: <**ENTER**>
> Text does not fit.
> Enter leader length for text: **4**
> Dim:

Note the apostrophe before the zoom. This executes the transparent version of the command which means that it can be run in the middle of other commands including DIM commands. This command is located in the DISPLAY pull-down menu from the menu bar at the top of the screen. The leader is the arrow and line leading from the object to the text. If you accept the default text offered by the radius command, the letter "R" is automatically prefixed to the number. This command also draws a cross at the centre of the circle. The size of the cross is determined by the value of the DIMCEN and DIMSCALE variables. If your dimension text appears inside the circle it probably means that you have not reset the DIMTIX value to "off". If this happens pick "undo", reset dimtix and repeat the radius command.

Before including the diameter for the internal diameter of the gland, use the transparent zoom to return to the previous magnification. You have to use the transparent version as the normal ZOOM command doesn't work within Dim:. Pick **diametr** from the DIM: menu or type "DIAM". Then pick the inside circle near the point (38,17). Accept the text offered by AutoCAD and give a leader length of 6.

> Dim: **'ZOOM**
> \>\>Center/Dynamic/Left/Previous/Window/\<Scale(X)\>: **P**
> Resuming DIM command.
> Dim: **DIAM**
> Select arc or circle: **38,17**
> Dimension text \<8.0000\>: **\<ENTER\>**
> Text does not fit.
> Enter leader length for text: **6**
> Dim:

This time accepting the default text causes the greek letter φ to appear in front of the text. This is the standard symbol for indicating a diameter dimension. Again the point picked on the circle controls the position of the dimensions.

To draw the centre mark for the right hand bolt hole pick **center** from the screen menu and pick the circle near the point (46,19).

> Dim: **CENTER**
> Select arc or circle: **46,19**

As before, the size of this mark is dictated by the value of dimscale multiplied by dimcen. One variation is possible by specifying a negative value for the variable, dimcen. The negative value causes centre-lines to be drawn which intersect the circle itself. In that case the size depends on the diameter of the circle. A dimcen value of zero suppresses the drawing of centre marks with the radius and diameter commands.

To conclude the gland drawing (Figure 7.11) put a leader line to indicate that the sloping line is tangential to the arcs. The **leader** command allows you to place pointers with text on the drawing. Once you have picked **leader** from the menu you will be prompted for the leader start point. This is where the point of the arrow will be drawn. Use the object snap **intersec** to locate the intersection of the arc and line near the point (47,18). The prompt changes to the familiar "To point:" request similar to the LINE command. Pick the point (51,16). You can make the leader line consist of as many line segments as necessary by

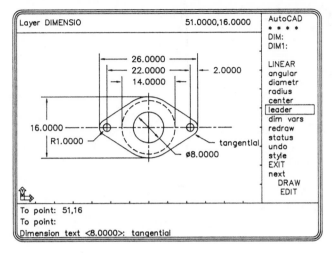

Figure 7.11 The dimensioned gland

picking points. When the line is completed press <**ENTER**> to exit the "To point:" prompt. Then type the desired text, which is the word "tangential".

> Dim: **LEADER**
> Leader start: **INTERSEC** of **47,18** (or pick a point near to this)
> To point: **51,16**
> To point: <**ENTER**>
> Dimension text <8.0000>: **tangential**
> Dim:

Even though you gave only two points on the leader line, a final horizontal line segment is drawn automatically. The previous dimension text is offered as the default but in this case it is not suitable. The only real problem that can occur with drawing leader lines is if the distance between the start point and the first point is not long enough to draw the arrow. If this happens the command continues as normal but no arrow is drawn.

Now that all the dimension lines and text have been added you can explore some of the editing facilities for associative dimensions. These commands are found by picking **next** towards the bottom of the DIM: menu. Of these commands, NEWTEXT and UPDATE are the more useful with HOMETEXT having only limited value. HOMETEXT is used to reposition the dimension text to whatever its default location should be and might be used after a STRETCH command. NEWTEXT allows you to change any dimension text on the drawing. For example, to change the "2.0000" text to "R2.00" you would use the following command sequence. You first give the new text to be used and then select all the dimension lines to alter.

Dim: **NEWTEXT**
Enter new dimension text: **R2.00**
Select objects: **53,34** (Point near the text "2.0000")
1 selected, 1 found.
Select objects: <**ENTER**>
Dim:

The result of this alteration is shown in Figure 7.12. The other alterations shown in the diagram are the result of a combination of changes in the dimension variables, the drawing units and the UPDATE command. These will now be described in detail. This is a good time to save your drawing and take a break.

Standard dimension variable settings

There are a number of undesirable features in the current dimension lines, as shown in Figure 7.11. Firstly, there is no real need for the text to be written to four places of decimals when it is all whole numbers. The other changes are a matter of style or convention. With the AutoCAD default settings, all the text is horizontal and is placed in breaks in the dimension line. While these are acceptable, they do not comply with the recommendations given in British Standards for engineering drawing practice.

To comply with BS308 the dimension variables should be set as given in Table 7.2. This gives a commentary on the meanings of the values. Where possible the AutoCAD Release 10 default values are used. As these are different from the defaults given in Release 9 it is worth going through the values fairly carefully.

The first four variables are concerned with settings for alternate units to be included in the drawing. As the international system of units is in millimetres a second system is rarely required. However, some disciplines are in a transition from imperial units to metric and so may wish to include both measurements. The values given in Table 7.2 assume that if alternate units are to be used, then the main units are millimetres and the secondary units are inches.

Make sure that all your dimension variables are set to the values given in Table 7.2. The quickest way of doing this is by typing **STATUS** at the Dim: prompt. Any variables that differ can be changed by typing their name and then giving the appropriate value. These variables may also be selected from an icon menu by picking **Dim** from the menu bar and then picking Variables from the bottom of the pull-down menu. This is available in the enhanced ACADUK menu.

As 4 places of decimals is a bit excessive for the current drawing, you can change it to two using AutoCAD's UNITS command. To do this **EXIT** from

Table 7.2 Dimension variable settings for BS308

Variable name	BS308 setting	Explanation
DIMALT	Off	Alternate dimensions not used.
DIMALTD	2	Decimal places for alternate units.
DIMALTF	0.039	Factor for alternate units (number of inches in 1mm).
DIMAPOST	"	Will suffix the inches symbol after alternate units.
DIMASO	ON	Enables associative dimensioning.
DIMASZ	3.00	Size of arrow to be used to terminate dimension lines.
DIMBLK		Name of block to be used in place of the arrows.
DIMBLK1		Block to be used at first extension line instead of arrow or tick. See DIMSAH.
DIMBLK2		Block to be used at second extension line instead of arrow or tick. See DIMSAH.
DIMCEN	-3.00	Size of centre mark. Negative value gives centre-lines.
DIMDLE	0.00	Extend dimension line. For use with DIMTSZ.
DIMDLI	10.00	Distance between dimension lines drawn using CONTINUE or BASELINE
DIMEXE	1.50	Length of extension line beyond arrows. AutoCAD default is too large.
DIMEXO	2.50	Extension line offset.
DIMLFAC	1.00	1 drawing unit = 1 dimension unit.
DIMLIM	OFF	Limit dimensions not required. See DIMTOL.
DIMPOST		Unit suffix for dimensions. None required.
DIMRND	0.00	Rounding off value for dimesnions. Not required.
DIMSAH	Off	Disables DIMBLK1 and 2. Release 10.
DIMSCALE	0.40	Overall scaling factor for size of arrows and text. Depends on drawing size. Text should be 3mm on plots.
DIMSE1	Off	Disable suppression of first extension line. Would turn on for running dimensions.
DIMSE2	Off	Disable supression of second extension line.
DIMSHO	Off	Turn off dynamic display of dimension value. You need a fast computer for this to work well.
DIMSOXD	Off	Disable supression of dimension line drawn outside the extension lines. Release 10.
DIMTAD	On	Draw dimension text above dimension line.
DIMTIH	Off	Makes text inside extension lines parallel to dim line. If on, the text will be drawn horizontally.
DIMTIX	Off	If this is on, it forces text inside extension lines. Release 10.
DIMTM	0.00	Minus value for tolerance dimensions. See DIMTOL.
DIMTOFL	Off	If this is on, it forces text outside extension lines. Release 10.
DIMTOH	Off	Makes text outside extension lines parallel to dim line. Otherwise text will be drawn horizontally.
DIMTOL	Off	If on, this enables tolerance dimensions.
DIMTP	0.00	Plus value for tolerance dimensions. See DIMTOL.
DIMTSZ	0.00	Tick size. If non-zero, oblique ticks are drawn in place of the arrows.
DIMTVP	0.00	Vertical position of text. Only effective if DIMTAD is OFF. Release 10.
DIMTXT	3.00	Size of dimension text.
DIMZIN	1	For use with feet and inches units (Release 9). In Release 10, a value of 4 causes all leading zeros of decimal units to be supressed. See Reference Manual.

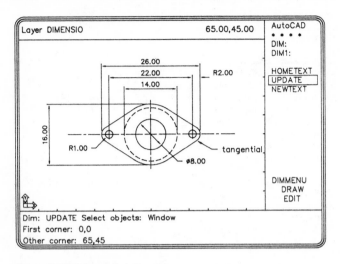

Figure 7.12 The updated dimensions

Dim: and type **UNITS**. Accept all the defaults except the number of digits to the right of the decimal point.

Dim: **EXIT**
Command: **UNITS**
Enter choice, 1 to 5 <2>: <**ENTER**>
Number of digits to right of decimal point (0 to 8) <4>: **2**
Systems of angle measure:
Enter choice, 1 to 5 <1>: <**ENTER**>
Number of fractional places for display of angles (0 to 8) <0>:
   <**ENTER**>
Enter direction for angle 0 <0>: <**ENTER**>
Do you want angles measured clockwise? <N>: <**ENTER**>
Command:

Now to update all the dimensions to the new environment type **DIM1** (Figure 7.12). This works exactly like DIM but executes just one dimension command and then returns to the "Command:" prompt. Use a window to select all the dimension lines.

Command: **DIM1**
Dim: **UPDATE**
Select objects: **Window**
First corner: **0,0**
Other corner: **65,45**
31 found.
Select objects: <**ENTER**>
Command:

Drawing a pentagon

To illustrate the remaining dimension commands and a couple of new drawing commands, you will now create a pentagon and find out the internal angle between two adjacent sides. To save time in setting up a new drawing environment just change to the POLYGON layer and freeze the others. This will allow you to use all the current dimension variable settings. Some of these will be altered temporarily to create tolerant dimensions.

Command: **LAYER**
?/Make/Set/New/ON/OFF/Color/Ltype/Freeze/Thaw: **S**
New current layer <DIMENSIONS>: **POLYGON**
?/Make/Set/New/ON/OFF/Color/Ltype/Freeze/Thaw: **F**
Layer name(s) to Freeze: *
Cannot freeze layer POLGON. It is the CURRENT layer.
?/Make/Set/New/ON/OFF/Color/Ltype/Freeze/Thaw: **<ENTER>**

The **POLYGON** command can be found in the DRAW pull down menu or on the second part of the DRAW screen menu. When you select this command you are first prompted for the number of sides. Use 5 sides for a pentagon (Figure 7.13). You can then either specify a circle to be inscribed or circumscribed by the polygon or you can give the position and length of one side.

Command: **POLYGON**
Number of sides: **5**
Edge/<Center of polygon>: **EDGE**
First endpoint of edge: **20,10**   (A)
Second endpoint of edge: **@20,0**   (B)

This actually draws a closed polyline, calculating the vertices from the geometrical properties of equilateral polygons. It can be edited in the same way as any other closed polyline.

The **CHAMFER** edit command can be used to cut off the top corner. This command is similar to the FILLET command but draws a straight line between the chamfer points. For this command you give the length by which each of a pair of lines is to be trimmed back. If a polyline is to be chamfered then you have the further option of trimming all the corners. For example, to chamfer the corners of the pentagon by trimming 3 units from each end of the line segments you would get the shape given in Figure 7.13. You first have to give the sizes of the chamfer and then the polyline to be edited.

Command: **CHAMFER**
Polyline/Distance/<Select first line>: **DISTANCE**
Enter first chamfer distance <0.00>: **3**
Enter second chamfer distance <3.00>: **<ENTER>**
Command:CHAMFER Polyline/Distance/<Select first line>:
    Polyline
Select polyline: **30,10**

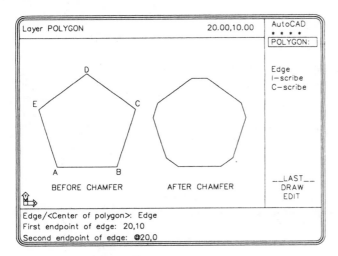

Figure 7.13 The chamfered pentagon

Chamfer can also be used with unequal distances and be applied to individual pairs of lines. If a polyline to be chamfered contains an arc then the arc will be deleted and replaced with a straight line.

Wrapping up dimensions

The "angular" option in the DIM: menu allows the dimensioning of angles between lines. To draw the angle between the longer lines AB and BC, enter the Dim: environment and pick angular. Then pick points on lines AB and BC. Indicate where the dimension arc is to be located and accept the default dimension text and text location.

> Command: **DIM**
> Dim: **ANGULAR**
> Select first line: **30,10**   (Line AB)
> Second line: **43,20**   (Line BC)
> Enter dimension line arc location: **31,10**
> Dimension text <108>: **<ENTER>**
> Enter text location: **<ENTER>**
> Dim:

Accepting the default text location causes the "108°" to be positioned in the middle of the arc. Giving any other location response will put the text at that location.

With aligned dimensions the length is measured parallel to the line joining the two extension line origins. To find the new length of the line between C and

D pick **aligned** from the LINEAR sub-menu. Instead of picking the origin points press <**ENTER**> and pick the line CD at the point (38,35). Put the dimension line at (42,39) and accept the default text.

> Dim: **ALIGNED**
> First extension line origin or RETURN to select: <**ENTER**>
> Select line,arc, or circle: **38,35**
> Dimension line location: **42,39**
> Dimension text <14.00>: <**ENTER**>

The dimension line is aligned with the line segment and gives the correct length. The original length was 20 from which 3 was taken from each end.

To dimension the chamfer at the point E use the **rotated** dimensions at an angle of 198 degrees. This angle is perpendicular to the line AE. Pick **rotated** from the LINEAR sub-menu, then press <**ENTER**> and pick the short line at point e. Place the dimension line at (13,30) and accept the default text.

> Dim: **ROTATED**
> Dimension line angle <0>: **198**
> First extension line origin or RETURN to select: <**ENTER**>
> Select line,arc, or circle: **15.5,28.5**
> Dimension line location: **13,30**
> Dimension text <2.85>: <**ENTER**>
> Dim:

Note that rotated dimensions with angle zero are the same as horizontal dimensions and angle = 90 gives vertical dimensions.

Finally to produce dimensions with a tolerance level built in change the following dim vars and use **horiz** to dimension the line AB.

> Dim: **DIMTOL**
> Current value <Off> New value: **ON**
> Dim: **DIMTM**
> Current value <0.00> New value: **.3**
> Dim: **DIMTP**
> Current value <0.00> New value: **.5**
> Dim: **DIMTIX**
> Current value <Off> New value: **ON**
> Dim: **DIMTAD**
> Current value <On> New value: **OFF**
> Dim: **horiz**
> First extension line origin or RETURN to select: <**ENTER**>
> Select line,arc, or circle: **30,10**
> Dimension line location: **30,3**
> Dimension text <14.00>: <**ENTER**>

The first three variables control the tolerance values, the other two control the display. This should give the display as shown in Figure 7.14. If you don't

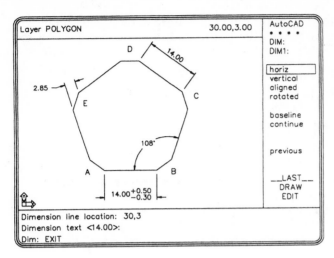

Figure 7.14 Final dimensions

accept the default dimension text the tolerance values will not be drawn.
To finish up, **exit** from the Dim: environment and **END** the drawing.

Dim: **EXIT**
Command: **END**

Summary

In this chapter you have encountered some advanced drawing and editing commands. Some of these, such as TRIM and CHAMFER allow you to dispense with having to draw preparatory construction lines. Others like POLYGON and DIVIDE draw multiple objects. By far the most important component covered in this exercise has been the dimensioning sub-system. AutoCAD changes when you are in Dim: and many new commands are made available while at the same time most of the drawing and editing commands are withdrawn.

Dimensions are calculated automatically from the current drawing units. It is important to choose suitable units and accuracy levels for sensible dimension values. The dimension environment can be tailored to your specific needs by setting up the relevant dimension variables.

You should now be able to:

Insert dividing markers.
Draw lines tangential to two circles.
Draw equilateral polylines.
Trim circles and chamfer polylines.
Use ZOOM center with a magnification.
Use the transparent zoom.
Use all the commands on the DIM: screen menu.
Add horizontal and vertical dimension lines.
Draw aligned, rotated, angular and tolerant dimensions.
Set up the dimension variables.

Chapter 8 ADDING DEPTH TO YOUR DRAWINGS WITH 3D CAD

General

Since the early days of AutoCAD, the programmers have been striving to produce full three-dimensional capability for the PC-CAD user. With Release 10 they can justifiably claim to have done just that. Earlier versions of AutoCAD allowed only use of isometric projection techniques or a pseudo-3D known as 2.5D. This chapter will take a brief look at all three techniques to produce some simple drawings.

The opening up of the Z axis brings new and exciting aspects to AutoCAD use. Things can be constructed on the computer screen at full scale and depth. Once the object has been drawn it can be viewed from above (plan), from the front and side (elevation) and in either isometric or perspective projection. You can "walk" around the AutoCAD image and even through it. These facilities are particularly useful for disciplines where it is necessary to have a full appreciation and visualisation of the design.

As a cautionary note, one should not get carried away with the novelty and hype associated with 3D CAD. Architects and engineers have successfully managed to develop the most complex of projects over hundreds of years using simple 2D drawings. Thus, for a lot of design projects the 2D representation is adequate. Any changeover to 3D CAD must justify the extra effort required. You should also be aware of what AutoCAD 3D can and can't do.

AutoCAD models solid objects as wire frame skeletons. As such you can see through the objects that are drawn. You can tell AutoCAD to HIDE the lines at the back of the object to give the impression of solidity.

All the commands you have used up to now also work in 3D, although some special commands are needed (eg 3DPOLY line). There is a whole new vocabulary of terms relating to 3D geometry and a set of completely new functions. Let the work commence.

Isometric projection

Isometric projection is still the standard method of conveying three-dimensional engineering information on a two-dimensional sheet of paper. To produce anything other than simple shapes in isometric projection requires considerable expertise in drafting techniques. It is not my purpose to introduce such drawing construction methods but I do wish to display the special features within AutoCAD for isometric projections. To demonstrate these features and the basics of isometric projection we will create a drawing of the cooker that was used in Chapter 6.

Start up AutoCAD and create a new drawing called "COOKISO". Set the LIMITS to (0,0) and (3250,2250) and the UNITS to Decimal. Set the GRID to 100 units. To set up the isometric axes use the **SNAP** command and pick the **Style** option and a vertical spacing of **50**. You are then given the choice of "Standard" or "Iso". Pick **Iso** and watch the cursor cross-hairs change when you move them back into the drawing area. The grid also changes to give the projection axes.

C:**ACAD**

Main menu

Enter selection: **1**

Enter NAME of drawing: **COOKISO**

Command: **LIMITS**
ON/OFF/<Lower left corner> <0.00,0.00>: <**ENTER**>
Upper right corner <420.00,297.00>: **3250,2250**
Command: **ZOOM**
All/Center/Dynamic/Extents/Left/Previous/Window/<Scale(X)>:**W**

Setting units gives a lot of dialogue which is truncated below.

Command: **UNITS**

System on units:...
Enter choice, 1 to 5 <>:**2**
Number of digits to right of decimal point (0 to 8) <2>: **0**

System of angle measure:...

Enter choice, 1 to 5 <>:**1**
Number of fractional places for display of angles (0 to 8) <4>:**2**
Direction for angle 0.00 <0.00>:<**ENTER**>
Do you want angles measured clockwise? <N> <**ENTER**>

Command: **GRID**
Grid spacing(X) or ON/OFF/Snap/Aspect <10.00>: **100**

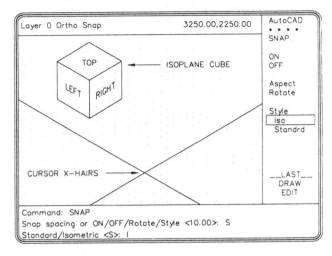

Figure 8.1 Isometric screen

These settings will be useful for the other two drawings in this chapter. To keep them safe, SAVE the drawing twice with the filenames EXP-NY and EXP-GIZA.

> Command: **SAVE**
> File name <COOKISO>: **EXP-NY**
> Command: **<ENTER>**
> SAVE File name <COOKISO>: **EXP-GIZA**

Now to switch on the isometric projection pick SETTINGS from the AutoCAD screen menu and then SNAP.

> Command: **SNAP**
> Snap spacing or ON/OFF/Aspect/Rotate/Style <10>:**S**
> Standard/Isometric <S>: **I**
> Vertical spacing <10>: **50**

The three isometric projection planes are shown in Figure 8.1 but won't appear on your screen display. The X,Y and Z axes are at 150, 30 and 90 degrees from the horizontal. The orientation of the cursor cross hairs depends on which plane you want to work in. The effect of ORTHO also depends on the plane. The isoplane cube shown in Figure 8.1 defines the planes as LEFT, RIGHT and TOP. You can switch between the planes by using the ISOPLANE command. This doesn't appear in any screen menu but can be found in the pull-down menu under "Settings" followed by "Drawing aids".

Make sure that ortho and coordinate display are ON (^O, ^D) and switch to the right hand plane to draw the front of the cooker shown in Figure 8.2. You will find it easier to drag the line points than to key them in. Watch the coordinate display for the correct lengths.

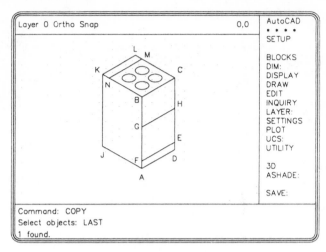

Figure 8.2 An isometric cooker

Command: **ISOPLANE**
Left/Top/Right/<Toggle>: **R**
Command: **LINE**
From point: pick a snap point in the vicinity of (1689,475)   (A)
To point: @**950<90** or drag the point on the Z axis   (B)
To point: @**500<30** or drag the point on the Y axis   (C)
To point: @**950<270**   (D)
To point: **C**
Command: <ENTER>
LINE From point: @**0,100**   (E)
To point: @**−500<30**   (F)
To point: <ENTER>
Command: <ENTER>
LINE From point: @**0,450**   (G)
To point: @**500<30**   (H)
To point: <ENTER>

Now switch to the left hand plane to draw the side. You can use the ISOP-
LANE again or use the toggle key ^**E**. Pressing ^E once changes to the left
plane, once again and the top plane is set. You can cycle through all the planes
quickly using ^E. This toggle is also transparent so you can switch in the middle
of another command.

Command: ^**E** <Isoplane left> <ENTER>
LINE From point: **int** of pick point A using object snap.   (A)
To point: @**600<150**   (J)
To point: @**950<90**   (K)
To point: **int** of pick point B.   (B)
To point: <ENTER>

Use ^E to toggle to the top plane to finish the cooker.

```
Command: ^E <Isoplane top> <ENTER>
LINE From point: int of pick point K.                        (K)
To point: @500<30                                            (L)
To point: int of pick point C                                (C)
To point: <ENTER>
Command: <ENTER>
LINE From point: @500<150 A point on CN 100 from N           (M)
To point: @−500<30                                           (N)
To point: <ENTER>
```

To draw the heating elements you have to distort the circles. Luckily, the ELLIPSE command is just right for the job. The elements are at 200mm centres. The centre of each circle is 150mm from the nearest edge. First, change the entity colour to red.

```
Command: COLOUR
New entity color <BYLAYER>: RED
Command: ELLIPSE
<Axis endpoint 1>/Center/Isocircle: I
Center of circle: pick the snap point near (1516,1675)
<Circle radius>/Diameter: 75          (The back left heating ring.)
Command: COLOUR
New entity color <1 red>: BYLAYER                 (Reset to normal.)
```

AutoCAD uses the isoplane setting to calculate the correct amount of distortion and the orientation of the ellipse. This is a special feature of the ELLIPSE command, triggered when the SNAP style is isometric. Unfortunately, the ARRAY command does not support the isometric planes and so you have to use the straightforward COPY command.

```
Command: COPY
Select objects: LAST
1 found.
Select objects:
<Base point or Displacement>/Multiple: M
Base point: 0,0                             (Any point will do.)
Second point of displacement: @200<30
                                  (The back right heating ring.)
Second point of displacement: @200<−30
                                  (The front left heating ring.)
```

Second point of displacement:
Command: <**ENTER**>
COPY
Select objects: **LAST**
1 found.
Select objects:
<Base point or Displacement>/Multiple: @**200<30**
Second point of displacement: <**ENTER**>
(The front right heating ring.)
Command: **END**

The absolute coordinates that appear on the status line don't mean much when you are working in isometric projection. What is important is the relative position from the last point. Remember that the lines with <150 are parallel to the X axis, those at <30 are supposed to represent the Y axis and the vertical direction is Z. The cooker in Figure 8.2 is only a projection of the 3D information, it is not a 3D object.

The usefulness of AutoCAD's isometric projection will depend on the user's skill in that drafting technique. In general, you will have to use many construction lines to locate key points in the isometric view. Ortho, grid, snap and isoplane are very effective, while typing coordinates is not.

The Express State Building in 2.5 dimensions

It's time for a change of scene for all you out there, slaving over hot stoves. The next stop for the AutoCAD Express is the Big Apple where the skyline is about to be committed to the PC. In this example you will use the conventional 2D operations to draw a plan view. By also assigning a thickness and elevation in the vertical direction (Z axis) the shapes will have body (Figure 8.3). Edit the drawing "EXP-NY" that you created above. If you didn't do the previous exercise, start a new drawing and follow the AutoCAD commands given above, down as far as the SAVE "EXP-NY" line.

Main menu

Enter selection: **2**

Enter NAME of drawing: **EXP-NY**

To give depth to the drawing entities use the ELEV (elevation) command. This allows you to set the altitude of the drawing plane and also the thickness or height of the entities. This command can be reached via the "SETTINGS" screen sub-menu or the pull-down menu followed by "Drawing aids" or by

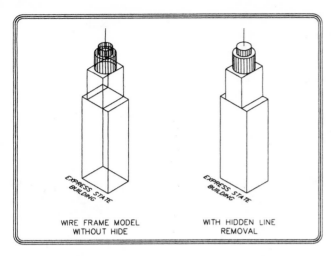

Figure 8.3 Express State Building

typing "ELEV". The main tower of the building is a massive 500 units by 400 units and has a height of 1350 units. The height to the top of the mast is 2500 units.

> Command: **ELEV**
> New current elevation <0>: **<ENTER>**
> New current thickness <0>: **1350**

Setting the elevation to zero means that the base of the tower is at ground level. Now ZOOM in to the construction area and draw a rectangle for the main tower (Figure 8.4).

> Command: **ZOOM**
> All/Center/Dynamic/Extents/Left/Previous/Window/<Scale (X)>: **W**
> First corner: **700,700**
> Other corner: **1800,1500**
> Command: **LINE**
> From point: **1000,1000**   (A)
> To point: **@500,0**   (B)
> To point: **@0,400**   (C)
> To point: **@−500,0**   (D)
> To point: **C**   (A)

The next part up is not quite as large but is 500 units tall. Therefore the elevation and thickness must be changed. By setting the elevation to 1350 the new entities will be drawn at the top of the main tower.

```
Command: ELEV
New current elevation <0>: 1350
New current thickness <1350>: 500
Command: LINE
From point: 1100,1000                                    (E)
To point: @300,0                                         (F)
To point: @0,400                                         (G)
To point: @−300,0                                        (H)
To point: C
```

As the construction reaches skyward the elevation must be updated for the new elements. Climb to the top of the last object and draw a cylinder. A vertical cylinder is just a circle with a thickness.

```
Command: ELEV
New current elevation <1350>: 1850
New current thickness <500>: 250
Command: CIRCLE
3P/2P/TTR/<Center point>: 1250,1200                      (J)
Diameter/<Radius>: 150
```

And again.

```
Command: ELEV
New current elevation <1850>: 2100
New current thickness <250>: 100
Command: CIRCLE
3P/2P/TTR/<Center point>: @          (The last point, ie J.)
Diameter/<Radius>: 100
```

Now to draw the mast on top use a POINT with a thickness of 300 units. Of course you must first go to the new elevation.

```
Command: ELEV
New current elevation <2100>: 2200
New current thickness <100>: 300
Command: POINT
Point: @                             (1250,1200 again.)
```

When you are finished working above ground level it is good practice to reset the elevation and thickness back to zero. This will help prevent user confusion if the drawing is made over a number of sessions. You can then add the title text.

```
Command: ELEV
New current elevation <2200>: 0
New current thickness <300>: 0
```

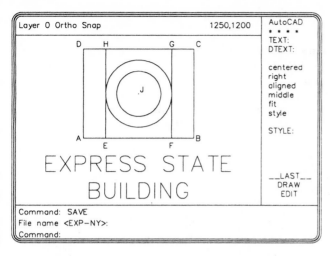

Figure 8.4 Plan view of skyscraper

Command: **TEXT**
Start point or Align/Center/Fit/Middle/Right/Style: **C**
Center point: 1250,850
Height <>: **70**
Rotation angle <0>: **<ENTER>**
Text: **EXPRESS STATE**
Command: **<ENTER>**
TEXT Start point or Align/Center/Fit/Middle/Right/Style: **<ENTER>**
Text: **BUILDING**
Command: **SAVE**
File name <EXP-NY>: **<ENTER>**

Your picture should now look like Figure 8.4. If the POINT appears as an X or
+ or small circle, then you will have to change the setting of the PDMODE
variable to zero and REGENerate the picture. The effect of setting PDMODE
to different values can be seen by picking DRAW, next, POINT:, and example: in that order from the screen menu.

Command: **SETVAR**
Variable name or ? <>: **PDMODE**
New value for PDMODE <current>: **0**
Command: **REGEN**

Finally, to see the 3D effect of Figure 8.3 you will have to change the view point
from which AutoCAD is looking. To get the solid effect you can remove the
lines at the back. The commands VPOINT and HIDE do these jobs.

HAZARD WARNING!

Always SAVE the drawing before a HIDE operation. The HIDE command can take a long time to calculate all the hidden lines to remove. Don't get impatient and start hitting the <ENTER> key. This only re-executes the last command, ie HIDE, and you will have even longer to wait. Use the cancel key, ˆC, if you want to interrupt. As there are only about 25 lines to be hidden in this drawing it shouldn't take more than a few seconds.

Views and more views

The parallel projection view shown in Figure 8.3 is achieved by changing the view point to $(1,-1,1)$. The actual viewing direction is parallel to the line joining this point to the drawing's TARGET point. The default TARGET point is the origin. Note that the plan VPOINT was $(0,0,1)$, ie looking down the Z axis from that point to the origin. A front elevation of the building could be generated with a view point of $(0,-1,0)$, a back elevation by $(0,1,0)$ and a side view by $(1,0,0)$.

> Command: **VPOINT**
> Rotate/<View point> <0,0,1>: **1,−1,0**
> Command: **SAVE**
> File name <EXP-NY>: <**ENTER**>
> Command: **HIDE**
> Regenerating drawing.
> Removing hidden lines: 25

This should give the required picture. It is a bit of a fraud, really. If you zoom in to the cylinders on the roof and redo the HIDE you should see that one of the lines at the top of the upper rectangular block is not correctly hidden. The reason for this is that the 2.5D lines produce an open ended rectangular box and not a solid block. The thick circles give solid cylinders though.

If you need to store particular view points you can use the VIEW command. This allows you to save the current display settings (VPOINT, ZOOM etc) for later retrieval. This is a help when trying to remember the VPOINT coordinates.

> Command: **VIEW**
> ?/Delete/Restore/Save/Window: **S**
> View name to save: **ISOMETRIC-P**

You can also store the front view settings. This time, instead of picking VPOINTS: use the pull-down icon menu (Figure 8.5). Pick **Display** from the menu bar and then **3D Viewpoint**. On some menus you will have to pick **3D**

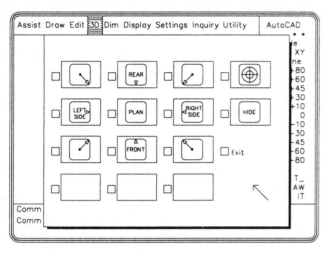

Figure 8.5 View point icon menu

followed by **3D View**. Then pick the small box on the left side of the "FRONT" icon. If you don't have the icon menu on your version use VPOINT (0,−1,0).

> Command: **VPOINT**
> Rotate/<View point> <1,−1,1>: **R**
> Enter angle in X-Y plane from X axis <315>: **270**
> Enter angle from X-Y plane : **0**
> Regenerating drawing.

Picking the icon runs the VPOINT command with the "Rotate" option. The first rotation angle is set automatically to give the front view and you are prompted for a vertical angle from the XY plane. If you give a positive angle here the view will be looking down on the object. A zero angle means that you will be looking straight at it. The overall result is the same as setting VPOINT to (0,−1,0). When you are happy with the display save the VIEW.

> Command: **VIEW**
> ?/Delete/Restore/Save/Window: **S**
> View name to save: **FRONT**

When you want to retrieve the view, type **VIEW** followed by **R** and the view name. Try to save a plan view and side view.

> Command: **VIEW**
> ?/Delete/Restore/Save/Window: **R**
> View name to restore: **ISOMETRIC-P**

There will be more about VIEW in the next chapter.

Multiple views

You can even see all these views on the one screen with the multiple view port facility introduced in Release 10. The easiest way to set up the multiple views is to use the icon menu. Pick **Display** followed by **Set Viewports** (or just "Viewports" on some menus). This gives you a screen full of possible configurations as shown in Figure 8.6. Pick the box for the three vertical divisions. This runs a short program using the VPORTS command.

Whatever was on the screen prior to selecting the viewports will now be shown in triplicate (Figure 8.7). The cursor cross-hairs will only appear when the cursor is in the active viewport. A cursor arrow appears if it is in any other viewport. Display commands such as ZOOM, VIEW, REDRAW and coordinate selection apply only to the active viewport. Two new commands, REDRAWALL and REGENALL, cause all the viewports to be redisplayed. To make another viewport active move the cursor arrow to it and press the pick button. Make sure that the far right viewport is active and use the following sequence to create a fourth one.

Command: **VPORTS**
Save/Restore/Delete/Join/SIngle/?/2/<3>/4: **2**
Horizontal/<Vertical>: **H**

This divides the right viewport into two, the upper half becoming active. Change to the plan view and in the two long viewports change to the front and side views. Do a **ZOOM All** if the picture doesn't fill the viewport.

Command: **VPOINT**
Rotate/<View point> <1,−1,1>: **0,0,1**   (Plan)

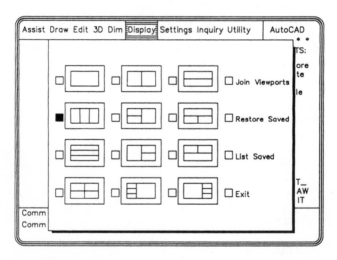

Figure 8.6 Viewport icon menu

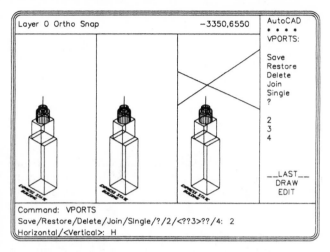

Figure 8.7 Three viewports

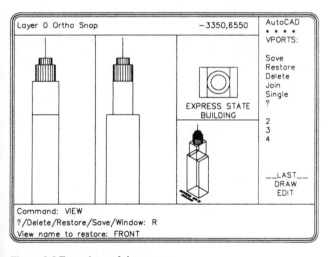

Figure 8.8 Four views of skyscraper

Pick the viewport on the left of the screen.

> Command: **<ENTER>**
> VPOINT Rotate/<View point> <1,−1,1>: **1,0,0**   (Side)

Pick the middle viewport.

> Command: **VIEW**
> ?/Delete/Restore/Save/Window: **R**
> View name to restore: **FRONT**   (Front)

When you are ready you can END the drawing.

> Command: **END**

The other options available in the VPORTS sub-menu allow you to: save and name the current viewport configuration so that it can be recalled later; restore a named configuration; delete a configuration from the list; Join two adjacent viewports as long as the resultant shape is rectangular; revert to a SIngle viewport configration; divide the current viewport into 2, 3 or 4 sections. By combining different configurations with the Join and the divide options you can create a wide variety of shapes and sizes. You are restricted to a maximum of four viewports on the screen at any one time. If you try to exceed four you will get the message: "The specified division would create too many viewports." and nothing would happen.

Viewports are very useful for 3D CAD by giving you an instant update of new entities in all the views. You can also switch between the viewports for the selection of entities or construction points in the middle of other commands. Their usefulness is not confined to 3D work and they can help speed up 2D drafting considerably. One viewport can be used to show a small-scale picture of the whole drawing, while other viewports can contain various details for working on.

The pyramids of Giza in glorious 3D

Pack your bags and board the AutoCAD Express for your next destination, the ancient and three-dimensional land of Egypt. You have probably recognised from the previous section that there is a new level of complexity when trying to control points in 3D. In this section you will learn how to master this and construct a fully three-dimensional object, the Cheops pyramid.

The most difficult aspect of working in 3D is the optical illusion you encounter because the screen is only two-dimensional. To help with this problem you can set up a viewport for visualisation and give it a suitable VPOINT. You will also use the coordinate filters, those .x, .y, .z, .xy etc that now appear on the LINE sub-menu.

Edit the EXP-GIZA drawing and draw the plan for the pyramid. Then set up three viewports on the screen to watch the 3D take off.

Main menu

Enter selection: **2**
Enter NAME of drawing: **EXP-GIZA**

Command: **LINE**
From point: **1000,1000**   (A)
To point: **@600,0**   (B)
To point: **@0,600**   (C)
To point: **@−600,0**   (D)
To point: **C**   (A)
Command: **VPORTS**
Save/Restore/Delete/Join/SIngle/?/2/<3>/4: **3**
Horizontal/Vertical/Above/Below/Left/<Right>: **<ENTER>**

This makes the larger viewport appear on the right hand half of the screen. This is also the new active viewport. Use ZOOM W to make better use of the display.

Command: **ZOOM**
All/Center/Dynamic/Extents/Left/Previous/Window/<Scale (X)>: **W**
First corner: **700,700**
Other corner: **2000,1800**

Make the lower left viewport active by moving the cursor into it and pressing the pick button. Then change the VPOINT to give a frontal view. Move the the upper left and set up an isometric type of view.

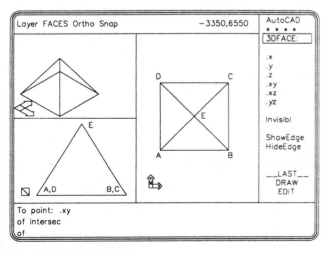

Figure 8.9 Cheops' pyramid

Pick lower left viewport.
Command: **VPOINT**
Rotate/<View point> <0,0,1>: **0,−1,0**
Regenerating drawing.
Grid too dense to display

Pick upper left viewport.
Command: **<ENTER>**
VPOINT Rotate/<View point> <0,0,1>: **1,−1,1**

With these views you should be able to see if the lines to the apex of the pyramid are being drawn correctly. There are four sloping lines to be drawn from the corners, A,B,C and D, to the apex, E which is 475 units above the centre point. To explain the facilities a number of coordinate definition methods are used. (If you are using Release 9 you will have to use the 3DLINE command instead of LINE.)

Command: **LINE**
From point: **1000,1000**   (A)
To point: **@300,300,475**   (E)

If the Z ordinate is not specified it is taken as the current elevation setting. The point E is 300 units along the X axis, 300 along the Y axis and 475 units up the Z axis from the point A. As the second point is input the line should appear in all three viewports. For the next point use object snap intersection to locate B in the right hand viewport.

To point: **intersec**
of Pick the right hand viewport and then pick the point B.   (B)
To point: **<ENTER>**

The object snap is also able to pick up the full XYZ coordinates as demonstrated by the next sequence.

Command: **<ENTER>**
LINE From point: **intersec**
of Pick point C.   (C)
To point: **intersec**
of Pick point E.   (E)

If you are not sure of the elevation of a particular point on the plan view you can use the .XY filter to use just those coordinates and type in Z separately.

To point: **.xy**
of intersec
of Pick the point D.   (D)
(Need Z): **0**
To point: **<ENTER>**

The complete pyramid should now appear similar to Figure 8.9 but without the letters A to E.

Making the faces solid

The pyramid shown above is but the first step in construction. The 3D lines form only the frame on which we can hang the fabric. To make the slopes solid we will create 3DFACEs on each of the triangles. Making the 3D faces is like stretching fabric over the wire frame. Faces are opaque when the HIDE command is executed. At present, if you move to the upper left viewport and try HIDE, all the lines will still be visible.

Create a new layer with a different colour so that the faces are distinguishable from the original lines. Make sure that the right hand viewport is active before starting on the faces. Then make a 3D face for the bottom of the pyramid and a face for each of the other four sides.

> Command: **LAYER**
> ?/Make/Set/New/ON/OFF/Color/Ltype/Freeze/Thaw: **M**
> New current layer <0>: **FACES**
> ?/Make/Set/New/ON/OFF/Color/Ltype/Freeze/Thaw: **C**
> Color: **red**
> Layer name(s) for color 1 (red) <FACES>: **<ENTER>**
> ?/Make/Set/New/ON/OFF/Color/Ltype/Freeze/Thaw: **<ENTER>**

To see the 3DFACE options pick 3D from the AutoCAD screen menu followed by 3DFACE. We will return to the other items on the 3D menu later. The 3DFACE sub-menu contains the .x, .y, etc, filters and also the options to make the edges of the face either visible or invisible. Whether you want the edges visible will depend on the drawing. To make any edge invisible you must pick "Invisibl" or type "I" before inputting the first point of that edge. Picking "ShowEdge" allows you to override previous "Invisibl" selections while "HideEdge" reverses this. The process of having to specify all the invisible edges at the time of drawing is tedious and can lead to phantom faces where all the sides are invisible. If this happens, use the SETVAR command to set the system variable SPLFRAME to a non-zero value. This will cause all invisible edges to become visible.

> Command: **3DFACE** First point: **1000,1000**   (A again.)
> Second point: **@600,0,0**   (B)
> Third point: **@600<90**   (C)

Let's use the filters for the last point, for fun. Point D has the same X value as A and the same Y as C.

> Fourth point: **.x** of **intersec**
> of Pick point A. (need YZ): **.y** of Pick point C.
> (need Z): **0**
> Third point: **<ENTER>**

You will be prompted for more third and fourth points to add more faces onto the last edge. In fact, the 3DFACE command is like a 3D version of the SOLID command. However, the order of point input (ABCD above) is more comprehensible than that for SOLID (ABDC). Note that only the edges of the face are shown. Faces are never filled but they are opaque when using HIDE. The four points defining the face should be on the same plane if possible. It is not an error to use non-coplanar points but it is sloppy 3D CAD.

```
Command: <ENTER>
3DFACE First point: 1000,1000                        (A)
Second point: @600,0                                 (B)
Third point: intersec of Pick point E                (E)
Fourth point: <ENTER>
Third point: intersec of Pick point C                (C)
Fourth point: intersec of Pick point D               (D)
Third point: <ENTER>
Command: <ENTER>
3DFACE First point: 1000,1000                        (A)
Second point: @0,600                                 (D)
Third point: intersec of Pick point E                (E)
Fourth point: <ENTER>
Third point: intersec of Pick point C                (C)
Fourth point: intersec of Pick point B               (B)
Third point: <ENTER>
Command: SAVE
File name <EXP-GIZA>: <ENTER>
```

Faces always have four points defining them. To make a triangle two of the points must have the same location (eg first and second or third and fourth). Note that the third and fourth points of the previous face are used as the first two points in the next.

Your pyramid should look much the same as before, but this time in red. To see the difference between the 3DFACE representation and the LINEs, move to the upper left viewport and issue the HIDE command. Then make the layer containing the lines the current layer and freeze layer, FACES. Try HIDE once more and you should still be able to see the all the lines. Thaw and Set the FACES layer again for the next part of the exercise.

Define your own coordinate system

The most important advance in 3D AutoCAD has been the introduction of user definable coordinate systems. This means that you can reset the position of the origin and also the orientation of the X, Y and Z axes. The default coordinates system that has been used up to now is the World Coordinate System (WCS). The WCS specifies the drawing origin and the directions of X,

Y and Z axes. Other coordinate systems are defined relative to this.

One possible point of difficulty can be deciding on which direction the positive Z axis points towards. AutoCAD uses the right hand rule to define all coordinate systems. Place your right hand near the screen with your palm facing you and extend the thumb to the right, forefinger up and middle finger towards you. These fingers show the positive directions of the X, Y and Z axes respectively. If you keep your fingers in that postiion and rotate your hand you will see how the axes of the new coordinate system relate to each other.

In this section you will draw an inscribed circle on the ABE slope. To try this in the WCS would be fruitless because AutoCAD circles are always drawn in the XY plane. You have to define a User Coordinate System (UCS) parallel to the slope. In fact you have to make a new UCS for every new plane you want to draw circles or other 2D entities in.

The UCS command appears on the AutoCAD screen menu. Pick it or type **UCS** at the keyboard. Try resetting the origin to the point A on the pyramid.

> Command: **UCS**
> Origin/Zaxis/3point/Entity/View/X/Y/Z/Prev/Restore/Save/Del/?/
>   <World>:**O**
> Origin point <0,0,0>: **1000,1000,0** or pick pt A in right viewport.

The little UCS icon should now move to A. The "W" disappears from the icon but a small "+" indicates that it is at the UCS origin. This shifting of the origin can be very useful even in 2D drawings. Note that all coordinate values are now relative to this new origin.

Now define the four slopes as new coordinate systems. The options for defining the plane are quite varied. You can align the UCS with an entity such as a 3DFACE, or you can specify three points in the plane. You can also select the XY plane or specify a new Z axis direction. The UCS can also be set to a particular VIEW or rotated about any of the XYZ axes. Different UCS definitions can be named and saved and restored like VIEWs.

> Command: <**ENTER**>
> UCS
> Origin/Zaxis/3point/Entity/View/X/Y/Z/Prev/Restore/Save/Del/?/
>   <World>:**E**
> Select object to align UCS: Pick the face ABE along edge AB.

The UCS icon should now take up its new orientation. Save this UCS as "ABE". The position of the origin is dependent on which point of the 3D face was originally drawn first. This method cannot be used with entities that contain non-coplanar points.

Now save this UCS.

> Command: <**ENTER**>
> UCS
> Origin/Zaxis/3point/Entity/View/X/Y/Z/Prev/Restore/Save/Del/?/
>   <World>:**S**
> ?/Name of UCS: **ABE**

Define the BCE plane by picking each of the points with object snap intersection and save it.

Command: <**ENTER**>
UCS
Origin/Zaxis/3point/Entity/View/X/Y/Z/Prev/Restore/Save/Del/?/
    <World>:**3**
Origin point <0,0,0>: **INT** of Pick point B.
Point on positive portion of X axis <601,0,0>:**INT** of Pick point C.
Point on positive portion of the UCS X-Y plane <599,0,0>:**INT** of
    Pick E.
Command: <**ENTER**>
UCS
Origin/ZAxis/3point/Entity/View/X/Y/Z/Prev/Restore/Save/Del/
    ?/<World>:**S**
?/Name of UCS: **BCE**

To demonstrate this method further restore the WCS and define a new UCS for the side CDE. Remember the right hand rule for positive axis directions.

Command: <**ENTER**>
UCS
Origin/ZAxis/3point/Entity/View/X/Y/Z/Prev/Restore/Save/Del/
    ?/<World>:**W**
Command: <**ENTER**>
UCS
Origin/ZAxis/3point/Entity/View/X/Y/Z/Prev/Restore/Save/Del/
    ?/<World>:**3**
Origin point <0,0,0>: **1600,1600,0**   (C)
Point on positive portion of X axis <1601,1600,0>:
    1000,1600,0   (D)
Point on positive portion of the UCS X-Y plane
<1600,1599,0>:**1300,1300,475**   (E)
Command: <**ENTER**>
UCS
Origin/ZAxis/3point/Entity/View/X/Y/Z/Prev/Restore/Save/Del/
    ?/<World>:**S**
?/Name of UCS: **CDE**

Finally, use the Entity option to make the fourth UCS for side DAE.

Command: <**ENTER**>
UCS
Origin/Zaxis/3point/Entity/View/X/Y/Z/Prev/Restore/Save/Del/
    ?/<World>:**E**
Select object to align UCS: Pick the face DAE along edge AD.

The UCS icon moves to point A since that was the first point used to originally draw the 3D face. The X axis is positive along the line AD as that was the original input order of the points. The positive Y axis is up the face. From the right hand rule this means that the Z axis is positive into the pyramid. All the other faces have UCS's with Z positive out from the pyramid. To make this last UCS consistent you should move the origin to D and make D to A the positive direction for the X axis. This latter task can be accomplished by rotating the UCS about the Y axis.

```
Command: <ENTER>
UCS
Origin/Zaxis/3point/Entity/View/X/Y/Z/Prev/Restore/Save/Del/
    ?/<World>:O
Origin point <0,0,0>: 600,0 Point D relative to current UCS.
Command: <ENTER>
UCS
Origin/Zaxis/3point/Entity/View/X/Y/Z/Prev/Restore/Save/Del/
    ?/<World>:Y
Rotation angle about Y axis 0.0: 180
Command: <ENTER>
UCS
Origin/ZAxis/3point/Entity/View/X/Y/Z/Prev/Restore/Save/Del/
    ?/<World>:S
?/Name of UCS: DAE
```

This effectively flips the UCS over. You should now see the icon at D with the X arrow pointing towards A and Y pointing up the slope.

To get a list of these defined coordinate systems use the "?" option from the UCS command:

```
Command: UCS
Origin/Zaxis/3point/Entity/View/X/Y/Z/Prev/Restore/Save/Del/
    ?/<World>:?
```

Table 8.1 UCS definitions

Current UCS: DAE

Saved coordinate systems:

ABE	Origin = <600,−0,−0>, X axis = <−0,1,−1>
	Y axis = <−1,1,0>, Z axis = <1,0,0>
BCE	Origin = <600,320,−507>, X axis = <−1,−0,0>
	Y axis = <0,0,1>, Z axis = <−0.1,−0>
CDE	Origin = <−0,320,−507, X axis = <0,−1,1>
	Y axis = <1,1,0>, Z axis = <−1,0,0>
DAE	Origin = <0,−0,0>, X axis = <1,0,−0>
	Y axis = <1,1,0>, Z axis = <−1,0,0>

The coordinates in the "<>" are relative to the current UCS. To see the definitions with respect to the WCS you will first have to select the **W** option and repeat the above command.

    Origin/Zaxis/3point/Entity/View/X/Y/Z/Prev/Restore/Save/Del/
      ?/<World>:**W**

You can restore any of the named UCS's, or delete ones that are no longer required. The "Prev" option restores the previous UCS setting.

The all seeing eye

You can now use these four coordinate systems to add bricks to the pyramid walls and to draw the "all seeing eye". Use the right hand viewport for the following constructions. Restore the "ABE" **UCS** and set up a plan view before drawing the eye. The **PLAN** command is a subset of VIEW and can be found on the DISPLAY sub-menu (Figure 8.10).

    Command: **UCS**
    Origin/Zaxis/3point/Entity/View/X/Y/Z/Prev/Restore/Save/Del/
      ?/<World>:**R**
    ?/Name of UCS to restore: **ABE**
    Command: **PLAN**
    <Current UCS>/Ucs/World: <**ENTER**>

This causes the view point to change so that you are now looking perpendicularly down on the face ABE. AutoCAD executes a ZOOM Extents automatically when a PLAN has been selected. This means that the edge lines will appear at the very edge of the viewport. To get a better picture use **ZOOM** to reduce the size. Then create two new layers on which to draw the wall pictures.

    Command: **ZOOM**
    All/Center/Dynamic/Extents/Left/Previous/Window/<Scale (X)>: **0.9X**
    Command: **LAYER**
    ?/Make/Set/New/ON/OFF/Color/Ltype/Freeze/Thaw: **N**
    New layer name(s): **EYE,WALLS**
    ?/Make/Set/New/ON/OFF/Color/Ltype/Freeze/Thaw: **C**
    Color: **BLUE**
    Layer name(s) for color 5 (blue) <FACES>: **EYE**
    ?/Make/Set/New/ON/OFF/Color/Ltype/Freeze/Thaw: **S**
    New current layer <FACES>: **EYE**
    ?/Make/Set/New/ON/OFF/Color/Ltype/Freeze/Thaw: <**ENTER**>

To inscribe a circle in the ABE triangle draw a three-point circle using object snap "TANgent".

Command: **CIRCLE**
3P/2P/TTR/enter point: **3P**
First point: **TAN** to Pick the line AB.
Second point: **TAN** to Pick the line AE.
Third point: **TAN** to Pick the line BE.

The circle should fit nicely in the triangle. You can now use two arcs to draw the eye shape. Use the quadrant points of the circle with object snap to locate the end and centre points. Then mirror the arc about the line FG (Figure 8.10).

Command: **ARC**
Center/<Start point>: **QUAD** of Pick circle near point F.
Center/End/<Second point>: **E**
End point: **QUAD** of Pick circle near point G.
Angle/Direction/Radius/<Centre point>: **300,0**   (H)
Command: **MIRROR**
Select objects: **LAST**
1 found.
Select objects: <**ENTER**>
First point of mirror line: **INT** of Pick point F.
Second point: @**1,0**   (A horizontal line.)
Delete old objects? <N>: <**ENTER**>

The pupil and iris will complete the all seeing eye. A doughnut makes a good pupil while a circular array gives the iris. Another circle encloses both.

Command: **CIRCLE**
3P/2P/TTR/<Center point>: **CEN** of Pick the inscribed circle.
Diameter/<Radius>: **70**
Command: **DONUT** (Can also be spelt "DOUGHNUT".)
Inside diameter <1>: **0**
Outside diameter <1>: **60**
Center of doughnut: @   (The centre of the circles.)
Center of doughnut: <**ENTER**>

Now draw the line from the doughnut to the small circle and ARRAY it.

Command: **LINE**
From point: @**30,0**
To point: @**40,0**
To point: <**ENTER**>
Command: **ARRAY**
Select objects: **LAST**
1 found.
Select objects: <**ENTER**>
Rectangular or Polar array (R/P): **P**
Center point of array: **300,180**   (The centre of the circles.)
Number of items: **36**
Angle to fill (+=ccw, −=cw) <360>: <**ENTER**>
Rotate objects as they are copied? <Y>: <**ENTER**>

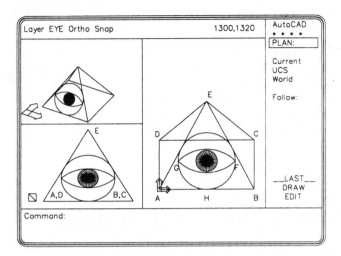

Figure 8.10 The all seeing eye

The all seeing eye of Cheops' pyramid should now look like that in Figure 8.10. The doughnut will appear fully solid only in plan views. Now is a good time to SAVE the drawing as the next task is to HATCH the walls with a brick pattern.

Command: **SAVE**
File name <EXP-GIZA>: <**ENTER**>
Command: **LAYER**
?/Make/Set/New/ON/OFF/Color/Ltype/Freeze/Thaw: **S**
New current layer <EYE>: **WALLS**
?/Make/Set/New/ON/OFF/Color/Ltype/Freeze/Thaw: <**ENTER**>
Command: **HATCH**
Pattern (? or name/U,style): **BRICK**
Scale for pattern <1.0>: **100**
Angle for pattern <0.00>: <**ENTER**>
Select objects: **300,360** or pick the large inscribed circle.
1 selected, 1 found.
Select objects: **140,0** or pick the face ABE along the line AB.
1 selected, 1 found.
Select objects: <**ENTER**>

The area outside the circle should now be hatched in all three viewports. If the wrong area has been bricked in use "ERASE, last" and try again.

To put the bricks on the other three walls you will have to restore each UCS with a PLAN view and execute the HATCH command. There is a special option with the PLAN command called "Follow". This causes AutoCAD to go automatically to the plan view whenever a UCS is restored or newly defined. This effect is dependent on the setting of a system variable, UCSFOLLOW.

Setting UCSFOLLOW to 1 enables this feature, 0 disables it. Pick **Follow:** from the PLAN menu (part of the DISPLAY sub-menu).

```
Command: 'SETVAR Variable name or ? <>: UCSFOLLOW
New value for UCSFOLLOW 0: 1
```

Picking it from the menu saves you a bit of typing. Of course you can always do it the long-hand way with the SETVAR command.

```
Command: UCS
Origin/Zaxis/3point/Entity/View/X/Y/Z/Prev/Restore/Save/Del/
    ?/<World>:R
?/Name of UCS to restore: BCE
Command: HATCH
Pattern (? or name/U,style) <BRICK>: <ENTER>
Scale for pattern <100.0000>: <ENTER>
Angle for pattern <0.00>: <ENTER>
Select objects: 140,0 or pick the face BCE along the line BC.
1 selected, 1 found.
Select objects: <ENTER>
```

Note how the display goes straight to the plan view. Now do the remaining two sides.

```
Command: UCS
Origin/Zaxis/3point/Entity/View/X/Y/Z/Prev/Restore/Save/Del/
    ?/<World>:R
?/Name of UCS to restore: CDE
Command: HATCH
Pattern (? or name/U,style) <BRICK>: <ENTER>
Scale for pattern <100.0000>: <ENTER>
Angle for pattern <0.00>: <ENTER>
Select objects: 140,0 or pick the face BCE along the line BC.
1 selected, 1 found.
Select objects: <ENTER>
Command: UCS
Origin/Zaxis/3point/Entity/View/X/Y/Z/Prev/Restore/Save/Del/
    ?/<World>:R
?/Name of UCS to restore: DAE
Command: HATCH
Pattern (? or name/U,style) <BRICK>: <ENTER>
Scale for pattern <100.0000>: <ENTER>
Angle for pattern <0.00>: <ENTER>
Select objects: 140,0 or pick the face BCE along the line BC.
1 selected, 1 found.
Select objects: <ENTER>
```

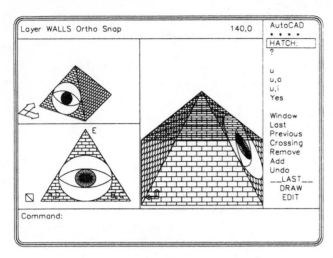

Figure 8.11 The brick-built pyramid

If you execute a HIDE on the upper left viewport, your picture should look like Figure 8.11. This may take a minute or two as approximately 2575 lines have to be removed.

>   Command: **HIDE**
>   Regenerating drawing.
>   Removing hidden lines: 2575

A dynamic view point on visualisation

Another of the goodies included in Release 10 is the Dynamic View command, DVIEW. This is quite an advance on the VPOINT command as it allows you to see the object as you move and twist it in full 3D. DVIEW effectively combines ZOOM, VPOINT, and a perspective view option with a powerful user interface. The emphasis is on 3D visualisation and much of the terminology comes from photography. To use DVIEW you have to imagine yourself looking through a camera lens at a target point.

To see the pyramid in all its glory let's use the full screen and revert to the World Coordinate System. It is advisable to do a zoom such that the object to be viewed appears near to the centre of the screen at a low magnification. If the object is near the edge or fills the screen the dynamic view may cause it to go off screen completely.

Command: **VPORTS**
Save/Restore/Delete/Join/SIngle/?/2/<3>/4: **SI**
Command: **UCS**
Origin/Zaxis/3point/Entity/View/X/Y/Z/Prev/Restore/Save/Del/
    ?/<World>:**W**
Command: **ZOOM**
All/Center/Dynamic/Extents/Left/Previous/Window/<Scale (X)>: **A**

Now pick **DVIEW:** from the DISPLAY sub-menu. This command has two
pages of screen menu. The first relates mainly to the "Select objects" options.
This allows the usual methods of selection with an extra option to select all the
objects on any layer. Once the selection has been completed you can pick
"Dview Options" to manipulate the display.

Command: **DVIEW** Pick from the screen menu.
Select objects: **W**
First corner: **900,900**
Second corner: **1700,1700**
58 found.
Select objects: **R**
Remove objects: Pick **By Layer** from the screen menu.
Layer name: <WALLS>: **0**
8 found, 8 removed
Remove objects: <**ENTER**>

Only the selected objects will be shown in the dynamic previews. When the
final view has been chosen, all the drawing will be displayed. You could have
included the construction lines from layer 0 but they wouldn't add much to the
visualisation. The command prompt changes to give all the display options.
The display will be calculated relative to a given camera position and the target
position. The target is the point where the camera is focussed on and will always
end up in the centre of the screen. The camera can be placed anywhere in 3D
space either inside or outside the pyramid. To find the current target position
select the **POints** option.

CAmera/TArget/Distance/POints/PAn/Zoom/TWist/CLip/Hide/
    Off/Undo/<eXit>: **PO**
Enter target point <1625.00, 1179.18, 247.38>: **1300,1300,0**
Enter camera point <1625.00, 1179.18, 248.38>: **1300,900,237**

The Z value in the defaults may differ slightly from yours. The new coordinates
put the target at the centre of the pyramid base and the camera in front of and
looking down on the eye. That was a static type of operation. To use the
dynamic view select the "CAmera" option. This allows you to specify the angle
from the XY plane (the base ABCD of the pyramid). A positive angle puts the
camera above the target, a negative angle below. A plan view can be generated

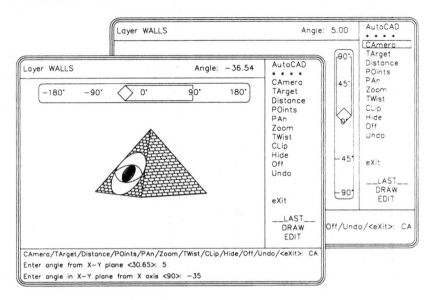

Figure 8.12 DVIEW's Camera slider bars

by using an angle of 90 degrees. You are then asked to put in a camera direction angle relative to the X axis (line AB). This angle rotates the camera in a horizontal plane while keeping it focussed on the target point.

When you select the **CA** option you are prompted for new angles with the current values as defaults. You can enter the angle by typing a value or by using the slider bars that appear on the screen (see Figure 8.12). These slider bars allow you to see the effect of different angles dynamically. As you move the cursor up and down the bar, the pyramid will be rotated and shown in preview mode. The preview image is shown in only one colour and is updated continuously. The speed of the update will depend on the number of objects displayed. Make sure that SNAP is OFF or the slider bar action may appear jumpy (Use **^B**).

> CAmera/TArget/Distance/POints/PAn/Zoom/TWist/CLip/Hide/
> Off/Undo/<eXit>: **CA**
> Enter angle in X-Y plane <30.65>: Use slider slowly and pick **5**
>   degs.
> Enter angle in X-Y plane from X axis <90.00>: Use slider and
>   pick **-35**

The TArget option works very like CAmera except that it is the target point that moves relative to the camera position. Remember, the target point will always end up in the middle of the screen. If you move the target up then the objects will appear lower in the display.

CAmera/TArget/Distance/POints/PAn/Zoom/TWist/CLip/Hide/
    Off/Undo/<eXit>: **TA**
Enter angle in X-Y plane <−5.00>: Use slider slowly and press
    <**ENTER**> to avoid changing the angle.
Enter angle in X-Y plane from X axis <145.00>: Use slider and
    press <**ENTER**>

PAn and Zoom options work similarly to the normal commands. The zoom is, however, a restricted version of the normal command. It only allows you to increase the magnification, similar to the ZOOM with Scale(X). You get a slider bar so you can see the effect before picking a scale factor. A scale factor less than 1 reduces the size and greater than 1 increases it. If you increase the scale too much the object might disappear. It hasn't gone anywhere, it's just that you are zoomed in on a single brick. Zoom back out to see the whole thing.

CAmera/TArget/Distance/POints/PAn/Zoom/TWist/CLip/Hide/
    Off/Undo/<eXit>: **Z**
Adjust zoom scale factor <1>: Use slider bar and press
    <**ENTER**> for default
CAmera/TArget/Distance/POints/PAn/Zoom/TWist/CLip/Hide/
    Off/Undo/<eXit>: **PA**
Displacement base point: Pick any point.
Second point: Move cursor around and enter ^C to cancel the pan.

TWist lets you rotate the view in the plane of the screen about the target point. This has the effect of rotating the camera on the line of sight. A rubber band appears from the target to the cursor cross-hairs and shows the current angle of twist. The angle is zero when the rubber band is horizontal and to the right. The camera is upright when the twist angle is zero, upside-down when the angle is 180 degrees and on its side for 90 degrees. The twist angle is an additional setting and does not affect the camera or target positions.

CAmera/TArget/Distance/POints/PAn/Zoom/TWist/CLip/Hide/
    Off/Undo/<eXit>: **TW**
New view twist <0.00>: Move cursor around and press
    <**ENTER**> for default.

You can generate cut-away images with the CLip option. This allows you to specify planes in front of and behind the target to cut through the object. Nothing between the camera and the front plane will be displayed. Similarly nothing behind the back plane is shown. This can be used to eliminate unnecessary foreground and background detail or to generate a cut-away view.

CAmera/TArget/Distance/POints/PAn/Zoom/TWist/CLip/Hide/
    Off/Undo/<eXit>: **CL**
Back/Front/<Off>: **F**
Eye/ON/OFF/<Distance from target> <464.94>: **215**

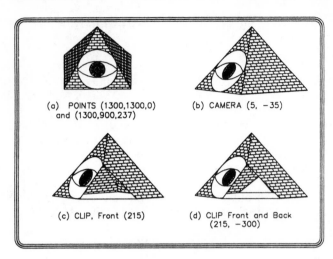

(a) POINTS (1300,1300,0)
    and (1300,900,237)

(b) CAMERA (5, −35)

(c) CLIP, Front (215)

(d) CLIP Front and Back
    (215, −300)

Figure 8.13 DVIEWS of Cheops with HIDE

The "Eye" option places the front plane at the camera point. This is useful for perspective views when clipping cannot be turned off. In normal dynamic viewing you can turn the front clip ON and OFF.

To get a better view of the front clip use the Hide option (Figure 8.13). This does a hidden line removal just like the HIDE command. Then clip a piece off the back and remove the hidden lines.

> CAmera/TArget/Distance/POints/PAn/Zoom/TWist/CLip/Hide/
>   Off/Undo/<eXit>: **H**
> Removing hidden lines: 1875
> CAmera/TArget/Distance/POints/PAn/Zoom/TWist/CLip/Hide/
>   Off/Undo/<eXit>: **CL**
> Back/Front/<Off>: **B**
> ON/OFF/<Distance from target> <−149.93>: **−300**
> CAmera/TArget/Distance/POints/PAn/Zoom/TWist/CLip/Hide/
>   Off/Undo/<eXit>: **H**
> Removing hidden lines: 1825

The minus indicates that the plane is to be behind the target. These clipping planes will remain in effect until CLip is disabled.

Getting things in persepective

To get a realistic view of objects you can generate a perspective view. When objects are in perspective the ones nearer the camera appear bigger than those further away. You can control the perspective view by choosing the "Distance"

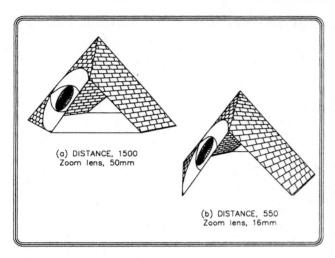

(a) DISTANCE, 1500
Zoom lens, 50mm

(b) DISTANCE, 550
Zoom lens, 16mm

Figure 8.14 Perspective views

option from DVIEW. You specify the distance from the camera to the target point and AutoCAD calculates the appropriate sizes of the objects. Again, a slider bar is available to input the distance via the mouse, and the status line gives a read-out of the current slider bar position.

> CAmera/TArget/Distance/POints/PAn/Zoom/TWist/CLip/Hide/
>   Off/Undo/<eXit>: **D**
> New camera/target distance <464.94>: **1500**

WARNING!

The UCS icon should change to a perspective view of rectangular block. Most of AutoCAD's commands do not work on perspective views, so keep your eye out for this icon.

Zoom operates slightly differently when a perspective view is displayed. Instead of asking you for a scale factor AutoCAD asks for a camera lens length. The default is 50mm which is the standard lens focal length for most cameras. Making the lens length longer is like using a telephoto lens and magnifies the image. A shorter lens length simulates a wide angle camera lens which accentuates the perspective (Figure 8.14). The slider bar gives the zooms in multiples of the current lens length.

> CAmera/TArget/Distance/POints/PAn/Zoom/TWist/CLip/Hide/
>   Off/Undo/<eXit>: **Z**
> Adjust lenslength <50.000mm>: **16**

To get an interesting fish-eye lens effect, shorten the perspective distance and do another hide.

> CAmera/TArget/Distance/POints/PAn/Zoom/TWist/CLip/Hide/
>   Off/Undo/<eXit>: **D**
> New camera/target distance <1000>: **550**
> CAmera/TArget/Distance/POints/PAn/Zoom/TWist/CLip/Hide/
>   Off/Undo/<eXit>: **H**
> Removing hidden lines: 2100

To round off the DVIEW command the "Off" option turns the perspective viewing off. "Undo" goes back to the previous view and "eXit" leaves the DVIEW command. The display retains the DVIEW settings on exit.

> CAmera/TArget/Distance/POints/PAn/Zoom/TWist/CLip/Hide/
>   Off/Undo/<eXit>: **X**
> Command: **END**

That concludes the AutoCAD Express stop in Egypt. It doesn't conclude the exploration of AutoCAD's third dimension. The next section covers the remaining exciting features.

AutoCAD's 3D box of tricks

You have already used the 3DFACE command and drawn lines in 3D space. AutoCAD contains a range of facilities for creating complicated 3D objects containing many sides and faces. You can also generate smooth surfaces and 3D polylines. You will find these in the 3D sub-menu.

The 3DPOLY command allows you to create a polyline in 3D space. The PLINE command is restricted to 2D. Points can be specified in the same way as for drawing a 3D line but the use of 3DPOLY is restricted to straight line segments. The line width is zero and cannot be changed. Neither can you draw a 3D polyarc. You can use PEDIT on a 3D polyline to change any of the vertices or to fit a spline curve to the points.

Start up a new drawing with limits (0,0) to (420,297). Call the drawing "EXP-3D". You will use this to draw examples of the 3D constructions.

> Main menu
>
> Enter selection: **1**
>
> Enter NAME of drawing: **EXP-3D**

Command: **LIMITS**
ON/OFF/<Lower left corner> <0.00,0.00>: <**ENTER**>
Upper right corner <420.00,297.00>: **840,594**
Command: **3DPOLY**
From point: 100,100,0   (A)
Close/Undo/<Endpoint of line>: @**125,0,25**   (B)
Close/Undo/<Endpoint of line>: @**0,125,25**   (C)
Close/Undo/<Endpoint of line>: @**−130,0,25**   (D)
Close/Undo/<Endpoint of line>: @**0,−130,25**   (E)
Close/Undo/<Endpoint of line>: @**135,0,25**   (F)
Close/Undo/<Endpoint of line>: @**0,135,25**   (G)
Close/Undo/<Endpoint of line>: <**ENTER**>

Use PEDIT to make this into a spiral (Figure 8.15).

Command: **PEDIT**
Select polyline: **LAST**
Close/Edit vertex/Spline curve/Decurve/Undo/eXit <X>: **S**
Close/Edit vertex/Spline curve/Decurve/Undo/eXit <X>: <**ENTER**>

Note that PEDIT recognised that the object is a 3D polyline and offers only the
relevant editing options. The accuracy of the fit is controlled by a system
variable "SPLINESEGS". If the system variable "SPLFRAME" is non-zero
then the original polyline is also shown. This gives an idea of how accurately the
curve fits the points. Do this and change the view point to see the graceful
spiral. Non-zero SPLFRAME also shows up any invisible 3DFACE edges.

Command: **SETVAR**
Variable name or ? **SPLFRAME**
New value for SPLFRAME <0>: **1**
Command: **VPOINT**
Rotate/<View point>: <0.00,0.00,1.00>: **1,−1,1**

Meshes

You can build up the surface of an object by using lots of 3DFACEs but it could
take a long time. A slight improvement is to use the 3DMESH command but
this still requires you to input the coordinates of each vertex. If the object has a
regular shape then the mesh can be generated from various control lines using
either EDGESURF, REVSURF, RULESURF or TABSURF.

To make a mesh you need to select "3DMESH" from the 3D sub-menu and
then specify the number of vertices. These are given in the length and breadth
directions (M and N, respectively).

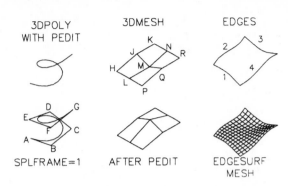

Figure 8.15 3D spiral and meshes

Command: **SETVAR**
Variable name or ? <SPLFRAME>: <ENTER>
New value for SPLFRAME <1>: **0**
Command: **3DMESH**
Mesh M size: **3**
Mesh N size: **3**   (This will make four faces in the mesh.)
Vertex (0,0): **300,100,50**   (H)
Vertex (0,1): **300,180,70**   (J)
Vertex (0,2): **300,250,70**   (K)
Vertex (1,0): **350,100,50**   (L)
Vertex (1,1): **350,180,50**   (M)
Vertex (1,2): **350,250,70**   (N)
Vertex (2,0): **400,100,50**   (P)
Vertex (2,1): **400,180,70**   (Q)
Vertex (2,2): **400,250,70**   (R)

You can use PEDIT on 3DMESHes as well (Figure 8.15). The edit options are different when a mesh is selected. You can smooth the mesh, close it in either M or N directions or change individual vertices. Use PEDIT to raise the middle vertex (1,1), M, by 40 units.

Command: **PEDIT**
Select polyline: **LAST**
Edit vertex/Smooth surface/Desmooth/Mclose/Nclose/Undo/eXit
    <X>: **E**
Vertex (0,0). Next/Previous/Left/Right/Up/Down/Move/REgen/
    eXit <N>: **U**

The Up/Down refers to movements in the M direction and Left/Right the N direction. When you get to the desired vertex you can "Move" it.

Vertex (1,0).Next/Previous/Left/Right/Up/Down/Move/REgen/
   eXit <U>: **R**
Vertex (1,1). Next/Previous/Left/Right/Up/Down/Move/REgen/
   eXit <R>: **M**
Enter new location: **@0,0,40**
Vertex (1,1).
Next/Previous/Left/Right/Up/Down/Move/REgen/eXit <R>: **X**
Edit vertex/Smooth surface/Desmooth/Mclose/Nclose/Undo/
   eXit <X>: **ENTER**

Note that the numbering of the vertices starts at (0,0) and so (1,1) is the second across and second up. Smoothing is only relevant when there are more than two faces in one of the directions. 3DMESH is a fairly tedious operation for larger meshes. It is, however, relatively easy to incorporate into AutoLISP programs. See Chapters 11 and 12 for more details.

Generated surfaces

The 3DPOLY is quite good for defining the edges of a surface. Once the edges are known, EDGESURF, RULESURF, TABSURF and REVSURF can be used to fill in the surface. TABSURF requires one edge and an extrusion direction, REVSURF needs a profile edge and an axis of revolution. RULESURF is defined by two edges, while EDGESURF is the most complicated, requiring four edge curves.

EDGESURF works by interpolating a Coons surface patch between four curves. The Coons patch is a mathematical technique using two cubic equations. The edges can be made up of lines, arcs, or open polylines and must touch at their end points. Use 3DPOLY to create four connected curves and then execute EDGESURF (Figure 8.15).

   Command: **EDGESURF**
   Select edge 1: Pick the first edge curve.
   Select edge 2: Pick the second edge curve.
   Select edge 3: Pick the third.
   Select edge 4: Pick the fourth.

This generates a polygon mesh which can be edited in the same way as the 3DMESH above. The vertices are numbered with the M direction along the first edge curve. The (0,0) vertex will be at the end point of the first edge nearest to the pick point used to select it. The number of faces that are created depends on the values of the two system variables, SURFTAB1 for the M direction and SURFTAB2 for N. The defaults for these are 12 each and they can be changed either using SETVAR or by picking Surftb1: or Surftb2: from the screen menu.

You must have four edges to define an EDGESURF mesh. If the shape requires only three curves then use BREAK to divide one of the sides in two.

If some of the sides can be defined by straight lines or regular shapes such as arcs and circles then the command TABSURF, RULESURF or REVSURF may be more appropriate (see Figure 8.16).

TABSURF is good for extruding objects in 3D space. It gives an effect similar to setting an entity THICKNESS but is more general. To generate a TABulated SURFace you require some object, called path curve in AutoCAD, to extrude and a line defining the direction of extrusion. In descriptive geometry jargon you need a *directrix* object and a *generatrix* vector. To make a leaning tower draw a circle in the WCS plan and a 3D line.

> Command: **CIRCLE**
> 3P/2P/TTR/<Center point>: **500,300,0**
> Diameter/<Radius>: **50**
> Command: **LINE**
> From point: **570,300,0**
> To point: **@0,40,100**
> To point: **<ENTER>**
> Command: **TABSURF**
> Select path curve: Pick the circle.
> Select direction vector: Pick the line.

This generates an open ended leaning tower. It is not cylindrical though, since the direction vector is not perpendicular to the plane of the circle. The extrusion direction depends on the point order used when the line was drawn.

A ruled surface is more general than the tabulated surface. You specify two boundary edges and RULESURF joins them together with straight lines to form a polygon mesh. You can use open or closed 2D and 3D polylines, circles, arcs, lines and points. However you cannot mix a closed object such as a circle with and open object such as a line. Points can be used with either open or closed paths. Make a surface from an arc to a line.

> Command: **ARC**
> Center/<Start point>: **800,300,0**
> Center/End/<Second point>: **C**
> Center: **750,300,0**
> Angle/Length of chord/<End point>: **A**
> Included angle: **270**
> Command: **LINE**
> From point: **800,500,0**
> To point: **@−220,0,30**
> To point: **<ENTER>**
> Command: **RULESURF**
> Select first defining curve: Pick the arc near the start point.
> Select second defining curve: Pick the line near (800,500,0).

PATH AND   2 CURVES   PATH AND
DIRECTION   AXIS

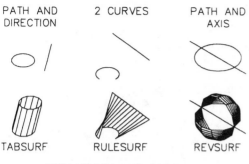

TABSURF   RULESURF   REVSURF

WITH HIDDEN LINE REMOVAL

Figure 8.16 3D generated surfaces

The two end points nearest the places where the curves are picked define the starting vertices of the mesh. If you pick one of the curves near the wrong end the surface will be twisted. If this happens use the UNDO command and try again, picking the points at the correct ends of the curves. The number of divisions for both TABSURF and RULESURF is determined by the SURF-TAB1 system variable.

The final surface generator in the 3D box of tricks is REVSURF. This produces a surface of revolution from a definition path and an axis to rotate it around. Common surfaces of revolution include wine goblets, spheres, torus shapes and power station cooling towers. REVSURF allows you to make either closed surfaces or open ones by controlling the angle of rotation. To make a part sphere draw a circle with an axis along one diameter.

> Command: **CIRCLE**
> 3P/2P/TTR/<Center point>: **570,150,0**
> Diameter/<Radius>: **100**
> Command: **LINE**
> From point: **400,300**
> To point: **@340,0**
> Command: **REVSURF**
> Select path curve: Pick the circle.
> Select axis of revolution: Pick the line.
> Start angle <0>: <**ENTER**>
> Included angle (+ccw −cw) <Full circle>: **90**

The positive direction of the axis depends on where the line defining the axis is picked. Angles are positive in the anti-clockwise direction as you look from the picked point to the furthest end point.

3D objects

AutoCAD comes with a number of extra programs to draw common 3D shapes including spheres, cones and pyramids. These can be used by picking "3D objects" from the 3D sub-menu or from the pull-down menu. The pull-down menu gives descriptive icons and is obtained by picking 3D from the menu bar followed by "3D construction". In some versions you will have to pick "DRAW" and "3D construction" from the menu bar.

When you use "3D objects" for the first time in an editing session you will get the message "Please wait . . . Loading 3D Objects". After a few seconds you will be able to use the extra commands: BOX, CONE, DISH, DOME, MESH, PYRAMID, SPHERE, TORUS and WEDGE. The prompts are self explanatory and don't need detailed description here. The operation of some of the commands is described in Chapter 12.

Summary

This chapter has covered the use of AutoCAD in isometric projection, 2.5D and full 3D. You have also encountered the display features of user coordinate systems and view points. The UCS and VPORT commands can be used in 2D drafting as well as 3D. Dynamic viewing is a powerful aid to visualising 3D spatial relationships.

The UCS facility is the most important tool in 3D computer aided drafting. Many objects are 2D (eg arcs, circles) and can only be drawn in plan. To draw a sloping circle you have to create a coordinate system so that the plane of the circle is the same as the plane of the UCS.

Using 3D CAD involves an extra level of difficulty above 2D drafting and requires much more discipline. You must keep track of where objects are and also what coordinate system and view point is being used. Vigilance helps to prevent troublesome errors caused by optical illusions.

You should now be able to:

Draw lines and circles in isometric projection.
Create objects with different elevations and thicknesses.
Use hidden line removal.
Set up multiple viewports.
View 2.5D and 3D objects from different view points.
Define new coordinate systems in 3D space.
Draw objects in 3D space.
Run dynamic visualisations and create perspective views.
Generate 3D surfaces.

Chapter 9 THE HARD COPY – PRINTING AND PLOTTING

General

The main purpose of producing drawings with AutoCAD is to communicate graphical information. Even at this late stage in the twentieth century the primary medium for such communication is with pictures on paper. Paper drawings are very user friendly in that they are easy to read and transport and also provide a useful framework for rough work and checking. With this in mind the current chapter is devoted to methods of translating the digital information in the AutoCAD drawing into black marks on paper.

A new order of activity is involved in producing plots and prints. That is you have to control another piece of equipment, be it printer, plotter or both. According to Murphy's Law this extra complexity inevitably leads to more things that will go wrong. To avoid the heartache and frustration associated with peripheral blues, stay calm and follow the guidelines laid out below.

Unless you have access to very expensive plotting equipment the generation of a hardcopy of a drawing takes time. The cheaper your plotter the longer it will take. In general you will not want to have to reproduce plots too often and so the aim is to get it right first time, if at all possible.

You will produce copies of some drawings from earlier chapters. Make sure that the drawing files BALLOON.DWG, from Chapter 4, and GLAND.DWG, from Chapter 7, are handy. If you don't have these files you can improvise with some other simple drawings. Avoid plotting bigger drawings until you have more experience.

It is assumed that AutoCAD has been configured correctly for your printer and plotter. If you are not sure if this has been done refer to Appendix A or the AutoCAD Hardware Installation Guide.

Printer-plotting

Drawings can be output on various types of printers, from humble 9-pin dot matrix to whizz-bang laser printers. Daisywheel printers do not support graphics and so are no good for AutoCAD. The quality of the printer plot depends on the resolution capability of the device. The printer produces the picture by converting all the graphics into a series of dots which are then inscribed on the paper. The crucial statistic for assessing resolution is the number of *dots per inch* (dpi) capability of the printer. The higher the dpi the better the picture quality. This is most noticeable when plotting arcs and other curved entities and shallow sloping lines.

With laser printers you must also check the maximum area that can be plotted at the highest resolution. A sneaky trick by some printer manufacturers was to advertise a high resolution of say 300dpi but conceal in the small print that this could only be achieved for drawings with a total area of less than 6 square inches. Most laser printers and inkjet printers being sold now will allow 300dpi for a full page or about 88 square inches.

The drawings reproduced below were generated on Epson LX-800, 9-pin dot matrix and Hewlett Packard Inkjet-Plus printers. Note that if you use different printers from time to time, you will have to reconfigure AutoCAD each time you change.

Printing the GLAND drawing

One of the quickest ways of obtaining a print is to use AutoCAD's main menu. Selecting item 4 from the menu starts the printer plot routine. This asks the user for some information about the drawing to be plotted, which part of the drawing to plot and so on. You can also control where on the page the plot is to be placed and what scale should be used.

    Main menu

    0. Exit AutoCAD
    1. Begin a NEW drawing
    2. Edit an EXISTING drawing
    3. Plot a drawing
    4. Printer plot a drawing

    5. Configure AutoCAD
    6. File Utilities
    7. Compile a shape/font description file
    8. Convert old drawing file

    Enter selection: **4**

    Enter name of drawing <>: **GLAND**

    What to plot – Display, Extents, Limits, View or Window <D>: **L**

Remember, the limits were set to (0,0) and (65,45) in Chapter 7. Everything within these limits is to be printed. AutoCAD then displays a message indicating the current printer plot settings and gives you the option of changing them if you desire. Window and Extents behave as with the ZOOM command. Extents finds the lower left and upper right corners of a window just big enough to enclose all the entities. Display will produce a plot of the display when the drawing was last SAVEd or ENDed.

> Plot will NOT be written to a selected file
> Sizes are in Millimeters
> Plot origin is at (0.00,0.00)
> Plotting area is 345.23 wide by 279.40 (MAX size)
> 2D Plots are rotated by 90 degrees
> Hidden lines will NOT be removed
> Plot will be scaled to fit available area

The first line indicates that the plot will not be directed to a file and will be sent to the printer. In some cases it is desirable to generate plot files which can be sent to the printer later. For example if you had a large number of drawings to print or if the printer was not available you could still generate the plot files, store them on disk and print them later. Examples of this are treated later.

The second line shows whether inches or millimetres are being used for the drawing units and print out sizes. The plot origin allows you to alter the position of the print out on the page. The plotting area indicates the size of the paper being used. I have assumed that a narrow carriage printer is being used, ie one where the page size is longer than it is wide. However, the GLAND drawing is wider that it is high. To get the largest print out you should specify that the plot be rotated by 90 degrees. The line about the hidden line removal really only applies to 3D plots. The extra processing involved in hidden line removal can take a long time and should be avoided if at all possible. The line, "Plot will be scaled to fit available area", means that AutoCAD will calculate a scale factor so that the chosen paper size will be used in full.

If all the settings appear as above then you can accept them and proceed. The plotting area may differ from one printer to the next. As long as the MAX size for your printer is being used you will get the largest plot possible. If any of the settings need alteration, answer Yes to the next question and follow the steps outlined under "Altering the printer parameters".

Make sure that the printer is switched on and that it is "ON LINE" and contains paper.

> Do you want to change anything? <N> <**ENTER**>
> Effective plotting area: 193.43 wide by 279.40 high
> Position paper in printer.
> Press RETURN to continue: <**ENTER**>

The printer works in rasters or line by line and the whole drawing must be translated to raster information before any actual printing takes place. This can take a number of minutes and, so that you know things are in progress, AutoCAD displays how many of the drawing vectors have been translated.

> Processing vector: xxxx

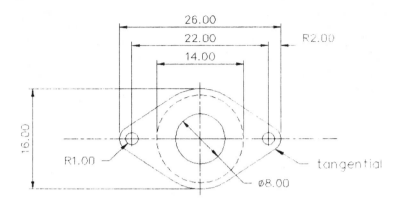

Figure 9.1 The GLAND printer plot (dot matrix)

Where the "xxxx" is the actual number of the vector and should increase rapidly. Unfortunately, AutoCAD only tells you how many vectors it has already processed and not how many are left. This means that you don't really know how much longer it will take. When sufficient processing has been completed the printer will start operating. On completion, you will get the output as in Figure 9.1, and the message:

Printer Plot complete.

Press RETURN to continue: <**ENTER**>

Pressing <**ENTER**> will bring back the main menu.

Altering the print parameters

While the method described above is a relatively quick way of getting output it has a number of unsatisfactory aspects. Firstly, the picture that is plotted is unseen. The user has to remember exactly what was visible when the drawing was last edited. Layers that were frozen or turned off will not be printed. It is far better to be able to see the picture on the screen before printing begins. This will help to reduce the number of incorrect plots produced. Another aspect worth considering is the lack of control over the scale factor that was used. While the proportions will be true it will be difficult to get a meaningful visualisation of the real sizes. Engineers and designers are used to reading drawings at specific scales (2:1, 1:1, 1:5 etc). Faced with a scale of say 3.567:1, difficulties arise.

In the next example a printer plot will be generated from within the AutoCAD editor and a second will be got ready for plotting at a later stage. You will take full control of the print parameters to produce hardcopy of the

BALLOON drawing. By saving a close up VIEW of the balloon itself you will be able to plot it later.

From the AutoCAD main menu, select 2. Edit an EXISTING drawing and enter **BALLOON** as the drawing name. Do a **ZOOM All** to get the display as shown in Figure 9.2. Before issuing any print or plot instructions from within the AutoCAD editor you should save the drawing. This is good CAD practice as a malfunction of the peripheral can cause the computer to hang up. If you have to reboot the system you will lose everything after the last SAVE command. After saving, pick **PLOT** from the screen menu and then pick **PRINTER** from the sub-menu. This executes the PRPLOT command and starts the same routine as given above. This time you can plot the display (which in this instance is the same as the limits).

> Command: **SAVE**
> File name <BALLOON>: <**ENTER**>
> Command: PRPLOT
> What to plot – Display, Extents, Limits, View or Window <L>: **D**
>
> Plot will NOT be written to a selected file
> Sizes are in Millimeters
> Plot origin is at (0.00,0.00)
> Plotting area is 345.33 wide by 279.40 (MAX size)
> 2D Plots are rotated by 90 degrees
> Hidden lines will NOT be removed
> Plot will be scaled to fit available area

Assuming you wish to use A4 size paper (210mm × 297mm) and want the output at a scale of 1mm on the plot to 0.25 units in the drawing file:

> Do you want to change anything? <N> **Y**
> Write the plot to a file? <N> <**ENTER**>
> Size units (Inches or Millimeters) <M>: <**ENTER**>
> Plot origin in Millimeters <0.00,0.00>: <**ENTER**>
>
> Standard values for plotting size

Size	Width	Height
A4	285.00	198.00
MAX	345.33	279.40

> Enter the Size or Width,Height (in Millimeters) <MAX>: **A4**

The page sizes available depend on the make and model of your printer. Standard sizes can be selected either by keying the mnemonic (eg A4) or giving the values for the width and height. The A4 could also have been chosen by keying "285,198". You can specify any paper size as long as you don't exceed the MAX values for your printer. A second point to note is that the actual plot

Figure 9.2 PRPLOT on inkjet printer

size may be less than the full page size. This occurs for printers that cannot print right up to the edges of the page and some allowance must be made for the margins. For example, the A4 size quoted is 285mm × 198mm while the actual paper size is 297mm × 210mm.

> Rotate 2D plots 90 degrees clockwise? <Y> <**ENTER**>

This causes the picture to be produced sideways on the page.

> Remove hidden lines? <N> <**ENTER**>
> Specify scale by entering:
> Plotted Millimeters=Drawing Units or Fit or ? <Fit>: **1=0.25**

Thus, if the drawing units are in metres then the scale is 1mm to 250mm. Keying ? at the last prompt gives a brief description of these options. AutoCAD then calculates the actual plotting area from the scale factor.

> Effective plotting area: 137.08 wide by 198.00 high
> Position paper in printer.
> Press RETURN to continue: <**ENTER**>
>
> Processing vector: xxxx
>
> Plot complete.
> Press RETURN to continue: <**ENTER**>

You should now be back to the original display with a copy of the drawing to hang on your wall (Figure 9.2).

Saving a VIEW

It is often necessary to produce a number of different plots of various parts of a drawing. You might want a large scale view of some detail as well a general layout. You can explore the drawing using ZOOM, PAN and VPOINT or DVIEW. Once you are happy with the display it can be stored as an AutoCAD VIEW. Such views can be quickly retrieved for redisplay or plotting. This saves you from having to remember what ZOOMs and other operations were used to get the desired effect. In this section you will create two VIEWs of the BAL-LOON drawing. The command is located in the DISPLAY sub-menu or can be typed at the keyboard.

> Command: **VIEW**
> ?/Delete/Restore/Save/Window: **W**
> View name to save: **PLOT-BALLOON**

This allows you to save a rectangular section of the display. Of the other options, "?" gives the names of previously defined views in the drawing; "D" allows you to delete a stored view; "R" causes a named view to be displayed; "S" stores the whole of the current display. If you have more than one VIEW-PORT on the screen only the active one can be stored as a VIEW. The rules for view names are the same as for layers, up to 31 numbers or letters but no spaces or full stops.

> First corner: **7,7**   (W1)
> Other corner: **32,42**   (W2)

Note that this is a tall, thin VIEW. When it is displayed on the screen, parts of the drawing to the left and right of the view's window may be displayed. However, when it is plotted only that portion within the window defined by W1 and W2 will be drawn. To see the view, restore it (Figure 9.3).

> Command: **VIEW**
> ?/Delete/Restore/Save/Window: **R**
> View name: **PLOT__BALLOON**

To generate the second view, ZOOM in to the lower right corner and use the "S" option.

> Command: **ZOOM**
> All/Center/Dynamic/Extents/Left/Previous/Window/<Scale(X)>: **W**
> First corner: **30,0**
> Other corner: **65,25**
> Command: **VIEW**
> ?/Delete/Restore/Save/Window: **S**
> View name: **MOUNTAIN__PLOT**

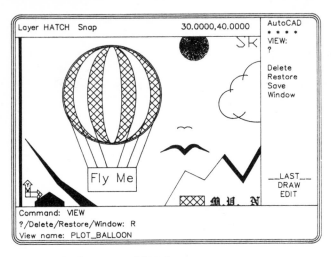

Figure 9.3 PLOT__BALLOON view

You now have two suitable views for plotting. Get your pen plotter ready and proceed to the next section. If you haven't used the plotter recently it is worth checking that there is ink in the pens and that they are all working smoothly.

Plotting

The procedure for outputting your drawings to pen plotters is very similar to the printer plotting described above. You have a bit more flexibility with plotters and you also get a higher quality hardcopy. The extra options available depend on how good your plotter is. With most devices you can have more than one pen and so vary the colours or line thicknesses. You can also vary the pen speed on some plotters to get darker or lighter lines.

Remember to save the drawing before plotting. To generate a plot of the mountain view pick **PLOT** from the screen menu and **PLOTTER** from the sub-menu. If the default settings are reasonable then accept them and let the plotting commence. If things go wrong you can always cancel the plot by pressing ^C. There may be a short time lag between issuing the cancel and actual processing/plotting being aborted.

> Command: **SAVE**
> File name <BALLOON>: <**ENTER**>
> Command: PLOT
> What to plot – Display, Extents, Limits, View or Window <L>: **V**
> View name: **mountain__plot**

It doesn't matter whether you use upper or lower case letters for the view name. All letters are automatically converted to upper case.

> Plot will NOT be written to a selected file
> Sizes are in Millimeters
> Plot origin is at (0.00,0.00)
> Plotting area is 285.00 wide by 198.00 (A4 size)
> Plot is NOT rotated by 90 degrees
> Pen width is 0.25
> Area fill will be adjusted for pen width
> Hidden lines will NOT be removed
> Plot will be scaled to fit available area
>
> Do you want to change anything? <N> <ENTER>
>
> Effective plotting area: 277.20 wide by 198.00 high
> Position paper in plotter.

AutoCAD then pauses to allow you to get the plotter and paper ready. If you press <ENTER> at the next prompt AutoCAD will send a plotter reset function and commence plotting. This "reset" clears the plotter memory buffer and may also clear any special plotter settings. Some plotters allow you to key in specific pen speeds and pressures using a control panel. To avoid the "reset" disturbing these settings you can press S at the prompt. This sends the "reset" but then pauses to allow the setup. When that is complete you press <ENTER> to begin the plot.

> Press RETURN to continue or S to Stop for hardware setup **S**
> Do hardware setup now.
> Press RETURN to continue: <**ENTER**>
>
> Processing vector: xxxx

Figure 9.4 Mountain plot (pen plotter)

The plotting begins almost immediately, unlike the printer plot. The pen movements are optimised to some degree by AutoCAD and so the order of items being plotted may appear strange. Indeed you might think bits of objects have been missed by the plotter. Be patient, all the gaps will be filled in before long. When the plot (Figure 9.4) is finished you will get the message:

> Plot complete.
> Press RETURN to continue: <**ENTER**>

This restores the graphic display and reloads the screen menu.

Plotter parameters – use of colours and pen thicknesses

In this section you will select specific plotter pens to reproduce the correct colours for the balloon view. Other parameters and their effects are explained. You should make sure that the plotter is set up with at least three pens: black in pen holder 1, red in 2 and blue in 3.

> Command: PLOT
> What to plot – Display, Extents, Limits, View or Window <L>: **V**
> View name: **BALLOON__PLOT**
>
> Plot will NOT be written to a selected file
> Sizes are in Millimeters
> Plot origin is at (0.00,0.00)
> Plotting area is 285.00 wide by 185 (A4 size)
> Plot is NOT rotated by 90 degrees
> Pen width is 0.25
> Area fill will be adjusted for pen width
> Hidden lines will NOT be removed
> Plot will be scaled to fit available area
>
> Do you want to change anything? <N> **Y**

To make any changes to the above settings or to the pen colour assignments you must reply "Y" to the prompt. This then gives a display of all the pen and colour assignments for alteration, if desired.

The actual linetypes shown depend on the plotter being used and your display may give more or less than the five variations given below. The AutoCAD Reference Manual recommends that only the plotter's CONTINUOUS line type be used. This helps to avoid confusion between the AutoCAD linetypes and the plotters' ones. The "continuous" type offered for the plotter means that the lines will be drawn exactly as they appear on the screen. In fact, it's difficult to see why this second set of linetypes is included at all.

When you reply to the last prompt with a "Y" or "YES" you will be prompted to make the appropriate changes. In this instance, change the red colour to pen number 2 and blue to pen number 3.

Entity Color	Pen No.	Line Type	Pen Speed	Entity Color	Pen No.	Line Type	Pen Speed
1 (red)	1	0	32	9	1	0	32
2 (yellow)	1	0	32	10	1	0	32
3 (green)	1	0	32	11	1	0	32
4 (cyan)	1	0	32	12	1	0	32
5 (blue)	1	0	32	13	1	0	32
6 (magenta)	1	0	32	14	1	0	32
7 (white)	1	0	32	15	1	0	32
8	1	0	32				

Line types: 0 = continuous line
1 = ...
2 = ...
3 = – – – – – – – – – – – – – – – –
4 = – – – – – – – – –
5 = – – –– – ––– –– –

Do you want to change any of these parameters? <N> **Y**

Enter values. blank=Next value,Cn=Color n,S=Show current values,X=eXit

Entity Color	Pen No.	Line Type	Pen Speed	
1 (red)	1	0	32	Pen number <1>: **2**
1 (red)	2	0	32	Line type <0>: **<ENTER>**
(red)	2	0	32	Pen speed <32>: **<ENTER>**

You might require a slower pen speed depending on the pens and paper being used in your plotter. Traditional ink drawing pens usually require slow speeds while felt tip and roller ball can use the fastest settings. If in doubt check the "Plotting pitfalls" section in Appendix B.

AutoCAD will cycle through all the options for each colour. To speed things up you can skip directly to any colour by replying to any of the prompts with "C" followed by the colour number. For example to jump to blue, type **C5** at the next prompt.

2 (yellow)	1	0	32	Pen number <1>: **C5**
5 (blue)	1	0	32	Pen number <1>: **3**
5 (blue)	3	0	32	Line type <1>: **X**

The "X" terminates the pen selection routine and AutoCAD moves on to select the rest of the plotter parameters.

Write plot to a file <N>: <**ENTER**>
Size units (Inches or Millimeters) <M>: <**ENTER**>
Plot origin in Millimeters <0.00,0.00>: <**ENTER**>

Standard values for plotting size

Size	Width	Height
A4	285.00	198.00
A3	396.00	273.00
A2	570.00	396.00
A1	817.00	570.00
MAX	1115.89	581.82

Enter the Size or Width, Height (in Millimeters) <A4>: <**ENTER**>

Rotate 2D plots 90 degrees clockwise? <N> **Y**

The balloon view is tall and thin. To get the biggest plot, you should use the paper in "portrait" mode. Then select a suitable pen width. This is the actual width of the nib in plotter units. Common pen widths are 0.25mm and 0.3mm which give good line thicknesses. The pen width is used by AutoCAD to calculate the number of movements required to fill in solids and polylines.

Figure 9.5 Balloon plot

Pen width <0.25>: **<ENTER>**
Adjust area fill boundaries for pen width? <Y>: **N**

This adjustment is used when the edges of the solids and polylines must be positioned very accurately. If the area is adjusted, then the pen strokes are moved in by one half the pen width at the boundaries. It saves AutoCAD some calculation time if the adjustment is not requested. If you specify a pen width larger than the actual size of the plotter's pens, then polylines and solids will not fill correctly. Text may also be drawn incorrectly.

Remove hidden lines? <N> **<ENTER>**
Specify scale by entering:
Plotted Millimeters=Drawing units or Fit or ? <FIT>: **<ENTER>**

Effective plotting area: 259 wide by 185 high
Position paper in plotter.

Press RETURN to continue or S to Stop for hardware setup **<ENTER>**

Processing vector: xxxx

Plot complete.
Press RETURN to continue: **<ENTER>**

Note that Figure 9.5 only includes those objects that were inside the view definition window. If you restore the view on the screen some items to the left and right of the window are also displayed. This is because AutoCAD always tries to fill the available screen area.

Plotting to a file

There are many reasons why you might want to output a drawing to a plot-file or printer-plot file. The plotter might not be available or you might have a lot of plots to generate. In either case you can still create your plots on disk. These plot files can be sent to the plotter from DOS or by using a DOS ".BAT" file. Thus the AutoCAD workstation doesn't have to be tied up in lengthy plotter–computer interactions. Any workstation with DOS can be used to get the actual hardcopy. Plot files can be queued and spooled in networks. This frees the AutoCAD workstation for more productive use.

Some laser and inkjet printers can emulate plotters. This normally requires special emulation software to be run outside of AutoCAD. To generate the plot you will probably have to have the plot files ready for input to the printer manufacturers software.

The AutoCAD procedure is exactly the same as the printing and plotting already described except for the one prompt "Write plot to a file <N>:". This time you reply with a "yes" and then give the filename. A default name, the same as the drawing name and with the extension ".PLT" can be selected. However, if you have a number of plots it is best to devise your own identification system (eg LAYOUT.PLT, DETAIL1.PLT etc).

To repeat the last plot but this time send the output to a file try the following AutoCAD sequence.

> Command: **PLOT**
> What to plot – Display, Extents, Limits, View or Window <L>: **V**
> View name: **BALLOON_PLOT**
>
> Plot will NOT be written to a selected file
> Sizes are in Millimeters
> Plot origin is at (0.00,0.00)
> Plotting area is 285.00 wide by 185 (A4 size)
> 2D plots rotated by 90 degrees
> Pen width is 0.25
> Area fill will NOT be adjusted for pen width
> Hidden lines will NOT be removed
> Plot will be scaled to fit available area
>
> Do you want to change anything? <N> **Y**

Entity Color	Pen No.	Line Type	Pen Speed	Entity Color	Pen No.	Line Type	Pen Speed
1 (red)	2	0	32	9	1	0	32
2 (yellow)	1	0	32	10	1	0	32
3 (green)	1	0	32	11	1	0	32
4 (cyan)	1	0	32	12	1	0	32
5 (blue)	3	0	32	13	1	0	32
6 (magenta)	1	0	32	14	1	0	32
7 (white)	1	0	32	15	1	0	32
8	1	0	32				

> Line types: 0 = continuous line
> 1 = ...
> 2 = ...
> 3 = – – – – – – – – – – – – – – – – –
> 4 = – – – – – – – – –
> 5 = – – – – – – – – – –
>
> Do you want to change any of these parameters? <N> **<ENTER>**
>
> Write plot to a file <N>: **Y**

You will then get the screen of information about the current pen settings. As these don't require any changes, answer **"N"** to the prompt. You will then be asked for filename to store the plot. This name can be any allowable DOS name, including the directory path. The file type ".PLT" is automatically added. The file type ".LST" is added for printer plots.

Enter file name for plot <BALLOON>: <**ENTER**>

The rest of the settings can be accepted by pressing <**ENTER**> to all the prompts.

Size units (Inches or Millimeters) <M>: <**ENTER**>

Rotate 2D plots 90 degrees clockwise? <N> **Y**

The balloon view is tall and thin. To get the biggest plot, you should use the paper in "portrait" mode. Then select a suitable pen width.

Pen width <0.25>: <**ENTER**>
Adjust area fill boundaries for pen width? <N>: <**ENTER**>
Remove hidden lines? <N> <**ENTER**>
Specify scale by entering:
Plotted Millimeters=Drawing units or Fit or ? <FIT>: <**ENTER**>

Effective plotting area: 259 wide by 185 high
Position paper in plotter.

Press RETURN to continue or S to Stop for hardware setup <**ENTER**>

Processing vector: xxxx

Plot complete.
Press RETURN to continue: <**ENTER**>

As the computer doesn't have to wait for the peripheral you should get the "Plot complete" message a lot quicker. To send the file to the plotter you will either have to SHELL or exit from AutoCAD and issue the DOS command. If the plotter is connected to the COM1 serial port you can COPY the file to that output device.

Command: **END**

Main menu

0. Exit AutoCAD
1. Begin a NEW drawing
2. Edit an EXISTING drawing
3. Plot a drawing
4. Printer plot a drawing

5. Configure AutoCAD
6. File Utilities
7. Compile a shape/font description file
8. Convert old drawing file

Enter selection: **0**

You will have to redirect your plotter output from COM1. This can be achieved with the MODE command. This command can also be used to set the correct communications parameters for your plotter.

C:> **MODE LPT1=COM1**
C:> **COPY BALLOON.PLT PRN**

If the plotter doesn't operate properly you may have to set the communications parameters using MODE once more. Check your plotter's documentation or the AutoCAD Installation Guide for the correct settings. If you have emulation or plot spooling software you should follow the supplier's instructions.

Always remember to match the AutoCAD configuration to the output device. If you are generating plot files for various plotters you must reconfigure AutoCAD each time you alter the hardware. Similarly you must reconfigure each time you change printer. It is the final output device that governs the AutoCAD settings.

Prplot ".LST" files can be copied directly to the PRN device without using the MODE command.

Postscript output

An increasing number of printers and electrostatic plotters accept the Postscript® command language. Postscript is a powerful plotting language. It is hardware independent and fast becoming the industry standard for plotting graphics and desk-top publishing. When using a Postscript device with AutoCAD you should use the configuration for "Postscript Laser Printers". The processing time for translating the drawing into Postscript commands can be quite long. The printer may "Time out" and disconnect if it has to wait too long between commands. You are recommended to send the plots to a file and then use the DOS "COPY" command. The chief advantage of using Postscript is that your plot file can be output on any make plotter that supports the language. Professional printing houses use Postscript photo plotters capable of up to 4000dpi. This means that you can plot lines as fine as 1/4000"! Most non-professional devices allow between 300 and 1200dpi.

Plotting 3D objects

There are a few special considerations for plotting 3D views. Firstly, you cannot rotate a 3D view by 90 degrees when plotting. You should adjust the screen viewpoint to achieve the desired plot.

Secondly, you can select hidden line removal. This usually makes the 3D object easier to visualise. Hidden line removal involves intensive calculations and can slow down the plot processing considerably. If you want a plot with hidden line removal you must select this option from the plot procedure prompts. The AutoCAD HIDE command only works on the screen display. It doesn't work for plots.

AutoCAD uses the WCS to calculate where to plot objects. Thus, when plotting 3D views try to ensure that you are in the World Coordinate System before plotting. If a UCS is being used you will find it difficult to position the picture sensibly on the paper. "What you see won't be what you get!"

The softcopy

In any drawing office, security and archiving are given great priority. This must be extended when drawings are stored on magnetic media. Some users will have access to sophisticated CAD management programs that take care of this. Many will just be relying on sensible practices.

The first sensible practice is to save the drawing regularly. In particular the drawing should be saved before "hazardous" operations such as plotting or using HATCH. AutoCAD provides one backup copy in the same directory as the drawing. You, the sensible user, should have another backup on another disk. A further safe copy should be stored in a separate and safe location. If one copy gets corrupted make sure it is replaced immediately, don't put it off.

Large volume archiving is best achieved by copying to a tape storage device. This normally requires specific hardware attached to your computer. Another device suitable for mass storage is the WORM (Write Once Read Many) laser disk system.

Summary

This chapter has covered the procedures for producing hardcopy output of AutoCAD drawings.

You should now be able to

Set up the printer plot parameters.
Produce printer plots on suitable printers.
Set up the plotter parameters.
Plot multi-coloured drawings on pen plotters.
Direct output to a file.
Copy plot files to the COM1 serial port.

Chapter 10   **BESPOKE AUTOCAD**

General

AutoCAD is a general drafting tool applicable to many disciplines. As such the software writers have avoided creating commands that are discipline specific or that don't have a wide appeal. It is more than likely that you will have certain routine AutoCAD tasks that have to be performed again and again. Wouldn't it be nice if AutoCAD had a command to do that specific task?

Well it does! Within AutoCAD you can write your own little programs or macros which string together a number of commands and values for the variables. In fact AutoCAD provides three ways of producing such macros. You can compose AutoCAD scripts, create your own screen menus or delve into AutoLISP, AutoCAD's built in fully functional programming language. It might take a bit of effort to automate your routine procedures but it is well worth the investment.

Inventing your own commands and macros isn't the only way to improve your AutoCAD efficiency. Other ways to speed up the AutoCAD Express include setting up prototype drawings, libraries of symbols and purchasing AutoCAD add-on software from third party suppliers.

In this chapter you will develop a prototype drawing and come across some of the easier ways to create macros and scripts. The blocks from Chapter 6 will be arranged into a symbols library with pull-down menu access. This chapter merely serves as a gentle introduction to the hidden power of AutoCAD. By the end you should be able to assess your scope for improvement and automation.

Ergonomics and the prototype drawing

Each time you start a new drawing with AutoCAD a prototype drawing is copied into the editor. The default for this is a drawing file called "ACAD.DWG". This contains all the default settings for all the AutoCAD system variables from the text font name to the dimensioning parameters. If these are not suitable for your application then it can be a bit annoying to have to alter them every time. You could edit the ACAD.DWG file itself and change the settings. The new settings would then become the new defaults. This has the added advantage of ensuring consistency in your drawings. However, it has the disadvantage that you can set only one set of defaults and you may require more depending on how many different types of drawing you produce. It is probably better to leave ACAD.DWG alone and create a number of other prototype drawings. These can be called up by using the "filename = prototype" method of giving the filename as was done in Chapter 4 (BALLOON=EXPRESS1).

As an exercise create a new drawing with the name "PRTYPE1" and set up the defaults outlined in Table 10.1. Set the dimension variables to the values given in Table 7.2. Items marked with "*" indicate changes from ACAD.DWG in European versions of AutoCAD (U.S. versions use imperial units). When you have completed this, "END" the drawing. The next time you create a new drawing add "=PRTYPE1" onto the filename. This will only be the starting point for your new drawing and can be altered as and when required.

Table 10.1 Prototype drawing settings

Key-word or variable name	Setting			
Limits	*0,0 to 420,297, On			
Units	Decimal, 4 places			
LTSCALE	* 10.0			
Layers	Name	Colour	Linetype	Status
	0	White	CONTINUOUS	On
	* CONST	Yellow	CONTINUOUS	On
	* TEXT	White	CONTINUOUS	On
	* CLINE	White	CENTER	On
Text style and font	* SIMPLEX			
Text height,rotation	3.0, 0			
Dimension variables	* See Table 7.2 (page 163)			
Coordinates	On			
Ortho	* On			
Axis	* 50.0			
Snap	* 5.0			
Grid	10.0			
ZOOM	All			

There isn't much point in making the first prototype drawing too sophisticated. It can be used as the basis for creating others which could also contain margins and an empty title box. Alternatively, the margins and title block could be stored as a WBLOCK and be inserted in the drawing. Only by analysing your own drawing output can you determine the best prototype drawings to develop. Defining all your layers in the prototype drawing helps to standardise the naming convention within your organisation. This will lead to easier drawing interchange between AutoCAD users and help to reduce layer related errors. Other things that can be added to the prototype drawing include standard views, viewport configurations and UCS settings.

Such things as text height and DIMSCALE will depend on the values of the limits and also on the plotter paper size. The values given in Table 10.1 are suitable for a 1:1 scale drawing plotted on A3 size paper. You could set up other prototypes for different scales and sizes.

Become an AutoCAD script-writer

An AutoCAD script is a text file that contains AutoCAD commands and suitable data in sequence. Any AutoCAD command can be included but you must furnish enough data in the script so that the command will execute successfully. The file has to be written outside AutoCAD and in ASCII text. The DOS editor, EDLIN, is suitable for this as is any wordprocessor that can be used in ASCII output mode.

The following simple script connects a series of points with a polyline. This type of script can be very useful if you are plotting graphs, particularly if the coordinates can be output from some other program. The filename must have the extension ".SCR". This file has been named "XY.SCR". The comments given in chain brackets, {comment}, are for clarity and are not part of the file. You don't type these.

```
PLINE                    {make sure there are no blank spaces}
0,0                             .{first point on polyline}
50,50                                    {second point}
100,50
100,100
200,0
                         {a blank line terminates the PLINE}

        XY.SCR, Script to draw a polyline
```

The end of line in a script file is the same as <ENTER> on the keyboard. There should be no blank spaces in XY.SCR. A blank space is the same as hitting the SPACE BAR during the command which in turn is the same as pressing <ENTER>. To run XY.SCR you must start up AutoCAD and create a new drawing or edit an old one. You can use the prototype drawing to set the default settings. Once in the drawing editor type **SCRIPT**. You are then prompted for the name of the file. Once the name has been entered, the script will begin. You don't add the ".SCR".

C:>ACAD

Main menu

0. Exit AutoCAD
1. Begin a NEW drawing
2. Edit an EXISTING drawing
3. Plot a drawing
4. Printer plot a drawing

5. Configure AutoCAD
6. File Utilities
7. Compile a shape/font description
8. Convert old drawing file

Enter selection: **1**

Enter name of drawing <>: **TESTSCRP=PRTYPE1**

Loading menu file . . .

Command: **SCRIPT**
Script file <dwg name>: **XY**

The PLINE command is executed and all the points are joined up. The script terminates at the end of the file or earlier if AutoCAD encounters any errors. Pressing ^C also stops the script. If your script didn't quite work press **F1** to see how far it got. The most likely error is a blank space in the wrong place. The unfortunate thing about a space out of place is that it is invisible and a bit of detective work might be called for.

A couple of AutoCAD commands specifically aimed at script control allow you to DELAY the program and to loop or re-run the script. Use your text editor and call the next script "BOXES.SCR". This one draws a box and then moves it upwards and to the right. In this case all the data for the LINE command are given on one line. This is the same as putting each pair of coordinates on separate lines, since the blank spaces are like pressing the SPACE BAR or <ENTER>. Some users prefer this compact form of writing scripts, but it is easier to make mistakes. The "RSCRIPT" at the end causes the script to be re-run. It will keep repeating until you interrupt it by pressing ^C or the backspace key.

When you run this script it should draw a series of squares along a 45 degree line. Note that all the data must be provided for the MOVE command. By using RSCRIPT and relative coordinates other interesting patterns can be generated.

```
LINE 10,10 30,10 30,30 10,30 close    {spaces act like <ENTER>}
DELAY 300                              {pause for 300 milliseconds}
MOVE
W                                      {select the "WINDOW" option}
0,0                                    {first corner}
420,297                               {other corner}
                                      {blank line to end object selection}
0,0                                    {base point}
10,10                                  {second point of displacement}
DELAY 300
RSCRIPT                                {re-run script from start}
```

BOXES.SCR, Repeating script of boxes

A useful application of scripts is to store your plot settings. If you have a particular type of plot that is done frequently then it can be automated. For example, the script given below produces plots on A3 size paper and at a scale of 1=1 with the black pen in holder 1, red in 2, blue in 3 and green in 4.

```
PLOT        {Start the plot routine}
L           {The drawing limits}
Y           {Yes, changes are required}
Y           {Yes, change the pen colours}
C1 2        {Colour 1, red, set to pen 2}
C3 4        {Colour 3, green, set to pen 4}
C5 3        {Colour 5, blue, set to pen 3}
C7 1        {Colour 7, white, set to pen 1}
X           {eXit from pen selections}
N           {Do not plot to a file}
M           {Sizes are in Millimetres}
0,0         {Plot origin}
A3          {Paper size}
N           {Plot not rotated by 90 degrees}
0.25        {Pen width}
N           {Do not adjust for pen width}
N           {Do not remove hidden lines}
1=1         {Plotted units=Drawing units}
            {Blank line will start plotter}
            {Another blank line to return to the drawing}
```

PLT1A3.SCR, Script for 1:1 plots on A3 size paper

You could set up a series of standard plotting scripts for all the paper sizes and the most common plotting scales. Any time you require a plot you just use the SCRIPT command and give the appropriate filename.

One of the best ways of finding out all the lines required for a script is to actually execute the command and write down all the replies that have to be typed at the keyboard. When composing the script avoid accepting default settings and set all the values for all the parameters. Otherwise, if the defaults get altered your script may no longer work. Remember to be careful with the use of *blank spaces* in your scripts.

Create your own screen menu

One of the major achievments of AutoCAD was to set the standard for use of screen menus in CAD. One of the factors in this success is that AutoCAD users can create their own screen menus and tailor them to their own needs. By creating your own menu you can convert single commands and even complicated sequences into one press of a button.

Menu macros allow more flexibility than scripts and as such are that bit more difficult to write. Menus are ASCII text files which, like script files, must be created using a text editor outside of AutoCAD. The default file is called ACAD.MNU and contains all the screen menus and pull-down menus. This is loaded into the computer each time you start the AutoCAD drawing editor. If you try listing it on the screen you can see how long it is (over 2000 lines). It is not the aim of this section to explain the full workings of AutoCAD menus and menu writing. You will be shown the main features and how easy it is to write a simple screen menu.

Create a text file and call it EXPRESS1.MNU, and type the lines given below. Items within the square brackets will actually be displayed on the screen and can be picked with the mouse. Whatever is to the right of the brackets will be executed if that item is picked. You will notice that "^C^C" is included directly after the right hand bracket. This issues the "CANCEL" command twice just in case you were in the middle of another command when you picked the item from the menu. Two cancels are needed to fully exit from some commands (eg dimensioning). Again, comments are given in chain brackets, {}, and should not be included in the EXPRESS1.MNU file.

You can have up to 20 menu items per screen. Some of the characters in the menu file have special meanings. The ";" is used to indicate <ENTER>. You have to press <ENTER> twice to get out of the LAYER command as evidenced by the TEXTL entry above. Blank spaces have the same effect as in script files so beware the invisible gremlin! Use the semicolon rather than a space whenever <ENTER> is required.

A new character is introduced in the "TRIANGLE" line. The backslash,\ , is used to tell AutoCAD to take some user input from the keyboard or mouse. Three backslashes are used, one for each vertex of the triangle. The "C" then closes it.

```
[EXPRESS    ]                           {Menu title. Nothing happens}
[MENU       ]
[           ]                     {Leaves a blank line on the screen}
[TEXTL:     ] ^C^CLAYER;S;TEXT;;TEXT   {Sets layer for TEXT}
[CONSLIN:   ] ^C^CLAYER;S;CONST;;LINE    {do. for const lines}
[CENTLIN:   ] ^C^CLAYER;S;CLINE;;LINE     {do. for cent lines}
[TRIANGL:   ] ^C^CLINE; \\\ C    {Draws a triangle from user input}
[           ]
[ERASE-L:   ] ^C^CERASE;L;;                  {Erases the last object}
[ERASE-P:   ] ^C^CERASE;P;;    {Erases the previous SELECTion}
[ZOOM-AL:   ] ^C^CZOOM;A                      {Does a Zoom All}
[ZOOM-P:    ] ^C^CZOOM;P           {Zoom to previous display}
[           ]
[PLOT1A3:   ] ^C^CSCRIPT;PLT1A3        {Runs the plotting script}
[BOXES:     ] ^C^CSCRIPT; BOXES         {Runs the boxes script}
[           ]
[ACADMNU:   ] ^C^CMENU;ACAD        {Reloads the original menu}
```

EXPRESS1.MNU, A useful screen menu

The rest of the lines are fairly straightforward. You have to press <ENTER> twice when using the ERASE command. Once to select the object and the second to exit the selection procedure. Thus there are two ";" at the end of the ERASE-L and ERASE-P lines. The last line gives a clue about how to run the menu file.

To use EXPRESS1.MNU you have to start up AutoCAD and enter the drawing editor (Use PRTYPE1.DWG as your prototype). At the "Command:" prompt type **MENU** and give the menu filename.

Command: **MENU**
Menu file name or . for none <ACAD>: **EXPRESS1**
Compiling menu EXPRESS1.MNU...

AutoCAD compiles the menu, ie translates it into its own code for faster use. The compiled menu is stored with the same name but with the extension ".MNX" to distinguish it. Once compiled, the screen menu should appear as shown in Figure 10.1. Test the menu by picking each of its options.

If the menu doesn't function correctly then you will have to leave AutoCAD to edit it. The most likely cause for malfunction is a typing error or a misplaced blank space or missing semicolon. Once the corrections have been made you can re-enter AutoCAD and reload the menu. Every time you modify the menu

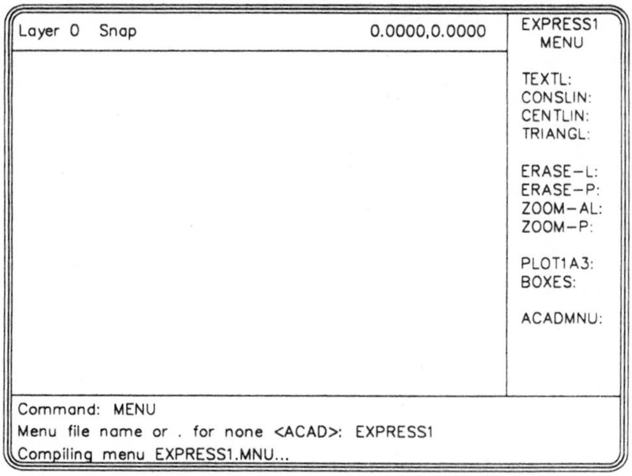

```
┌─────────────────────────────────────────────────────┬──────────────┐
│ Layer  0   Snap                      0.0000,0.0000   │  EXPRESS1    │
│                                                      │    MENU      │
│                                                      │              │
│                                                      │  TEXTL:      │
│                                                      │  CONSLIN:    │
│                                                      │  CENTLIN:    │
│                                                      │  TRIANGL:    │
│                                                      │              │
│                                                      │  ERASE−L:    │
│                                                      │  ERASE−P:    │
│                                                      │  ZOOM−AL:    │
│                                                      │  ZOOM−P:     │
│                                                      │              │
│                                                      │  PLOT1A3:    │
│                                                      │  BOXES:      │
│                                                      │              │
│                                                      │  ACADMNU:    │
│                                                      │              │
│                                                      │              │
├──────────────────────────────────────────────────────┴──────────────┤
│ Command: MENU                                                        │
│ Menu file name or . for none <ACAD>: EXPRESS1                        │
│ Compiling menu EXPRESS1.MNU...                                       │
└──────────────────────────────────────────────────────────────────────┘
```

Figure 10.1 EXPRESS1.MⁱⁿU

file you will have to reload it using the MENU command. It is particularly important to remember this if you are using the SHELL command or one of the External Commands to temporarily exit from AutoCAD. You can use the DOS EDLIN editor by typing "EDIT" at AutoCAD's "Command:" prompt.

The above menu is a rather crude example. It contains only one menu page and uses just one menu area. It is possible to write menus and macros for pull-down menus, mouse buttons, and tablets as well as having sub-menus. The next example contains a pull-down menu, a mouse button menu and a screen menu with two sub-menus (Figure 10.2).

To tell AutoCAD which parts of the menu file belong where you have to supply certain key-words at the start of each section. AutoCAD identifies each main section by a line starting with "***" followed by the key-word. The allowed key-words are SCREEN, POP1 to POP10, ICON, BUTTONS, TABLET1 to TABLET4 and AUX1. Sub-menus are identified by lines starting with "**" followed by the sub-menu name. Thus you can have screen menus, up to ten pull-down menus with icon sub-menus, up to four tablet areas (if you have a tablet) and assign functions to the mouse buttons. The "***AUX1" is used for an auxiliary function box if available.

This file demonstrates most of the important features of successful menu making. One of the mouse buttons must be used for picking. The others are programmed here to behave like the <ENTER> key and one to do a transparent redraw. Redrawing is a very common activity after erasing objects or to remove blips.

The pull-down (some people call this a pop-up) menu contains some of the lines from EXPRESS1.MNU. The text and line options are augmented so that the screen menu changes when the pull-down menu selection is made. This is good practice as it combines the two menu devices in a useful manner. Once you pick TEXTL from the pull-down menu, the screen menu automatically gives a handy list of TEXT command parameters.

```
***BUTTONS
;
'REDRAW
Ĉ Ĉ
***POP1
[DRAWING   ]
[TEXTL:     ] ^C^C$S=TEXTM;LAYER;S;TEXT;;TEXT
[COSLIN:    ] ^C^CLAYER;S;CONST;;LINE      {Layer and LINE}
[CENTLIN:   ] ^C^CLAYER;S;CLINE;;LINE       {do for cent lines}
[TRIANGL    ] ^C^CLINE; \\\C      {Draws a triangle from user input}
***SCREEN                                 {Start of screen menus}
**ROOTM                                {Name of first screen menu}
[ROOT       ]
[MENU       ]
[           ]
[LINE:       ] ^C^C$S=LINEM;LINE
[TEXT:       ] ^C^C$S=TEXTM;TEXT
[           ]
[ERASE-L     ] ^C^CERASE;L;;                 {Erases the last object}
[ERASE-P     ] ^C^CERASE;P;;      {Erases the previous SELECTion}
[ZOOM-AL:   ] ^C^CZOOM;A                       {Does a Zoom All}
[ZOOM-P     ] ^C^CZOOM;P              {Zoom to previous display}
[           ]
[PLOT1A3:   ] ^C^CSCRIPT;PLT1A3        {Runs the plotting script}
[BOXES      ] ^C^CSCRIPT;BOXES          {Runs the boxes script}
[           ]
[ACADMNU:  ] ^C^CMENU;ACAD       {Reloads the original menu}

**TEXTM
[TEXT:       ] ^C^CTEXT
[TEXTL:      ] ^C^CLAYER;S;TEXT;;TEXT
[DTEXT:      ] ^C^CLAYER;S;TEXT;;DTEXT


aligned
[centred      ]C                    {Avoids confusion with object snap}
fit
middle
right
style


[FONTS       ]
[TXT:        ] ^C^CSTYLE;TXT;TXT;0;1;0;N;N;N          {Sets font}
[SIMPLEX:    ] ^C^CSTYLE;SIMPLEX;SIMPLEX;0;1;0;N;N;N
[COMPLEX:    ] ^C^CSTYLE;COMPLEX;COMPLEX;0;1;0;N;N;N
[STYLE:      ] ^C^CSTYLE
[CHANGE:     ] ^C^CCHANGE
```

```
[ROOTMENU]$S=ROOTM
**LINEM
[LINE:        ] ^C^CLINE

[continue     ] ^C^CLINE;;
close
undo
.x
.y
.z
.xy
.xz
.yz
[ONELINE:     ] ^C^CLINE; \\;
[ORTHLIN:     ] ^C^CORTHO;ON;LINE
[A3MARGN:     ] ^C^CLINE;10,10;@400,0;@0,277;@-400,0;C
[A4MARGN:     ] ^C^CLINE;10,10;@277,0;@0,190;@-277,0;C

[ERASE        ] ^C^CERASE

[ROOTMENU]$S=ROOTM
```

EXPRESS2.MNU, a sample menu

The root menu again contains some lines from EXPRESS1.MNU and also has routes into the two sub-menus. If you pick TEXT you get the same as picking TEXTL without the layer change. The TEXTM sub-menu contains three macros for quickly changing the text style. The CHANGE command is also included as it can be useful for editing the drawn text. At the bottom of the menu is the escape route back to the ROOT MENU. You must provide adequate paths between parent and offspring menus.

The LINEM sub-menu can be accessed by picking LINE: from the root menu or by picking CONSLINE or CENTLINE from the pull-down menu. It contains all the valid key-words for use with LINE. If you are using a Release 9 version of AutoCAD you should include an extra line in this menu for the 3DLINE command. The ordinary LINE command works in 3D in Release 10 and higher. This sub-menu has a couple of macros for drawing margins around the page, A3MARGIN and A4MARGIN. The ONELINE: option draws one line segment between two points and returns you to the Command: prompt. ORTHLIN: turns the ortho mode on before executing the line command.

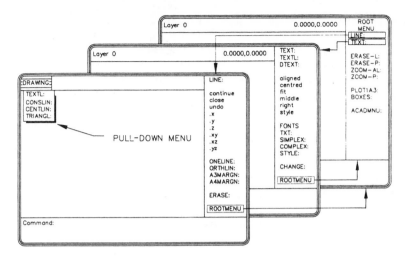

Figure 10.2 EXPRESS2.MNU

ERASE is probably the most useful edit command and so it too is included. Finally the sub-menu allows you to get back to the root menu.

When you are designing your menu you should take note of your own working practices. The logic behind the grouping of certain commands should mirror the way *you* work. One might be tempted to try to include lots of similar commands in one menu on the off chance that they might be needed. Resist this and only include those commands you use most frequently. Macros are worth including if they can store standard settings such as plot parameters. Let the computer store those difficult to remember facts. More sophisticated macros, than those given above, can be created. They can be made to do calculations and all sorts of numerical manipulations. However, they require a knowledge of AutoLISP which is described in the next chapter.

A final note on menu writing. Don't try to do too much too soon. Build up your library of menus slowly but steadily. When the new menus are fully tested they can be added to the ACAD.MNU, but make sure that you have a safe copy of the original ACAD.MNU just in case.

An icon symbol library

With the introduction of AutoCAD's Advanced User Interface (AUI) you not only have the ability to generate pull-down menus but you can create icon menus too. The icon menus use graphical symbols to prompt the user for input. They are particularly useful for selecting high level graphical entities like hatch patterns or text fonts. Release 10 also uses icons to help you select the dimension variables by giving you a picture of what each variable controls.

Obviously to create an icon menu you need icons. When all the pictures for the icons have been stored, they can be addressed from an ICON MENU. The actual menu looks very like the menus already discussed but includes an extra piece of information, the name of the icon to display. In this section you will use the KITCHEN.DWG from Chapter 6 and make a menu to help with the insertion of the BLOCKS.

Icons are AutoCAD slides

An AutoCAD slide is a pixel picture of the display. As the term, slide, suggests, it is like a photograph of the screen, a photograph that can be stored on disk. To make a slide you just get the screen display to show the required objects and issue the MSLIDE (make slide) command. You then supply a filename and it's done. You can review the slide with the VSLIDE (view slide) command.

Start AutoCAD and at the main menu enter selection 1. Give the drawing name as "ICON-EXP=KITCHEN". The display should be like Figure 10.3. Make sure that ATTDISP is on so that all the attributes are visible. The main point of interest for us now is the names of the blocks. Use the BLOCK command followed by a "?" to get a list.

> Command: **ATTDISP**
> Normal/ON/OFF <>: **ON**
> Command: **BLOCK**
> Block name (or ?):**?**
> Defined blocks.
> DOOR
> SINK
> FFREEZER
> COOKER
> APPLIANCE
> CUPBOARD
>
> 6 user blocks, 0 unnamed blocks.

Now ZOOM to a suitable working area in the lower right corner of the drawing. This will the display area for creating your slides.

> Command: **ZOOM**
> All/Center/Dynamic/Extents/Left/Previous/Window/<Scale(X)>: **W**
> First corner: **4500,0**   (W1)
> Other corner: **6500,1450**   (W2)

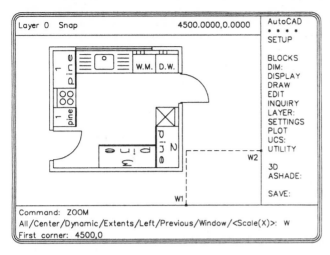

Figure 10.3 ICON-EXP=KITCHEN

INSERT the DOOR block, add text to show the insertion point and make the slide. Use the **DIM** command and **LEADER** to indicate the insertion point.

Command: **INSERT**
Block name (or ?): **DOOR**
Insertion point: **5200,400**
X scale factor <1>: **<ENTER>**
Y scale factor (default=X): **<ENTER>**
Rotation angle <0>: **<ENTER>**
Command: **DIM**
Dim: **LEADER**
Leader start: **5200,400**
To point: **4900,200**
To point: **5200,200**
To point: **<ENTER>**
Dimension text <>: **INS PT**
Dim: **EXIT**
Command: **TEXT**
Start point or Align/Center/Fit/Middle/Right/Style: **C**
Center point: **5600,1200**
Height <>: **140**
Rotation angle <0>: **<ENTER>**
Text: **DOOR**

You could now make a slide of this display if you wished. However, one more task is necessary before a suitable icon slide can be made. You must turn off the "FILL solids" option. When this is OFF only the outlines of solids and polylines are drawn. Commands such as REDRAW and REGEN work faster when FILL is OFF as there is less to draw on the screen. To capitalise on this, AutoCAD requires that it be OFF for icon menu slides.

    Command: **FILL**
    ON/OFF<ON>: **OFF**

The screen is now set for making the slide. The menu can be found by picking **UTILITY** from the AutoCAD root menu and then **SLIDES**. Pick **MSLIDE:** and give the name **DOOR-EXP**.

    Command: **MSLIDE**
    Slide file <c:\acad\icon-exp>: **DOOR-EXP**

And that's all there is to it. The file is stored on disk with the name "DOOR-EXP.SLD". To see the slide pick **VSLIDE** and give the slide name.

    Command: VSLIDE
    Slide file:<c:\acad\icon-exp>: **DOOR-EXP**

You must do a **REDRAW** or **REGEN** to restore the drawing screen before proceeding. To make the slides for the rest of the blocks, **ERASE** the door and its text. Then insert the appropriate block at the head of the leader arrow and add the text at the top.

    Command: **REDRAW**
    Command: **ERASE**
    Select objects: **6000,400**   (Point on DOOR block)
    1 selected, 1 found.
    Select objects: **5600,1200**   (Point on DOOR text)
    1 selected, 1 found.
    Select objects: <ENTER>
    Command: **INSERT**
    Block name (or ?): **FFREEZER**
    Insertion point: **5200,400**
    X scale factor <1>: <ENTER>
    Y scale factor (default=X): <ENTER>
    Rotation angle <0>: <ENTER>
    Command: **TEXT**
    Start point or Align/Center/Fit/Middle/Right/Style: **C**
    Center point: **5450,1200**
    Height <140>: <ENTER>
    Rotation angle <0>: <ENTER>
    Text: **FRIDGE FREEZER**
    Command: **MSLIDE**
    Slide file <c:\acad\icon-exp>: **FFRE-EXP**

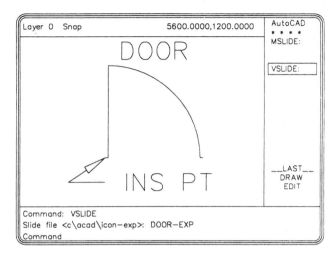

```
┌─────────────────────────────────────────────┬──────────┐
│ Layer  0   Snap         5600.0000,1200.0000  │ AutoCAD  │
│                                               │ * * * *  │
│              DOOR                             │ MSLIDE:  │
│                                               │          │
│                                               │┌────────┐│
│                                               ││VSLIDE: ││
│                                               │└────────┘│
│                                               │          │
│                                               │          │
│                                               │          │
│                                               │          │
│                                               │          │
│                                               │  __LAST__│
│         ⟋   INS  PT                          │  DRAW    │
│                                               │  EDIT    │
├───────────────────────────────────────────────┴─────────┤
│ Command:  VSLIDE                                         │
│ Slide file <c\acad\icon−exp>:  DOOR−EXP                  │
│ Command                                                  │
└──────────────────────────────────────────────────────────┘
```

Figure 10.4 The DOOR-EXP slide

Repeat this proceedure for the COOKER, APPLIANCE, CUPBOARD and SINK blocks giving slide names COOK-EXP, APPL-EXP, CUPB-EXP and SINK-EXP respectively. Accept the default attributes for APPLIANCE and CUPBOARD. Make sure that the cupboard attributes are visible when making CUPB-EXP. You will have to redo the leader arrow for the SINK-EXP slide.

Using the slides in the icon menu

The icon menu can be added onto EXPRESS2.MNU with your text editor. You must make one addition to the root screen menu to allow the icon menu to be called up. The start of the icon menu is designated by the key-word "***ICON". It can have up to 16 items but more can be accessed using sub-menus. Icon sub-menus start with "**" followed by the menu title, just like other sub-menus. They can be accessed using "$I" followed by the menu title as shown in the example below. A special menu command, "$I=*", actually activates the icons. In this listing, only the root menu and the icon menus are given. The other menus are exactly as EXPRESS2.MNU. Once again comments are included in {} but should not be typed by you.

The items in the square brackets are the names of the slides. What follows the brackets is the action or commands to be executed. If the first character in the brackets is a *space* it indicates to AutoCAD that the following text is to be used in place of a slide. Thus the last menu item above will cause the word "Exit" to appear on the icon menu and if it is picked a "^C" or "CANCEL" will be issued.

```
***SCREEN
**ROOTM
[ROOT      ]
[MENU      ]
[          ]
[LINE:     ]  ^C^C$S=LINEM;LINE
[TEXT:     ]  ^C^C$S=TEXTM;TEXT
[          ]
[ERASE-L:  ]  ^C^CERASE;L;;
[ERASE-P:  ]  ^C^CERASE;P;;
[ZOOM-AL:  ]  ^C^CZOOM;A
[ZOOM-P:   ]  ^C^CZOOM;P
[          ]
[PLOT1A3:  ]  ^C^CSCRIPT;PLT1A3
[BOXES:    ]  ^C^CSCRIPT;BOXES
[          ]
[KITCHEN   ]  ^C^C$I=KITCHEN $I=*        (Opens icon menu}
[          ]
[ACADMNU:  ]  ^C^CMENU;ACAD
```

```
***ICON                          {Indicates the start of the icon menus}
**KITCHEN                        {The name of the first icon sub-menu}
[KITCHEN FITTINGS]               {Menu title that will appear on screen}
[DOOR-EXP  ] ^CINSERT DOOR       {Display the slide and insert the block}
[SINK-EXP  ] ^CINSERT SINK
[FFRE-EXP  ] ^CINSERT FFREEZER
[COOK-EXP  ] ^CINSERT COOKER
[CUPB-EXP  ] ^CINSERT CUPBOARD
[APPL-EXP  ] ^CINSERT APPLIANCE
[EXIT      ] ^C                  {An escape route from the icon screen}
                                 {Blank line indicates end of sub-menu}
```

EXPRESS2.MNU with addition of icon pop-up menu

To use the new version of the menu start up AutoCAD and edit the ICON-EXP drawing. Use the MENU command to load it and pick **KITCHEN**: from the screen menu. The icons should be displayed as shown in Figure 10.5. If you move the arrow cursor into one of the small boxes to the left of one of the icons it should become highlighted. If you pick one of the small boxes the icons will disappear and the INSERT command will commence. The icon screen will also disappear if either the "Exit" box is picked or the "ESC" key is hit.

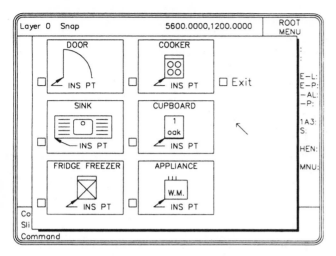

Figure 10.5 Kitchen icons

Tips for creating icon menus

Icon menus are rather awkward to create. They are also troublesome to maintain and update. Therefore they should only be used instead of screen or pull-down menus when real benefits can be achieved by their graphic nature. Some good examples can be found in the ACAD.MNU where icons are used for HATCH (see Figure 2.7, p.14), text fonts and the dimension variables.

EXPRESS2.MNU and the slides shown in Figure 10.5 demonstrate the features of a good icon menu. The graphic of the block gives the user a good idea of what to expect when inserting it. You can also see the orientation of the block and the insertion point from the icon. The window for making the slides was chosen so as to fill the screen area with useful information. Therefore the objects and text are as big as possible for the icon screen. Furthermore, the icons are simple and uncluttered. If you put too much information into the slide it will be illegible on the icon screen. Finally, every icon menu should reserve one box for an escape route which must be clearly labelled (eg Exit, Cancel).

A final note on slides

AutoCAD slides have more uses than just for icon menus. In fact they have been around for many versions prior to Release 9 when the icon was born. These other uses include making a slide show for demonstration purposes and exporting graphics to desk-top publishing software. The restriction that FILL must be OFF is only for slides to be used in icon menus. All other slides can have FILL turned ON. Slides cannot be edited. If you want to change one you have to re-make it.

When you have a lot of slides they can be grouped together to form a library. A utility program, SLIDELIB, provided on the AutoCAD Support disk does this. To run the program to make a library of the kitchen slides you should first create a text file containing the slide names. You could then type the following at the DOS prompt:

C:>SLIDELIB KITCHLIB <SLDLIST.TXT

SLIDELIB 1.1 (2/10/88)
(C) Copyright 1987,1988 Autodesk, Inc.
All rights reserved

Here SLDLIST is an ASCII text file containing the lines given below.

DOOR-EXP
SINK-EXP
FFRE-EXP
COOK-EXP
CUPB-EXP
APPL-EXP

SLDLIST.TXT

This will result in a file, called KITCHLIB.SLB, containing all the slides. The slides can be viewed with AutoCAD's VSLIDE command and used in icon menus but you have to use a slide name such as "KITCHLIB(DOOR-EXP)" in place of "DOOR-EXP". The original slides and the SLDLIST file can then be archived. The chief advantage of using a slide library is related to the tidyness of one larger file over lots of little ones. You can also achieve some saving of disk space (if you delete the original slides after archiving). The main disadvantage is that you cannot update the library or decompose it into its components. You have to make a new one even if you only want to change one slide. This isn't too difficult provided you have kept the originals and the slide list.

Summary

This chapter has covered a number of ways of tailoring AutoCAD to your own work practices, from the simple idea of a prototype drawing to creating your own macros. This has been an introduction to the techniques of simple menu writing. More complicated applications are dealt with in the next chapter and also in the AutoCAD Reference Manual.

It is the simple macros that save the most time. They save time because they can be written on the spot in response to new situations. If you ever find yourself repeating a task too often you can now say "I think I'll automate that" and a "Holy macro" and it's done.

You should now be able to

Create a prototype drawing.
Write scripts.
Make screen menus and sub-menus.
Write your own pull-down menu.
Generate slides and slide libraries.
Use slides to produce an icon menu.

Chapter 11 **AUTOLISP AS A PRACTICAL TOOL**

General

Must I really write programs? The answer is "No, but...". You can get by with AutoCAD as it is. The program is already so versatile that you might think that it is almost perfect. A large number of AutoLISP programs have already been written. The section on "The AutoLISP program library", below, introduces some useful titles ready for use. To use these you only need to know how to load an AutoLISP program. A host of AutoCAD third party software suppliers produce customising programs for all disciplines. You can probably find something suitable there. See Chapter 12 for more details on available software.

The "but" indicates that there is probably some aspect of your CAD work that can benefit significantly from a bit of parametric programming. If you found SCRIPTs useful but too limited then AutoLISP can be of even more use. AutoLISP is a powerful tool for creating macros containing variables and complicated functions.

Most users will not want to become experts in programming and so this chapter is aimed at showing how to create simple programs. You will also see how to modify some of the AutoLISP library routines to make them more useful. Space is too limited for an in depth description of all the facilities of AutoLISP. Only the main concepts and commands are described in abstract, others are treated by way of example programs. The reader is referred to the *AutoLISP Programmer's Reference Manual* for a full account of all the features.

What is AutoLISP?

AutoLISP is a derivative of one of the oldest computer languages that is still extant, LISP. LISP takes its name from an acronym of "LISt Processing" and was invented in 1959. AutoLISP is based on XLISP, one of the many dialects of LISP in the computing community, but contains many extra features related to the graphical capabilities of AutoCAD.

LISP is quite different from other programming languages such as BASIC or FORTRAN. It is far more flexible for handling different data types but it has a syntax that makes some mathematical expressions seem somewhat strange. For people who have some programming experience with the more conventional scientific languages this syntax will take getting used to.

One of the features of LISP is that variables can contain any nine types of data. Furthermore, a variable can switch from containing one type to another. This means that a particular variable can contain text data at one point and numeric data at another stage of the program. Compare that with the rigid rules of FORTRAN where all text variables must be declared at the start of the program and can never change from containing text data to numeric.

The main data types available in AutoLISP are: lists, symbols, text strings, real numbers, integers, AutoCAD commands and functions.

AutoLISP grammar and conventions

The first rule of AutoLISP grammar is that every expression must start with a left parenthesis and end with a closing parenthesis. The second imperative is that the function comes first and the operands second. Thus the AutoLISP expression to add two numbers would be written:

   (+ 3.5 4.7)

In this case the "+" is the addition function and the two numbers are the operands. This expression would return the value "8.2".

Another rule was demonstrated in the above expression, namely that the space is used to separate each of the elements of the list. Dedicated lispers call these individual elements "atoms". The use of spaces is very important in AutoLISP. A space is not required at the start or end of the list but it doesn't matter if you include one. If in doubt put spaces in.

Variable names can be any length and contain letters and numbers and other characters except ().';" and spaces. Symbols are the same as variables. You must avoid using the name of an AutoLISP function as a variable name or it will be redefined. A suitable expression to set a value for a variable would be:

   (SETQ my-first-variable 99.0)

The "SETQ" function is short for "set equal" and is similar to the BASIC command "LET variable = value". Upper or lower case letters are acceptable, they are all converted to upper case. To make the functions stand out from variables the former are typed in capitals and the latter in lower case.

Real numbers should always be written with a decimal point or in scientific notation (eg 9.9E1 which is the same as 9.9×10^6). The "99.0" above ensures that my-first-variable is a *real* number. If you used "99" or even "99." the variable would be stored as an integer. "What' the problem?", you might ask. Well the danger comes with the differences between real and integer arithmetic. With real numbers fractions are handled correctly but with integers everything after the decimal point is disregarded. Two examples of the division of 2 by 3 demonstrate this:

(/ 2 3) would return a value of 0
(/ 2.0 3.0) would give 0.6666

Another limitation of integers is that their values must be in the range from −32768 to +32767. You must also be careful with fractions. "0.9" would be handled correctly but ".9" would be confused with another AutoLISP structure. All numeric values can be preceded by a plus or minus sign.

Text strings must begin and end with double quotes. A number of characters take on special meaning when in double quotes. These special cases always start with a backslash, eg \n means send a new line. These will be dealt with later.

My first AutoLISP expression can add!

That's enough of the technical stuff. We can now get down to making it work. In this section you will meet a number of AutoLISP functions as a series of oneliners. The expressions can be typed within AutoCAD at the command prompt for an instant response. It is assumed that your copy of AutoCAD has been configured with AutoLISP enabled and that your AUTOEXEC.BAT start up file contains the lines:

set lispheap=40000
set lispstack=5000

These lines can be input at the DOS prompt anytime before starting AutoCAD. If you are not sure about your set up read the section on hardware configuration in Appendix A.

Start up AutoCAD with a new drawing called "LISPTEST".

Main menu

Enter selection: **1**

Enter name of drawing: **LISPTEST**

At the command prompt you can enter your first AutoLISP expression to add three numbers. The answer should come back instantaneously.

Command: (**+ 1 2 3**)
6   (This is what AutoLISP echos)

Note that the function is applied to all the elements (atoms) giving 1+2+3=6. Try the following expressions using the other arithmetic operations.

Command: (+ 3.0 (* 5.0 2.0))
13.000
Command: (/ 3.0 (* 5.0 2.0))
0.3000

These two have used nested operations. The innermost expression is evaluated first and then the outer. They also demonstrate that you can replace any element by an expression that can be evaluated. The restriction on this is that the data type must be consistent with the expressions, eg you cannot add a number to a text string.

Multiple expressions

You can build up an effect with AutoLISP by inputting a number of expressions. The order of evaluation is the same as the input order. You can store the values of the expressions in variables (symbols) and use them later. The next example uses a series of oneliners to build up the data to draw a line.

You can use the "SETQ" to store the answers to your calculations. These variables can then be used by AutoCAD to draw things.

Command: (SETQ x1 130.0)
130.0
Command: (SETQ y1 100.0)
100.0

Even the SETQ function returns a value. Every valid AutoLISP expression has a value. Now to collect the x1 and y1 values to form a pair of coordinates you must use the "LIST" function.

Command: (SETQ pt1 (LIST x1 y1))
(130.0 100.0)

The SETQ function requires a pair of operands, the variable name and its value. The value has been replaced by an expression and so must be enclosed in parentheses. The LIST function allows you to group items together in an orderly fashion. In LISP jargon, the above expression has created a symbol called "pt1" made up of a list containing two atoms. Atoms are indivisible items. Lists, on the other hand can be decomposed into their constituent elements. A list can contain atoms, sub-lists, symbols or variables or even AutoLISP expressions.

The variable "pt1" is now in a suitable form to draw a 2D line. To use the value of pt1 or any other variable, type !pt1 or "!variable name". The exclamation mark can also be used just to see the value of any AutoLISP variable. Now try out the line command.

Command: **LINE**
From point: **!pt1**
To point: **@100,100**
To point:

You should now have a line on the screen from the point (130,100) to (230,200).

The previous example has illustrated how you can build up a list to give the X and Y coordinates of a point. It has also shown how you can use that information interactively with an AutoCAD command. In the next example you will see how to decompose a list into its elements. The function "car" extracts the first element of a list while "cadr" takes the second. Finally, the "GETPOINT" function allows you to pick a point from the screen and store its coordinates. You can also include suitable prompt text with the "GETPOINT" function. Use object snap to pick the mid point of the last line.

Command: **(SETQ pt2 (GETPOINT "\nPick a point now:"))**
Pick a point now: **mid** of Pick the line. (180.0 150.0)
Command: **!(CAR pt2)**
180.0
Command: **!(CADR pt2)**
150.0

Note the use of "\n" to get the line feed before the "Pick . . ." prompt. There are a number of "GET-" type commands. These allow you to input data in the same way as you would to AutoCAD itself.

AutoLISP contains a full set of mathematical and trigonometric functions such as +,−,*,/,LOG, ALOG, EXP, EXPT, SQRT, SIN, COS, ATAN. Relational operators, such as >, <, <= (less than or equal), >=, /= (not equal) and logical functions, "IF", "OR" and "AND". There are file handling functions to OPEN a file, READ-LINE, WRITE-LINE and so on. You can also gain access to AutoCAD's database of entities to create or modify the drawing. To get a full list of all the function names and the names of currently declared variables you can examine the ATOMLIST.

Command: **!ATOMLIST**
(PT2 PT1 Y1 X1 INTERS GRREAD GRTEXT GRDRAW
    GRCLEAR . . . etc

The first few members of the atomlist are the variables already declared. The rest from "INTERS" to "ATOMLIST" are AutoLISP functions. Avoid using any of these names as variable names.

Examining AutoCAD's database using AutoLISP

One last example of a one-liner demonstrates how complicated an expression can get. It also shows how to get at the AutoCAD drawing database. The expression, below, tells you what layer a chosen object is on. Be careful when typing this one and remember to separate each item with a space. There are five right parentheses at the end.

Command:**(CDR (ASSOC 8 (ENTGET (CAR (ENTSEL "\nPick object:")))))**
Pick object: Pick a point on the line. "0".

If you pick an object on layer 0 then "0", including the quotes, will be displayed. Text strings are always in double quotes.

Working from the inside out on this one, the innermost expression is the ENTSEL function. This prompts you to pick an entity and returns a list containing the AutoCAD database number and also the coordinates of the point picked. Taking the CAR of this extracts the entity number. ENTGET retrieves the list containing all the information on relating to that entity number. The ASSOC function searches the list for a dotted pair containing the number "8", which is AutoCAD's code for layer in the database. A dotted pair is a special type of list containing two elements which are separated by " . " eg (8 . "0"). Finally, the CDR function takes the second item from the dotted pair and so returns the layer name, "0". Dotted pairs are special lists that contain only two atoms. AutoCAD uses them for certain drawing database entries as they use less memory than a normal list.

Try this example step by step. The actual entity name will differ from computer to computer and from one drawing to the next.

Command: **(ENTSEL "\nPick object:")**
Pick object: (<Entity name: 60000014> (160.0 130.0 0.0))
Command: **(CAR (ENTSEL "\nPick object:"))**
Pick object: <Entity name: 60000014>
Command: **(ENTGET (CAR (ENTSEL "\nPick object:")))**
Pick object: ((−1 . <Entity name: 60000014>) (0 . "LINE") (8 . "0")(10 130.0 100.0 0.0) (11 230.0 200.0 0.0) (210 0.0 0.0 1.0))

This is the full database entry for this line. It is an example of an "association list". Special codes are used by AutoCAD for various types of information. In the association list each element starts with its code and then contains the value. The codes 10 and 11 indicate the end points, 0 the entity type, −1 the entity name.

If you are using an earlier version than Release 10 the association list will contain X and Y coordinates but no z value. The last list, (210 0.0 0.0 1.0), will also be missing. This is used only for 3D work. If you are using Release 10 and the extra bits are still missing, check the setting of the FLATLAND variable. Use the AutoCAD command "SETVAR" to set it to 0 (zero). FLATLAND is used to switch AutoLISP into 2D mode so that you can run programs developed with earlier versions of AutoCAD. The 2D mode set by FLATLAND will not be available after Release 10, so all new programs should be developed with FLATLAND set to 0.

Command: **(ASSOC 8 (ENTGET (CAR (ENTSEL ' \nPick object:"))))**
Pick object: (8 . "0")

And finally, adding the CDR will extract the "0" from this pair.

This topic will be covered again later when it is incorporated into full AutoLISP programs. The technique of extracting the database information from an entity is quite an important one and will be used frequently. For example, to find out what type of entity has been picked you would use:

Command:**(CDR (ASSOC 0 (ENTGET (CAR (ENTSEL "\ nPick object:")))))**
Pick object: Pick a point on the line.

and get the response, "(0 . "LINE")".

Error messages

When things are not going quite right there can be many reasons for Auto-LISP's rejection of your imperatives. Here are some of the more popular "unexpected happenings".

The most common mistake to make is to omit a bracket or to include an extra one. If you have too many right parentheses you will get the message:

error: extra right paren

If you have too few the message will read simply:

1>

This indicates that there is one right parenthesis missing. If some number, n, parentheses are missing the message will be "n>". The moral is, always balance your brackets. Type the required number of ")" and press <ENTER>.

The next most common message to appear is "error: bad function". This means that the first item in the expression is not a valid function. This might occur if you forget to define a list. For example "(1 9)" is a bad function but "(LIST 1 9)" returns the value "(1 9)".

If you try to multiply a text string by a number you will be told that you have a "bad argument type". This tells you that the data type being used is incompatible with the function. Leaving out the double quotes when defining text strings also results in this.

It's not really an error, though sometimes it might not be desired, but if a function has no value, or a variable is empty the message is "nil". There are many occasions when "nil" can be useful. More of this later.

Two errors are related to the "lispheap" settings. If the lispheap is not big enough "insufficient string space" will be displayed. You will probably only get this when running relatively large programs. It can be rectified by exiting AutoCAD and increasing the lispheap setting. The problem can be alleviated if the variable names are kept below six characters. Also, if the lispheap is too small you might get the unwelcome message "insufficient node space" (not enough memory available). Again you can exit and increase the size or you can recover some node space by clearing out old functions. When you run an AutoLISP function it stays in the node space. Say the function was called "BIGFUNCTION"; to release its node space you can set the function to "nil", ie (SETQ BIGFUNCTION nil). You can also help matters if you run a special function called VMON. When the node space gets full, VMON causes the least used of the functions to be dumped to hard disk. The syntax is simply (VMON).

"LISPSTACK overflow" indicates that the environment variable setting is too low. It can also happen if the function has a large number of arguments. There is an absolute maximum of 45,000 for the sum of the lispheap and lispstack values. Normally values of 30,000 to 40,000 are suitable for the heap and 15,000 to 5,000 for the stack. If your computer has an extended memory board this can also be used by AutoLISP. See the AutoCAD Installation Guide for the details.

AutoLISP programming

My first program can subtract!

Having attacked the keyboard with all the above AutoLISP you will be pleased to know that you can run programs from ASCII text files. All that typing can be done in the user friendly environment of your wordprocessor. Once written and saved you can start up AutoCAD, load the new AutoLISP program and run it as many times as you like. Use your text editor to create a file containing the lines below. Call the file "EXPMINUS.LSP".

```
(DEFUN MINUS ()
    (SETQ a (GETREAL "\nEnter the first number:"))
    (SETQ b (GETREAL "\nEnter the number to subtract:"))
    (SETQ answer (− a b))
)
```

                    EXPMINUS.LSP

The program reads in two numbers and stores the sum in a variable called "answer". The last expression to be exaluated in a program is returned, ie it will appear on the screen. Two new functions are introduced.

DEFUN is the LISP for "define function" and allows you to give the function a name, "square". This name will be used to activate the function once the program has been loaded. Note that the function name is not the same as the program filename. Very often one file may contain many functions. The DEFUN command must be the first executable expression of the function. The two brackets after the function name must be included.

GETREAL is similar to the GETPOINT command and allows you to input a single real number. The prompt in double quotes will be displayed when the program is run. The "\n" is the code for a new line to be used for the prompts.

The actual position of the parentheses in the lines makes no difference to AutoLISP. However, the indentation convention is used to help get the position of closing parentheses correct. The rule is that whenever a line has an unclosed parenthesis then the subsequent lines are indented. When the parenthesis is closed the indentation is discontinued.

Loading and running programs

To run the EXPMINUS.LSP program you must be in the AutoCAD drawing editor. When the "Command:" prompt is displayed you can load your AutoLISP file. The syntax is similar to inputting other AutoLISP expressions directly.

>Command: **(LOAD "EXPMINUS")**
>MINUS

You don't have to include the .LSP file extension but the double quotes must be included. The name of the function is returned. You can now run this function like any other AutoLISP function.

>Command: **(MINUS)**
>Key in first number: **33.3**
>Key in number to subtract: **4**
>29.3
>Command: **(MINUS)**
>Key in first number: **3**
>Key in number to subtract: **5**
>−2.0

To see the value of the variables you can use the "!" facility.

>Command: **!A**
>3.0
>Command: **!B**
>5.0
>Command: **!ANSWER**
>−2.0

You can use this function again and again to subtract numbers. Each time you have to key in the full **(MINUS).** Each time you start a new AutoCAD session you will have to reload the AutoLISP file.

If you want to load a program from another directory you will have to include the DOS path with the filename. The backslash, "", character is reserved in AutoLISP for giving line feeds etc and cannot be used in the normal way to give the path name. You must use the forward slash, "/" or two backslashes, "\\", instead. For example, to load a .LSP file from the directory C:\LISP you would enter either, **(LOAD "C:\LISP\EXPMINUS")** or **(LOAD "C:/LISP/EXP-MINUS")** at the "Command:" prompt.

Making a new AutoCAD command

A small alteration to the DEFUN line in EXPMINUS.LSP will save having to include the brackets every time you want to run the program. Go back to your text editor and change the first line in EXPMINUS.LSP to:

(DEFUN C:MINUS ()

When the modified program is loaded it will create a new AutoCAD command called MINUS. You can use it by keying MINUS, without the brackets.

Command: **(LOAD "EXPMINUS")**
C:MINUS
Command: **MINUS**
Key in first number: **30.5**
Key in number to subtract: **5**
25.5

Note that you must reload the .LSP file every time you modify it. If you don't you will be using the old version.

If you do not wish to proceed with more AutoLISP programming you can jump to the next chapter. You can make use of AutoLISP programs without having to understand much more about the programming language. The next chapter explores the store of ready made programs supplied with AutoCAD.

The rest of this chapter contains programs which illustrate a number of aspects of AutoLISP. The programs introduce new functions and techniques when the occasion arises. Working through these examples will give you enough background to generate useful short programs. Again, you will have to use your text editor to create these files.

A program that draws

The first program uses the DEFUN function to specify local variables to be used to draw a square. A local variable is one that exists only when the function is being used. This saves memory and helps to keep control of the number of active symbols. The "/" is used to indicate that the following symbol names are local to the function.

```
;Program to draw a square from a given point and length of side
(DEFUN square(/ pt1 pt2 pt3 pt4 side)
    (SETQ pt1 (GETPOINT "\nPick lwr lft corner of square:")
        side (GETDIST "\nEnter the length of one side:")
        pt2 (POLAR pt1 0.0 side)
        pt3 (POLAR pt2 (/ PI 2.0) side)
        pt4 (POLAR pt1 (/ PI 2.0) side)
    );End of setq
    (COMMAND "line" pt1 pt2 pt3 pt4 "close")
);End of defun
```

EXPSQR.LSP

Other new bits in this program are ;, GETDIST, POLAR, PI and COM-MAND.

The SETQ function is used repeatedly for pt1 to pt4 and side. It evaluates each pair of operands in turn. Most AutoLISP functions can be used repeatedly in this fashion. You could of course use five separate SETQ's if you wished.

The semicolon tells AutoLISP that the rest of that line contains comments. Such comments are to help the programmer and are ignored by AutoLISP when the program is run.

GETDIST is similar to GETPOINT except that it requires you to input a distance. This can be done by typing the value or by picking two points on the screen. All the usual AutoCAD facilities for point picking can be used when inputting the length of the side. As with GETPOINT you can include a suitable prompt in double quotes.

(POLAR pt ang dist) returns the XYZ coordinates of the point with the relative polar position from the point, pt. The angle is measured in *radians* from the positive direction of the X axis in the current User Coordinate System.

PI is a special variable which evaluates to 3.141592654. This is the mathematical constant, π, and equals the number of radians in 180 degrees. Thus (/ PI 2.0) is the equivalent to 90 degrees. Never use PI as a variable name except in this context.

COMMAND allows you to put any AutoCAD command into an AutoLISP program. Note that all the literal text must be enclosed in double quotes. This example uses LINE to connect the four points and the "close" option to finish the job.

Programs that use arguments

Convert inches to millimetres Some functions require arguments and variables to be listed in the DEFUN expression. The following program takes one argument, a number to be converted from inches to millimetres. The list in parentheses after "DEFUN" gives the names of arguments and local variables to be used within the function. The "/" is used to separate the arguments from the local variables. An argument is also a local variable but it is special in that its value must to be supplied to the function.

```
;A function to convert inches to millimetres
;Requires one argument to be supplied at
(DEFUN intomm (inch / mm)
      (SETQ mm (* inch 25.4));There are 25.4mm in 1 inch.
);End of defun
```

IN-MM.LSP

You can load this function in the usual way. When you want to run it you have to supply the AutoLISP brackets and the number to convert.

```
Command: (LOAD "IN-MM")
INTOMM
Command: (INTOMM 4)
101.6
Command: (SETQ a (INTOMM 5.5))
139.7
```

The INTOMM function can now be used just like any other AutoLISP function but it always requires one argument. If you forget to supply the number or supply too many numbers you will get the message, "error: incorrect number of arguments to a function".

Convert degrees to radians Another utility function is DTOR given below. This can be used to convert decimal angles from degrees to radians. This can be particularly useful as AutoLISP's trigonometric functions all require angles in radians. The new program, UTILITY.LSP contains a snappier version of IN-TOMM as well as DTOR.

When you load UTILITY.LSP both of the functions, DTOR and INTOMM will be available. You can add more snappy utility programs to this file. It is a lot more convenient to have to load only one .LSP file than lots of little ones.

```
;A function to convert inches to millimetres
;Requires one argument to be supplied at
(DEFUN intomm (inch)
     (* inch 25.4);There are 25.4mm in 1 inch.
);End of defun

;Convert a number from decimal degrees to radians
(DEFUN dtor (degs)
     (/ (* pi degs) 180.0)
);End of defun
```

UTILITY.LSP

Find the mid-point of two 3D points   A final utility program uses the CAR, CADR and CADDR functions to extract the X, Y and Z components of two points. The respective components are then averaged and assembled to give the 3D mid-point. The controlling function C:3DMIDPT requests the user for two points and passes them to MIDPT and returns the answer. The program repeats until the user gives a null response ie until you hit <ENTER> without giving a point.

```
;function to find the mid-point of two 3D points
(DEFUN midpt (pt1 pt2 / x1 y1 z1)
     (SETQ x1 (/ (+ (car pt1) (car pt2)) 2.0)
          y1 (/ (+ (cadr pt1) (cadr pt2)) 2.0)
          z1 (/ (+ (caddr pt1) (caddr pt2)) 2.0)
     );End of setq
     (list x1 y1 z1); the new point is returned
);end of midpt

;Controlling function
(DEFUN c:3dmidpt ()
     (SETQ p1 (GETPOINT "\nPick first point:"))
     (SETQ p2 (GETPOINT "\nPick second point:"))
     (midpt p1 p2)
);End of defun
```

MIDPT.LSP

To run this program, load it and enter 3DMIDPT. You can also call "MIDPT" from other programs or from the keyboard. Note that you must always supply a 3D point to MIDPT, otherwise you will get an error with the CADDR function.

> Command: **(LOAD "MIDPT")**
> C:3DMIDPT
> Command: **3DMIDPT**
> Pick first point: **20,20,20**
> Pick second point: **40,60,80**
> (30.0 40.0 50.0)
> Command: **(MIDPT (LIST 20.4 3.5 0.0) (LIST 10 4 0.0))**
> (15.2 3.75 0.0)

A program to draw graphs

You have already seen how you can import data and draw graphs using AutoCAD script files. The first program, XYGRAF.LSP is not much more advanced than the script file but the second, 3DGRAF.LSP, allows a lot more flexibility.

```
;Program to read in pairs of numbers from an ASCII text file
;and draw lines between all the points
(DEFUN C:xygraf ()
        (PROMPT "Program to draw an x-y graph")
        (SETQ filnam (GETSTRING "\nEnter file name (incl ext):")
                data (OPEN filnam "r")                  ;opens file for reading
                pt1 (READ-LINE data)
                pt2 (READ-LINE data)
        );End of setq
        (WHILE pt2 ;while pt2 is not "nil"
                (COMMAND "line" pt1 pt2 "")
                (SETQ pt1 pt2)                          ;pt1 takes the value of pt2
                (SETQ pt2 (READ-LINE data))
        );End of while loop
        (CLOSE data)
);End of defun
```

XYGRAF.LSP

XYGRAF.LSP demonstrates some file handling techniques to read in a series of X,Y coordinates from an ASCII file. The relevant functions are OPEN, READ-LINE and CLOSE. The other new functions here are PROMPT,

GETSTRING and WHILE which allows the program to repeat for each new line in the ASCII data file.

PROMPT simply displays the message in double quotes on the screen. It returns "nil" to AutoLISP. Use it to display helpful information to whoever is running your program.

GETSTRING is another function from the GET . . . stable. It pauses for you to key in some text. The text is terminated by either <ENTER> or SPACE. If you want to include spaces in the text you can use GETSTRING in the following format:

> (GETSTRING T "\nEnter text now:")

Here, the "T" indicates that spaces are allowed in the text. To terminate the text you must press <ENTER>. If the "T" is missing or replaced by "nil" then spaces are not allowed as in the above program.

When using external files you must first open them and then tell AutoLISP what you intend to do with it. The expression, (OPEN filnam "r"), tells DOS that the file is to be opened for reading. The other options are "w" to write to a file and "a" to write appending the data to an existing file. NB: The "r", "w" and "a" must be in lower case.

HAZARD WARNING!

Be very careful when using OPEN with "w". If the file already exists it will be overwritten. Keyboard mistakes when giving the file name could cause the wrong file to disappear.

(OPEN filnam "r") returns a file descriptor which must be stored for use with the READ-LINE function. (READ-LINE data) returns the contents of one line in the file described by the descriptor stored in the variable, "data". The contents are returned as a string in double quotes and the AutoLISP moves to the start of the next line. If the end of file marker is encountered then READ-LINE returns "nil".

When you are finished with any input or output file it should be closed using "(CLOSE file-desc)". There is a limit to the number of files that can be open simultaneously.

The WHILE loop construction is a very important facility in AutoLISP. It allows you to repeat a number of lines of program many times. The format, (WHILE (test) (task)) is simple, yet flexible. As long as (test) evaluates to something other than "nil" the (task) expression will be evaluated. In the above example the test expression is simply the value of "pt2" which is non-nil until the end of file is reached by READ-LINE. The task expression spans over a number of lines and draws the line and reads the next line.

HAZARD WARNING!

Always ensure that the WHILE loop has a definite end. It is very easy to write an infinite loop which will cause your computer to apparently hang up. An example of an infinite loop might be "(WHILE T (PROMPT "nI'm in an infinite loop")". You can normally get out of it by pressing "^C".

Another technique for creating loops exists for the situation when you know exactly how many times you want to go round the loop. The REPEAT function does things a specified number of times. "(REPEAT 4 (PROMPT "\nAGAIN")", for example, would cause the word "AGAIN" to appear on 4 lines on the screen. The advantage of WHILE is that you don't have to specify the number of times to go around the loop.

To be compatible with XYGRAF.LSP, the data in the ASCII file must be in the format "xxx,yyy" with two numbers separated by a comma on each line. There should be no blank lines in the data file. The program will automatically halt when it reaches the end of the file. Use your text editor to create the data file, XYDATA.DAT. If you are using Release 10 or later this program can take 3D points, XYZDATA.DAT for example.

100.0, 100.0	100.0, 100.0, 0.0
150.0, 120.0	150.0, 120.0, 10.0
200.0, 150.0	200.0, 150.0, 10.0
250.0, 110.0	250.0, 110.0, 20.0
300.0, 125.0	300.0, 125.0, 25.0
350.0, 150.0	350.0, 150.0, 0.0
XYDATA.DAT	XYZDATA.DAT

The main advantage of XYGRAF.LSP over the script technique given in the previous chapter is that the AutoLISP program is less sensitive to blank spaces in front of and behind the numbers.

Command: **(LOAD "XYGRAF")**
C:XYGRAF
Command: **XYGRAF**
Program to draw an xy graph
Enter file name (incl ext): **XYDATA.DAT**
AutoCAD draws the five lines and returns "nil".
Command: nil
Command:

A fancy graph program

The previous program demonstrated the fundamentals of connecting points read from an external file. The next program does much the same thing with a few embellishments.

```
(DEFUN C:3Dgraf ()
    (PROMPT "Program to draw an xyz graph")
;user input
    (SETQ filnam (GETSTRING "\nEnter file name (including extension):"))
    (SETQ origin (GETPOINT "\nPick point for graph origin <0,0,0>:"))
    (INITGET "Red Yellow Green Cyan Blue Magenta White BYLayer")
    (SETQ colr (GETKWORD "\ nWhat colour for graph? <BYLAYER>:"))
    (SETQ points nil);initialise variable
      ;Set up graph origin and colour
        (IF (NULL origin)
            (SETQ origin (list 0.0 0.0 0.0))                    ;set default origin
        );End of if block
        (COMMAND "ucs" "o" origin)              ; set new ucs origin position
        (IF (NULL colr)
            (SETQ colr "BYLAYER")
        );End of if block
        (COMMAND "color" colr)
      ;Data input
        (SETQ data (OPEN filnam "r"))                       ;opens file for reading
        (SETQ pt (READ-LINE data))
        (WHILE pt                                           ;while pt is not "nil"
            (SETQ points (APPEND points (list pt)));makes list of all ;pts
            (SETQ pt (READ-LINE data))
        );End of while loop
        (CLOSE DATA);closes file
      ;Now draw the graph
        (SETVAR "pdmode" 3)                         ;sets point style to X shape
        (SETVAR "pdsize" −3)                        ;sets point size on screen
        (FOREACH xyz points (COMMAND "POINT" xyz));draws
        ;"point" at each pt.
        (COMMAND "3DPOLY"
            (FOREACH pt points (COMMAND pt)) "";  uses each point ;in
        turn
    )
      ;Reset system variables
        (COMMAND "ucs" "p")                     ; reset original origin location
        (COMMAND "color" "by
layer");reset colour to BYLAYER );End of defun
```

3DGRAF.LSP

3DGRAF.LSP uses the same techniques as XYGRAF.LSP for file handling but that's about all. The new program allows you to input where you want your graph's origin to be and also what colour to use. This can be useful when plotting more than one graph on the same screen. Rather than plotting the points as soon as they are read in, 3DGRAF.LSP stores all the point coordinates in one long list called "points". This list is then used twice, once to draw the 3D polyline and once to put an X at each point.

There are quite a few novelties brought into 3DGRAF.LSP. In the "user input" section the combination of INITGET and GETKWORD are used to select a colour. IF blocks are used to set up the default values. The command "UCS" is used to relocate the origin, and restore it to the previous setting at the end. APPEND is used to build up the list of points while FOREACH is used to extract them for plotting. The SETVAR function acts like the AutoCAD command to change the system variables.

INITGET is used to establish valid responses to the next GETxxx function. However, it doesn't work with either GETVAR or GETSTRING. GETKWORD, short for get keyword replaces GETSTRING when INITGET is being used. Only responses that are specified in the INITGET list are accepted by GETKWORD. This prevents the program from aborting if you give an inappropriate response. Instead you get the message "Invalid option keyword." and you are prompted to try again.

The format of (INITGET "Red Yellow Green Cyan Blue Magenta White BYLayer") used in the program means that any of the keywords within the double quotes are acceptable. The capital letters indicate valid abbreviations. Thus "R" or "red" would be valid responses. "BY" would be invalid as it doesn't contain all capitals. A null response is also valid. The general format of the function is "(INITGET <control bits> "string"). The control bit settings are summarised below. To get a combined effect add the values in the left hand column. For example, you might want to restrict the range of numbers to positive and non-zero for use with the LOG function.

(INITGET 7)
(SETQ ans (LOG (GETREAL "Input number for log function:")))

Here the optional string is omitted from INITGET.

Control bit	Description
1	Do not accept null response
2	Do not accept zero values
4	Do not accept negative values
8	Do not check limits
16	Points must be 3D
32	Draw dashed line when rubber banding or windowing

INITGET control bit settings

GETKWORD is similar to GETSTRING but you cannot have spaces in the text. The format is (GETKWORD "prompt string"). It must be preceded by a suitable (INITGET control bits "string") though the control bits are optional. The INITGET operates only for the next GETxxx function.

IF offers you the option of doing one task or another, depending on the value of some test expression. This function corresponds to the IF-THEN-ELSE structure in FORTRAN. The format in AutoLISP is

(IF (test) (then-do-this) (else-do-this))

When the test expression is true it returns "T" and the expression (then-do-this) is evaluated. Otherwise test returns "nil" and (else-do-this) is evaluated. In 3DGRAF.LSP, IF is used to check if a null response has been given to either the origin or colour prompts. The null response means that the user has pressed <ENTER> to accept the default. The IF blocks perform this action. Let's look at the first IF expression in detail.

```
(IF (NULL origin)
      (SETQ origin (list 0.0 0.0 0.0))          ;set default origin
);End of if block
```

The test expression, "(NULL origin)", uses the null function which returns a "T" if "origin" is nil. Otherwise it returns "nil". If the origin is nil it means that the user has pressed <ENTER> to accept the default which was "0.0,0.0,0.0". The test expression returns "T" and the SETQ function is evaluated. If the origin has some non-nil value the (else-do-this) would be evaluated if it existed. As it doesn't, the program just moves on to the next expression. Thus, depending on the program, you can omit either the (then-do-this) expression or the (else-do-this), if you so wish.

You have already seen how to construct lists using the LIST function. APPEND allows you to tag on more elements onto the end of an existing list. The line "(SETQ points (append points (list pt)))" appears within the WHILE loop of the program. Each time round the loop a new set of XYZ values are appended to the "points" list. The up-dated list is then stored back in the "points" variable. If you want to add elements onto the beginning of a list, use the CONS function, eg "(CONS (list pt) points)". The new first element goes in front of the original list.

(FOREACH xyz points (COMMAND "POINT" xyz)) steps through the "points" list assigning each element in turn to "xyz", and then evaluating the last expression which executes AutoCAD's "POINT" command. The FOREACH construction is used in a similar way within the 3DPOLY command. The expression (COMMAND xyz) returns the value of "xyz".

(COMMAND "3DPOLY" (foreach xyz points (COMMAND xyz)) "")

SETVAR is an AutoLISP function as well as being an AutoCAD command. The syntax is (SETVAR "variable name" value). It allows you to alter

AutoCAD's system variables (apart from those that are read only). The system variable PDMODE has been set to 3 which means that the AutoCAD command "POINT" draws an X shape mark at xyz for each element. The point size is set by PDSIZE, −3 generates points whose size is 3% of the current display.

Finally, to run 3DGRAF.LSP you will need a data file with a number of 3D points such as XYZDATA.DAT given previously. The same rules apply for the format of the file as for XYGRAF.LSP except that 3 numbers are required per line this time. No blank lines are allowed.

Command: (**LOAD "3dgraf"**)
C:3DGRAF
Command: **3DGRAF**
Program to draw an xyz graph
Enter file name (including extension): **XYZDATA.DAT**
Pick point for graph origin <0,0,0>: **<ENTER>**
What colour for graph? <BYLAYER>: **R**
AutoLISP draws the lines and points and returns "nil".
Command: nil
Command:

Automatic loading

If you have useful programs that you require in most editing sessions you can arrange for them to be automatically loaded. When the AutoCAD editor is invoked it searches for the file ACAD.LSP. If the file exists it is loaded automatically. You can check if you have a file called ACAD.LSP using the DIR command in AutoCAD or DOS.

Command: **DIR**
File specification: ACAD.LSP
Volume in drive C is EXPRESS-TMC
Directory of C:\ACAD

File not found.

If you already have ACAD.LSP make sure to take a safe copy of the original on floppy disk, just in case things go wrong. You can append your own functions to the ACAD.LSP file using the DOS COPY command with the "+""option. Remember one AutoLISP file can contain many functions.

C:\ACAD>**RENAME ACAD.LSP OLDACAD.LSP**
C:\ACAD>**COPYOLDACAD.LSP+EXPMINUS.LSP+UTILITY.LSP ACAD.LSP**

If you don't already have ACAD.LSP use the DOS RENAME command.

C:ACAD> **COPY EXPMINUS.LSP+UTILITY.LSP ACAD.LSP**

You can add more functions into ACAD.LSP but it's best to include only those ones that are used frequently. There is little to be gained by loading large AutoLISP files which are used only rarely. Load the big files as and when they are required.

Programming pointers

Program repetitive tasks.

Make lots of short functions rather than a few large ones. Breaking large programs into smaller units makes it easier to write and to debug (remove errors).

Try out new commands interactively at AutoCAD's "Command:" prompt before using them in programs.

Keep variable names less than six characters long.

Use indentation to flag unclosed parentheses.

Use comments to label the closing parentheses.

Standardise your variable names. Using the same name in different functions keeps the size of the ATOMLIST down.

Use local variables wherever possible.

Close files when they are no longer required.

Make real numbers REAL by including the decimal point and at least one figure to the right of it (eg 4.0), or use scientific notation.

Integers must be between −32,768 and +32,767 (2 to the power of 15).

A useful function to include in your ACAD.LSP file is (VMON).

The next stage

You have now been exposed to many, though not all, of the facilities within AutoLISP. You can now decide how much effort you wish to devote to developing your own programs. If you are to progress then you will require some essential reading material. *AutoLISP Release 10 Programmer's Reference*, published by Autodesk is a must. If you feel confident with

AutoLISP then *Inside AutoLISP* by J. Smith and R. Gesner, published by New Riders Publishing will be helpful. For people with little programming experience *AutoLISP in Plain English* by G.O. Head, published by Ventana contains good descriptions of different AutoLISP techniques.

The most immediate benefits will come from altering existing programs to suit your own situation. Sources of such programs include the above books, the AutoCAD bonus disks, user groups and magazines. *CAD User* is the independent AutoCAD magazine in Europe, while *CADalyst* and *CADENCE* are available in North America.

A number of ready made programs supplied with AutoCAD are described in the next chapter.

Summary

This chapter has given an introduction to programming with AutoLISP. The more important AutoLISP functions have been described, with the emphasis on examples. Seven programs have been developed covering topics such as mathematical calculation, file and data handling and program repetition.

You should now be able to

Create new commands.
Develop short utility functions for automatic loading.
Interrogate the AutoCAD database.
Read data from the keyboard and mouse.
Read data from files.
Construct data lists.
Run commands repetitively.
Use AutoCAD commands within programs.
Understand the *AutoLISP Programmer's Reference Manual*!

Chapter 12 **ADD-ON PROGRAMS FOR AUTOCAD**

General

The previous chapter has demonstrated the flexibility of AutoLISP and the open nature of AutoCAD which allows new commands to be developed. AutoCAD owes much of its success to this openness as it has spawned a whole industry of third party software developers dedicated to enhancing and customising the package. The range of add-on software for AutoCAD is vast and covers most engineering and architectural disciplines. It includes simple things like extra text fonts and menus, to numerical control programs for machine tools.

This chapter describes the add-on programs that come supplied with AutoCAD as well as a selection of currently available third party software. The aim is to provide a flavour for the type of packages that are available and to give advice on selecting such programs. For a complete list of third party software the reader is referred to the current issue of *AutoCAD Applications and Services Catalogue* available from Autodesk. All relevant addresses are given at the end of this chapter.

The AutoLISP program library

Autodesk supply a number of utility programs with the AutoCAD package. Some of these programs are located on the SUPPORT disk, while others are on the BONUS disk. The SUPPORT disk contains the more important programs such as 3D.LSP and others that are used routinely by AutoCAD. Some of the listings available are in an unprotected form in the \ SOURCE directory. The programs on the BONUS disk are intended to be used as examples for you to build your own utilities around.

These programs provide a valuable store of labour saving devices as well as good examples of programming technique. In this section some of the more useful programs are described. All the descriptions are limited to what has to be done to get them to work. If you want to find out how they work you will have to print them out and study the AutoLISP Reference Manual.

The programs are grouped here under three headings. The text utilities give methods of importing and exporting large amounts of text to and from AutoCAD as well as clever text editing facilities. The 3D utilities include how to plot a 3D graph and rotate objects about any axis. A few miscellaneous programs are concerned with drawing and entity management. The name of the disk containing the individual program is given to help you find the files, if they are not already installed in your AutoCAD directory.

Text utilities (Figure 12.1)

ASCTEXT.LSP (Support disk): This program allows you to import an ASCII text file that has been created using a word processor. When using this you can specify the text height and spacing between the lines. This is useful if you have to input a lot of text or numbers (eg parts schedules) to a drawing.

To try this out, create a text file called "POEM.TXT" (you can use any valid DOS file name) with the following lines. Type the text such that is is left justified.

An AutoLISP user from Poole
Wrote a neat productivity tool.
Said the boss with some joy,
"Here's a pay rise, my boy.
Hiring you I was nobody's fool."

POEM.TXT

```
Command: (load "asctext")
C:ASCTEXT
Command: ASCTEXT
File to read (including extension): POEM.TXT
Start point or Centre/Middle/Right: C
Center point: 210,200
Height <>: 15
Rotation angle <0>: <ENTER>
Change text options? <N>: <ENTER>
```

This will then import the five lines and write them in the current text style. The first line will be centred on (210,200) and the distance between the lines will be calculated automatically by AutoCAD. Use some fancy text style to embellish the lyric!

To obtain more control over the imported text you could reply "Y" to the "Change text options?" question. This will give the following prompts which are self explanatory.

```
Command: ACSTEXT . . .
Change text options? <N>: Y
Distance between lines/<Auto>: 20
First line to read <1>: <ENTER>
Number of lines to read/<All>:<ENTER>
Underscore each line? <N>: <ENTER>
Overscore each line? <N>: <ENTER>
Change text case? Upper/Lower/<N>: <ENTER>
Set up columns? <N>: <ENTER>
```

If you are importing a long file you can specify to arrange the text in columns by replying "Y" to the last prompt. You will then be asked for the horizontal distance between the columns (centre to centre) and the number of lines per column.

WTEXT.LSP (Support disk): This is the reverse of the previous program. It is used to copy AutoCAD text strings from the drawing to an ASCII text file. If the file already exists you have the option to overwrite it or to add the text onto the end.

```
Command: (load "wtext")
C:WTEXT
Command: WTEXT
Filename to write to: POEM.TXT
File "POEM.TXT" already exists.
Append/Overwrite or <New name>: <ENTER>
File name to write to: NEW-POEM.DOC
Select objects: Pick the text using the usual methods, eg. Window.
Select objects: <ENTER>
Sorting −5
```

It doesn't matter what order you pick the lines of text for writing. The program sorts the text entities by location. The text whose insertion point has the largest Y value becomes the first line and so on. If two text entities are inserted at the same height in the drawing then the one with the larger X component gets written first. This latter result might be undesirable in some circumstances.

Text entity A   Text entity B   Text entity B
Text entity C   Text entity A
                                            Text entity C

Position in drawing   Position in output file

WTEXT.LSP Sorting Order

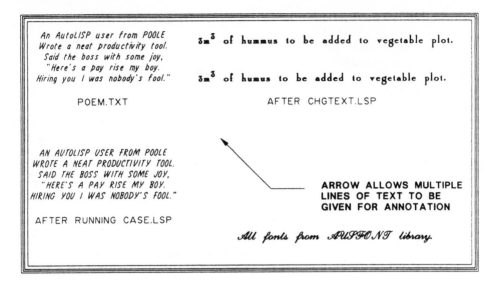

Figure 12.1 Text utilities

CHGTEXT.LSP (Support disk): This is a useful program for correcting spelling errors, particularly in long text strings. For example, suppose the following string appeared in your garden landscaping drawing. "3m³ of hummus to be added to vegetable plot". You would probably wish to change the "hummus" to "humus".

> Command: **(load "chgtext")**
> **C:CHGTEXT**
> Command: **CHGTEXT**
> Select objects: Pick the text string.
> Old string: **hummus**
> New string: **humus**

This is a lot easier than using AutoCAD's CHANGE command where you would have to re-enter the whole line of text.

CASE.LSP (Bonus disk): This program provides a programming example of the use of selection sets. It allows you to change a number of text entities to either upper or lower case. The program demonstrates how you can get AutoCAD to ignore all non-text entities in the selection. The following example uses CASE and the stored values of the limits to change all the text in a drawing to upper case.

> Command: **(load "case")**
> **C:CASE**
> Command: **CASE**

Change case to? Lower/<Upper>: **U**
Select objects: **W**
First corner: **0,0**
Other corner: **420,210**
5 found.
Select objects: **<ENTER>**

ARROW.LSP (Bonus disk): This acts very like the DIM:LEADER command but allows you to enter multiple lines of text. The arrow size is taken from the current values of DIMASZ and DIMSCALE. The text height is calculated from the current values of DIMTXT and DIMSCALE. ARROW can be entered at the "Command:" prompt.

Command: **(load "arrow")**
C:ARROW
Command: **ARROW**
Start point of arrow: Pick a point.
Next point: Pick point.
Next point: **<ENTER>** Press <ENTER> if no more points are needed.
Enter text: **First line of text**
Enter text: **Second line of text**
Enter text: **<ENTER>** Press <ENTER> if no more text is to be added.

The ARROW.LSP program is particularly useful for annotating drawings.

3D utilities (Figure 12.2)

3D.LSP (Support disk): The 3D objects, such as pyramid, cone etc are just clever AutoLISP programs which are loaded when you pick **3D objects** from the 3D screen menu. This program can also be accessed from the menu bar and icon menus or from the keyboard as follows.

Command: **(LOAD "3D")**
3D
Command: **3D**
Box/Cone/DIsh/DOme/Mesh/Pyramid/Sphere/Torus/Wedge:

You can select the appropriate object to draw and follow the prompts. 3D.LSP also defines the new commands BOX, CONE, . . . and WEDGE which can be typed at the "Command:" prompt. For example, to draw a pyramid you can type the command, input the corners of the base and the apex.

Command: **PYRAMID**
First base point: **100,100**
Second base point: **@100<0**
Third base point: **@100<90**
Tetrahedron/<Fourth base point>: **@100<180**

Replying, "T" will result in a triangular base and you will be prompted for the "Top/<Apex point>".

Ridge/Top/<Apex point>: **150,150,80**

If you choose "Ridge" you will get a shape resembling the roof of a house while "Top" allows you to make a truncated pyramid. The order of selecting the top and ridge points is important and may take some practice.

3DARRAY.LSP (Support disk): This works just like the ARRAY command but allows rectangular arrays on a 3D grid pattern. It also allows a polar array of objects about any rotation axis.

Command: **(LOAD "3DARRAY")**
Loading. Please wait . . .
C:3DARRAY
Command: **3DARRAY**
Select objects: Pick object for copying.
Select objects: <**ENTER**>
<Array>/Rotate: <**ENTER**> (This line may not appear with some versions).
Rectangular or Polar array (R/P): **R**
Number of rows (---)<1>: **3**   (Parallel to X axis of current UCS.)
Number of columns (|||)<1>: **2** (Parallel to Y axis of current UCS.)
Number of levels (...)<1>: **4**   (Parallel to Z axis of current UCS.)
Distance between rows: **110**
Distance between columns: **110**
Distance between levels: **95**

The rotate facility allows you to rotate an object about any axis. This is similar to AXROT.LSP which is described below. The polar array issues the following prompts.

Command: **3DARRAY**
Select objects: Pick object for copying.
Select objects: <**ENTER**>
Rectangular or Polar array (R/P): **P**
Number of items: **6**
Angle to fill <360>: **180**
Rotate objects as they are copied? <Y>: <**ENTER**>
Centre point of array: **100,100,0**
Second point on axis of rotation: **0,0,0**

AXROT.LSP (Bonus disk): This is a generalised version of the ROTATE command. Rotate is restricted to movements in the plane of the UCS (ie about an axis parallel to the Z direction) while AXROT allows rotations about axes parallel to any of X, Y or Z axes.

> Command: **(LOAD "AXROT")**
> C:AXROT
> Command: **AXROT**
> Select objects: Pick objects to be rotated.
> Select objects: **<ENTER>**
> Axis of rotation X/Y/Z: **X**
> Degrees of rotation <0>: **90**
> Base point <0,0,0>: Pick base point for rotation.

As the object is being rotated, the UCS is temporarily changed to the desired plane and the ROTATE command is employed before switching back to the original UCS.

CHFACE.LSP (Bonus disk): This is like PEDIT for 3DFACEs. CHFACE allows you to alter the location of any vertex of a 3DFACE. The vertex can be chosen by pointing to it, or from the order it was created in.

> Command: **(LOAD "CHFACE")**
> C:CHFACE
> Command: **CHFACE**
> Select entity to change: Pick the 3D face to edit.
> 1/2/3/4/Undo/Display/<Select vertex>: Pick vertex or type number.
> New location: @**0,0,10**
> 1/2/3/4/Undo/Display/<Select vertex>: **<ENTER>**

The numbers "1/2/3/4" refer to the four vertices of the face. As it is difficult to remember the order in which the individual points were input, it is probably safer to pick them with the cursor. The "Display" option executes a transparent REDRAW. Undo reverses the previous action.

FPLOT.LSP (Bonus disk): This is an interesting program that plots 3D graphs. You can supply the Z data in terms of any LISP function that returns a real number. You also need to specify the ranges for the X and Y coordinates. The function then calculates the Z value from X and Y and creates a 3D surface. The resolution of the surface must also be supplied. The format for using FPLOT is:

> (FPLOT <function of x and y> <range for x> <range for y> <resolution>)

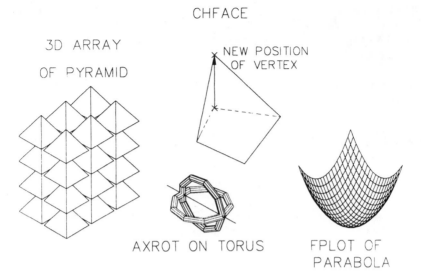

Figure 12.2 3D utilities

Probably the best way to define the function is to write a little LISP routine. The function given below defines a parabaloid surface. Use FPLOT to draw the graph of $z = 0.5(x^2 + y^2)$.

> Command: **(DEFUN parab (x y) (* 0.5 (+ (* x x) (* y y))))**
> PARAB
> Command: **(LOAD "FPLOT")**
> C:DEMO
> Command: **(FPLOT 'PARAB '(-2 2) '(-2 2) 20)**

The single quote is an AutoLISP function and must be included as shown. Use ZOOM to get in close to the parabola and DVIEW to get the 3D effect.

The "C:DEMO" that appears when you load FPLOT.LSP is a command to run a demonstration plot. This gives an impressive picture but takes a few minutes to generate. The demo is drawn for the X and Y ranges from -3 to 3 so you should MOVE or ERASE the parabola before running it.

> Command: **DEMO**

Miscellaneous utilities

SETUP.LSP (Support disk): This program can be loaded and run by picking Setup from the AutoCAD screen menu. It allows you to set up the drawing units and limits in relation to the paper size and final desired scale of the plotted output. It also draws a border at the drawing limits. This program must be used in conjunction with the screen menu. It also requires drawing called "BORDER.DWG" to be available for insertion as a global block. Unfortunately, the border is drawn at the limits and does not allow for the plotter's margin requirements. This can be easily modified by removing the line '"insert" "border" "0,0 × y "0"' from SETUP.LSP.

DELLAYER.LSP (Support disk): This program will erase all the entities on a given layer.

Command: **(LOAD "DELLAYER")**
C:DELLAYER
Command: **DELLAYER**
Layer to delete : Type layer name.

The layer still exists after this command but it is empty. To get rid of it completely you will have to PURGE it the next time you edit the file. The PURGE command only works if it is the very first command to be executed during an AutoCAD session.

Command: **PURGE**
Purge unused Blocks/LAyers/LTypes/SHapes/STyles/All: **LA**
Purge layer *layer name* <N>: **Y**

You will then be prompted with each unused layer name for purging. Replying with a "Y" causes the layer to be removed from the drawing database. This command can also be used to get rid of unused blocks, linetypes, text styles and shapes.

ATTREDEF.LSP (Support disk): This is a utility for updating block definitions. This is slightly more sophisticated than simple block redefinition using the BLOCK command. ATTREDEF also updates the attributes of all the previous insertions of the block being redefined. Before using ATTREDEF you must have the new block ready to define. For the KITCHEN drawing in Chapter 6, a typical modification might be as follows.

Command: **INSERT**
Block name (or ?): ***CUPBOARD** (This is like using EXPLODE on
CUPBOARD)
Insertion point: **0,0**
Scale factor <1>: **<ENTER>**
Rotation angle <0>: **<ENTER>**

Make any modifications to the geometry and define a new attribute.

Command: **ATTDEF**
Attribute modes – Invisible:Y Constant:N Verify:N Preset:N
Enter (ICVP) to change, RETURN when done: **<ENTER>**
Attribute tag: **COST**
Attribute prompt: **Enter cost of cupboard:**
Default attribute value: **100**
Start point or Align/Center/Fit/Middle/Right/Style: **C**
Center point: **250,200**
Height <140.0000>: **<ENTER>**
Rotation angle <0.00>: **<ENTER>**

Command: **(LOAD "ATTREDEF")**
C:ATTREDEF
Command: **ATTREDEF**
Name of block you wish to redefine: CUPBOARD   (For example)
Select new block . . .
Select objects: Pick the objects of *CUPBOARD plus the new attribute.
Select objects: **<ENTER>**
Insertion base point of new Block: **0,0**

The program will proceed to update all the occurrences of the CUPBOARD block. Old attributes that also appear in the new block retain their original values. New attributes are set to their default value. You can now use ATTEDIT to change the costs of the individual cupboards.

Third party software

What to look for in an add-on package

The first question must be "What hardware is required for the extra program?" Some programs work quite happily on humdrum equipment, while others need memory expansion boards and fast processors. You can normally check this out with your AutoCAD dealer. The golden rule is choose the software first and then get a computer that satisfies the requirements.

The next question is "How does the add-on interact with AutoCAD?" Some programs work wholly within the AutoCAD environment and are true extensions of the original drafting package. Others are stand alone programs that can exchange data with AutoCAD through either the DXB, DXF or IGES formats. These are usually larger and more powerful programs than those that run within AutoCAD and are capable of more complicated tasks. However, as they run externally from AutoCAD they cannot make use of the package's superb user interface of screen menus and pull-down icons. There may also be difficulties in translating from the add-on data format to AutoCAD. The IGES (Initial Graphics Exchange Standard) results in mammoth data files for drawings of any complexity. Programs that use this format to "talk" to AutoCAD are less desirable than ones that use DXB or DXF, which are both standards developed by Autodesk. The rule for assessing the true compatibility of an add-on program with AutoCAD is to get the supplier to do a demo with some of your own (large) drawing files and data sets.

Software upgrades are an important way of keeping up to date with the latest technology. You will want your add-on package to work with future versions of AutoCAD too. Some software suppliers offer reduced cost updates while others give "free" updates as part of a maintenance agreement. This long term commitment from the software supplier is worth assessing before you purchase anything.

Extensions to AutoCAD   The most straighforward types of add-on software are extra menu files, tablet menus, text fonts, shape files, block and symbol libraries. Most AutoCAD dealers offer consultancy services to get you started on producing libraries of standard symbols and customised menus. These are normally done on a once-off basis, though it is possible to purchase the more common drafting symbols. RIBA Services of London produce an architectural library called RIBACAD, while AutoCIM of Leamington Spa have a number of mechanical engineering libraries and tablet menus.

Graphics utilities

AutoCAD has the potential to be used for a range of graphic art applications. However, the text fonts look crude when used with a large text height as they are made up of straight lines. For sign writing, Graphic Computer Services of Western Australia supply SOLTEX, a program to produce solid lettering, with smooth curves at all magnifications. This program, written in AutoLISP works a bit like AutoCAD's text command but uses polylines and polyarcs to construct the characters. GCS also provide the programs, AUSFONT, ARCTEXT, and ARCSOL and a wide range of additional text fonts. AUSFONT combines the ASCTEXT.LSP facilities for importing ASCII files with text kerning. Kerning is a printing term and causes letters to be proportionally spaced in relation to the adjacent characters. ARCTEXT allows you to draw text along circular arcs. ARCSOL does the same for the SOLTEX characters.

AutoSHADE is a 3D visualisation package from Autodesk. It generates an "artist's impression" by shading in the solid objects. Realistic lighting and shadow effects can be achieved. This program works as a post-processor on the AutoCAD wire frame image. It is useful for creating "realistic" views of objects.

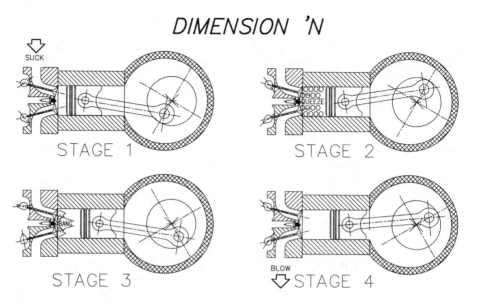

Figure 12.3 Parametric combustion engine

Parametrics

Parametric programming can be a bit of a chore but can yield considerable benefits. A parametric drawing is one where key dimensions can be made variable. On running the parametric you input the relevant sizes and the drawing is created automatically. This is ideally suited to situations where standard parts and symbols can be grouped into families by their shape. Only one parametric drawing is required for each family.

Dimension 'N from Aprotec International of Peterborough provides a graphic interface for creating parametric master drawings. It runs wholly within AutoCAD using the normal drawing facilities. When the master drawing is complete, with dimension lines if desired, Dimension 'N is invoked. The drawing is parametrised by defining a datum point of reference and a number of static and dynamic markers. The markers are used to define all the entities that will change or move when the parametric is being used. The marker location is given relative to the datum using an AutoLISP expression such as (+ A B) for the X and (− 100 B) for the Y coordinate where A and B are two variables specified at run time. When defining a marker you use the cursor to pick all the entities that are to move when the marker moves.

There are a number of programs available to generate parametrics. The particular strength of Dimension 'N is that you can attach boundary conditions to all the variables. These can be used to check that sensible values have been input or to check the values against some design criteria. You can also embed

AutoLISP statements in the parametric master which will be evaluated when the drawing is used. This means that you can use AutoLISP programs to carry out design calculation and feed the results directly to the drawing and alter the dimensions accordingly.

Dimension 'N works well with AutoCAD's screen menus. The command format and prompt sequences resemble the AutoCAD syntax. This is helpful – you know immediately what to expect when the familiar prompts appear.

A couple of special features make Dimension 'N even more versatile. Firstly, you can define parametric blocks whose insertion points, rotation and scale factors can be parametrised. You can also parametrise the block name to be inserted. This means that you can specify that one of a set of blocks can be inserted depending on some parametric variable. The actual block to be inserted is only finalised at run time. The second feature is that you can use programming loops in the drawing definition. This is excellent for testing mechanisms where a number of moving parts are related. By looping the parametric through a complete cycle, the parts can be tested for all possible configurations. Figure 12.3 demonstrates these features. The position of the piston, connecting rod and valves are all dependent on the angle of the crank shaft. Also dependent on the angle is whether the engine is in the SUCK or BLOW part of the cycle. The relevant block is inserted when the crank shaft angle is at the right value.

Drawing office management

Management of the AutoCAD drawing office can be a major headache. Book keeping and archiving procedures that worked well for manual drafting are often insufficient for keeping track of drawings on floppy disk. Indeed it is difficult to keep track of what each drawing contains.

AutoManager from CYCO is a valuable but inexpensive tool for flipping quickly through a lot of drawings. It can be run from inside AutoCAD to view a number of drawing files. The program is menu driven and is completely self explanatory. The only difficulty you might have is fitting it in memory if you run a number of memory resident DOS utilities.

CADMAN from SMC and DATECH and CADMASTER from Aprotec International offer two similar solutions to managing drawing production in a networked environment. Both programs control AutoCAD from a database management program. Management programs provide facilities to control access to drawings, record the revision history of drawings and streamline plot spooling. They can also be used to provide weekly and monthly reports of the time spent on different jobs. CADMAN is menu driven, allows up to 20 character drawing names and stores project information as well as the drawing title in its database. Database information is passed to AutoCAD for inclusion in the drawing. Changes in that information made in the drawing editor are passed back to the database, ensuring consistency. It also controls archiving of drawings onto tape or disk. CADMASTER offers similar features and also provides network hardware.

Scanning

Many users require to get old drawings from paper or blueprints into their AutoCAD system. This can be a costly and time consuming operation. The benefits accrue when modifications are required for old designs. Scanning bureaux provide services in which the original prints are scanned by an optical device which outputs the image in raster form to a computer. The rasterised image consists millions of dots making up the complete picture. The next stage in the operation is to translate the dots (pixels) into vectors recognisable by AutoCAD. This vectorisation accounts for about 90% of the cost of converting a drawing from paper to AutoCAD. It requires specialised hardware and software which can recognise patterns in the raster dots and convert them to lines, circles and text entities etc.

Another way to convert the raster image to a vector drawing is to trace over it. AutoVIEW, released by CAD-Capture of Blackburn allows you to import such a raster file into an AutoCAD drawing. It does this by converting all the pixels into line entities. At this stage the drawing consists only of hundreds of small lines. However, with the image already on the screen it is quite easy to use as an underlay and to trace over it with the relevant AutoCAD entities. You will need a scanner to generate the raster images or employ the facilities of a scanning bureau.

Architectural and civil engineering software

Packages available for the construction industry range from symbol libraries to structural detailing, surveying and mapping to drainage and earthworks.

SSDS and RCDS are a pair of programs from RADAN of Bath for structural steel and reinforced concrete detailing. Both are written in AutoLISP and use AutoCAD screen menus extensively. Different views and schedules are produced automatically. The steel detailing and scheduling package contains a library of standard beam and column cross section shapes. It supports notches, bolt holes, stiffeners, sloping members and automatic dimensioning. The reinforced concrete package supports the British Standard bar bending codes. Bills of materials can be output to files or included on the drawing.

AutoCAD's AEC Architectural package provides the discipline specific configuration for architectural work. This is the only industry specific add-on produced by Autodesk itself.

Bill of materials

Most applications packages contain some kind of bill of materials reporting. AutoBOM from AutoCIM is a general BOM program which reports quantities by attribute extraction. Other programs do similar functions outputting to popular database programs.

Other disciplines

There are a number of packages that can be used to generate piping diagrams with full schematics and BOM. Electrical and electronic schematics can also be automated and linked to design software. Full Computer Integrated Manufacturing can be accomplished by coupling AutoCAD to numerical control programs for tooling machines. Many of these packages are bigger, more powerful and more expensive than AutoCAD. In general, the highly specific design and control software packages run externally from AutoCAD and communicate with it through DXF or IGES data exchange files.

Finite element analysis

AutoCAD models objects as 3D wire frames. To generate solid 3D objects you would need to use a "solid modelling" package. AutoSOLID from Autodesk gives you this facility. It is a separate program but can import data from AutoCAD. AutoSolid and other such packages contain their own graphic commands for building up the 3D geometry and mass properties of objects. This information is then output to yet another package to do the finite element analysis (FEM). AutoSOLID can output data in formats compatible with the FEM packages ANSYS, NASTRAN and COSMOS-C. A special version of AutoSolid ANSYS is available for full integration. FEM programs are heavy number crunchers and require fast computers with large memory.

Wordprocessing and desk-top publishing

Some utilities which enable AutoCAD to import and export text have been described earlier. The corollary to this is to import AutoCAD graphics into a document. This can be done with most desk-top publishing (DTP) packages and with the better wordprocessing (WP) programs. The DTP program Ventura Publisher can use AutoCAD slides to produce graphics embedded in a document. Word-perfect 5.0, the popular WP program, uses DXF files for its AutoCAD importing. In most cases the DTP or WP programs give very limited graphic editing facilities such as simple scaling up or down of the image. The combination of AutoCAD's graphics and a good WP or DTP program is very powerful and results in impressive illustrated documents.

Summary

The message is clear: "Owning AutoCAD is just the start". There is a large amount of add-on software available. Some quite useful LISP files exist which can help to speed up awkward and repetitive tasks. Indeed the AutoCAD bonus files include some real gems. AutoCAD user groups distribute their members' utility programs and many more programs are printed each month in magazines. *CAD User* is the independent magazine for AutoCAD users in Europe while *CADalyst* and *CADENCE* are published in North America.

Larger and more discipline specific programs are available for most applications. Hundreds of packages use AutoCAD as the graphics engine and user interface. This has been a brief overview of just some of these. Finding the correct package for your situation will require some research. When you select possible contenders make sure that you see them in action with realistic demonstrations.

Products and addresses

AEC Architectural,
AutoSolid and
AutoCAD Applications
and Services Catalogue

Autodesk Ltd,
South Bank Technopark,
90 London Road,
London SE1 6LN

AutoBOM

AutoCIM,
St Alban's House,
Portland Street,
Leamington Spa,
CV32 5EZ

AutoManager

Cyco International,
1908 Cliff Valley Way,
Suite 2000, Atlanta,
Georgia 30329, USA

In UK: DATECH Ltd,
Central Court,
Knoll Rise,
Orpington,
Kent BR6 0JA

AutoVIEW

CAD-Capture Ltd,
Whitebirk Industrial Estate,
Blackburn BB1 5UD

CADMAN

SMC Ltd,
Enterprise Centre,
North Mall,
Cork, Ireland

CADMASTER and
Dimension 'N

Aprotec International,
137 Orton Enterprise Centre,
Bakewell Road,
Orton Southgate,
Peterborough PE2 0XU

CAD User Magazine

Compudraft Ltd,
24 High Street,
Beckenham,
Kent BR3 1AY

RIBACAD

RIBA Services Limited,
39 Moreland Street,
London EC1V 8BB

SSDS and RCDS

Radan Computational Ltd,
Ensleigh House,
Granville Road,
Lansdown,
Bath BA1 9BE

Appendix A **CONFIGURATION**

General

The configuration of AutoCAD to work on your particular hardware involves two stages. Firstly, you must set the computer's working environment and then tell AutoCAD about the various pieces of hardware it has to communicate with. The chief difficulty with describing system configurations is that they depend on many factors. Thus, comprehensive coverage of all the possible AutoCAD configurations is not feasible in a short book. The major considerations are outlined below though slight modifications may be required for your own installation. If in doubt, you should consult the AutoCAD Installation Guide.

The DOS environment

The computer's working environment on PCs is controlled through two files, CONFIG.SYS and AUTOEXEC.BAT. The first file contains parameters telling your computer how to utilise its memory and may also contain some default settings for its operation. AUTOEXEC.BAT is a list of DOS commands which are automatically executed when you turn the computer on. Both of these files are ASCII text files and can be created with EDLIN or a wordprocessor. The sample files given below are the ones I use on my own computer.

```
COUNTRY=044
SHELL=C:\DOS\COMMAND.COM C:\DOS  P  E:256
DEVICE=C:\DOS\ANSI.SYS
DEVICE=C:\DOS\RDISK.SYS
FILES=20
BUFFERS=24
```

CONFIG.SYS

The first line indicates that the English (Code 44) defaults should be used. The "SHELL" line extends the amount of memory to be reserved for running DOS. The first device drivers set up ANSI.SYS, a graphics standard, which is used by another package on my computer. RDISK.SYS is a short program that sets up any extended memory (above 640K) to behave just like a disk drive (RAM Disk). On some computers you will have to use VDISK.SYS instead of RDISK.SYS. The "FILES" tells the computer how many different files it will have to be able to handle simultaneously. The "BUFFERS" is also used for input/output control and specifies the amount of memory to be set aside for routine reading and writing to disk. Buffers must be greater than 10 for AutoCAD to run satisfactorily.

```
ECHO OFF
PATH D:\;C:\ACAD;C:\DOS;C:\PCWRITE;
TIMER/S
PROMPT $P$G  (Makes the DOS prompt display current directory
                                        eg C:  ACAD>)
KEYBUK
TURBOPC                        (Utility to speed up processor clock)
TON                            (Toggles high speed clock)
CGE350 SCRNSAV 10     (Utility to blank out screen if idle for 10
                                                minutes)
REM Set up AutoCAD environment.
SET ACADFREERAM=24        (This is also the default value)
SET LISPHEAP=30000              (Required for AutoLISP)
SET LISPSTACK=15000             (Required for AutoLISP)
SET ACAD=C:\ACAD\SUPPORT (Path for AutoCAD support
                                    files eg .SHX etc)
CD\MOUSE                     (Install MOUSE program)
MOUSE
MENU
CLICK
CD\ACAD                              (Run AutoCAD)
ACAD
C:\WORK
```

Example AUTOEXEC.BAT

The comments given in brackets are by way of explanation and should *not* be included in the file. The example AUTOEXEC.BAT file contains a number of useful utility programs as well as some DOS commands. The "ECHO" command prints comments on the screen, or if it is OFF it suppresses them. The PATH command gives DOS the names of the directories to search for programs: "D:" is the RAM (Random Access Memory) disk; "C:\DOS" is where I have all the MS-DOS programs; "C:\PCWRITE" is my wordprocessor.

The AutoCAD environment set-up starts with the statement "SET ACAD-FREERAM=24" which will be used by AutoCAD to control the size of the working memory store. In this example 24Kb will be reserved. If you get an error message "Fatal error: OUT OF RAM" then you will need to increase the ACADFREERAM setting. A maximum of 30 is allowed.

The sum of the values for the LISPHEAP and LISPSTACK variables must be less than or equal to 45,000 bytes. The heap is used to store AutoLISP variables while the stack is the AutoLISP working memory. (See Chapter 11.)

The final variable to be set is called "ACAD" and contains the path name for the location of AutoCAD's support files eg menus, LISP programs, text fonts etc. This is only required if those files are not in the same directory as the ACAD.EXE program file.

Configuring AutoCAD

The second stage of setting up AutoCAD on your computer is to tell the program about the hardware it has available to it. You must specify what kind of video display unit is installed, what type of printer and plotter and the make of your digitising or pointing device. This is done from AutoCAD's main menu by selecting option 5.

Main menu

0. Exit AutoCAD
1. Begin a New drawing
2. Edit an Existing drawing
3. Plot a drawing
4. Printer plot a drawing

5. Configure AutoCAD
6. File utilities
7. Compile shape/font description file
8. Convert old drawing file

Enter selection: **5**

AutoCAD then displays the current configuration, if one exists. For example, the configuration might appear as:

Configure AutoCAD.

Current AutoCAD configuration

Video display: IBM Enhanced Graphics Adapter
Digitiser: Microsoft Serial or Bus Mouse
Plotter: Hewlett-Packard 7580
Printer plotter: Epson FX-100 or 286

Press RETURN to continue: **<ENTER>**

Pressing the ENTER key then shows the configuration menu.

Configuration menu

  0. Exit to main menu
  1. Show current configuration
  2. Allow detailed configuration

  3. Configure video display
  4. Configure digitizer
  5. Configure plotter
  6. Configure printer plotter
  7. Configure system console
  8. Configure operating parameters

Enter selection: <0>:

You use this menu like the main menu. To select an option, type the appropriate number followed by **<ENTER>**. The options 0 – 2 don't cause any actual changes to the configuration and so are separated from the other selections. The rest are used to alter the set-up of individual devices.

Enter selection: <0>: **2**

Do you want to do detailed device configuration? <N> **Y**

Selection number 2 appears as "Allow I/O port configuration" in older versions of AutoCAD but does much the same thing. You must choose this option if you wish to alter the DOS MODE parameters for peripherals connected to the input/output ports on your computer. You will require some technical knowledge to do this though AutoCAD does offer sensible defaults. You should also use this option to tell AutoCAD to which port (Serial = COM1 or COM2 or Parallel = LPT1, LPT2 or LPT3) your plotter, printer and digitiser are connected. Consult the operating manual for your mouse, plotter or printer when using this option.

If you answer "Y" to the above question you will be shown the current configuration again and given the message "Port configuration questions will be asked during device configuration". You will also be asked much more detailed questions when configuring the display.

When you have made all the desired modifications you can exit the configuration menu by selecting "0". You will be asked if you want to keep the changes or to discard them.

Enter selection <0>: <**ENTER**>

If you answer N to the following question, all configuration changes you have just made will be discarded.

Keep configuration changes? <Y> <**ENTER**>

Altering devices

When you select any of the options 3 to 6 you will be told what your current device and its settings are. You then have the choice of simply altering the settings or of choosing a new device. Depending on the type of device to be configured, AutoCAD displays a list of makes and models that are acceptable. You simply type the number given for your device and answer a few questions about it. If your device does not appear on the list you should consult the device's operating manual. Many smaller manufacturers build their equipment to emulate better known makes. For example, IBM's EGA is emulated by many makes of video display unit, while Hewlett-Packard is the de facto standard for plotters.

Configuring the video display unit   As an example, to change the display configuration from EGA to match a new VGA monitor you might do the following:

Enter selection: <0>: **3**
Your current video display is: IBM Enhanced Graphics Adapter
Do you want to select a different one? <N> **Y**

If the AutoCAD device driver files (*.DRV) are not present in the current or ACAD directories you will be asked where they are. I keep the driver files on a backup floppy disk. This saves about 1Mb on the hard disk and these files are not used very often.

Enter drive or directory containing the Display device drivers: **A:**

Note, the colon is included. You will then be presented with an alphabetical list of over 40 different devices supported by AutoCAD. This takes up 3 screens with the ENTER key being used to move to the next screen.

Available video displays:

1. ADI display
2. BNW Precision Graphics Adapter
etc.

Select device number or ? to repeat list <18>: **21**

If you have previously measured the height and width of a "square"
on your graphics screen, you may use these measurements to correct the aspect ratio.

Would you like to do so? <N> **Y**

The number for EGA is "18" and VGA is "21". Answering "Y" to the last
question gives you the opportunity of getting AutoCAD to calculate a correc-
tion factor for the dot aspect ratio of your screen. To do this you will first have
had to display a drawing on the new screen. The aspect ratio problem is caused
by the screen pixels being taller than they are wide resulting in circles that look
like ellipses and squares that look like rectangles. If this happens on your
screen, measure the width and height of the object that should be square with a
ruler. You can then use these values as inputs for AutoCAD's configuration.
The units (mm or inches etc) of measurement don't matter as long as they are
the same for width and height.

Width of square <1.0000>: *Give measured value*
Height of square <1.0000>: *Give measured value*

After giving the square sizes or if you answered "N" to the previous question,
you will then be asked a number of questions about what to display. You can
also choose whether you want lines to appear as white on a black background or
vice versa.

Do you want a status line? <Y> <**ENTER**>
Do you want a command prompt area? <Y> <**ENTER**>
Do you want a screen menu area? <Y> <**ENTER**>
Do you want dark vectors on a light background field? <Y><**ENTER**>

This will mean that the colour number 7 (white) will actually appear as black on
the screen while the background will be white.

Do you want to supply individual colors for parts of the graphics
screen? <N> <**ENTER**>

Answering "Y" to the last question would allow you to specify the colours of
the menu text and background, pull-down menus etc. If you have previously

requested the detailed configuration, you will automatically be asked for all the colours. AutoCAD will then return to the configuration menu.

Configuring the digitiser   The term "digitiser" covers most forms of pointing device from the relatively cheap mouse and joystick to tracker balls and expensive A0 digitising tablets. The configuration procedure is quite simple. You enter selection number 4 and choose your device's number from the list displayed. You may also tell AutoCAD where the device is conected if you have previously requested the "Allow detailed configuration". The other important parameter to choose is the scale factor to use. This will link the degree of motion on the screen to movements of the pointing device.

To change from a Microsoft Mouse to a Logitech Logimouse you might do the following:

Enter selection: <0>: **4**
Your current digitizer is: Microsoft Serial or Bus Mouse
Do you want to select a different one? <N> **Y**

Available digitizers:

1. None
2. ADI digitizer
etc.

Select device number or ? to repeat list <21>: **20**
Do you want to adjust the Logimouse scaling parameters? <N> **Y**
Fast motion factor, 0 to 255 <3>: **5**
Fast motion threshold, 0 to 2047 <100>: **35**

The scaling parameters depend on your pointing device and you should consult your device's manual to get the appropriate values. The fast motion numbers cause the cursor to move extra fast when the mouse is moved quickly. Moving the mouse slowly allows greater precision. The threshold is the speed above which the fast motion factor is to be used. The values given above allow the mouse to be operated on a pad 150mm × 150mm.

If selection 2 had already been chosen you would have also been asked about the communication port being used. For example:

Connects to Asynchronous Communications Adapter port.
Standard ports are:

COM1
COM2

Enter port name, or address in hexadecimal <COM1>: **COM2**

Other makes of mouse and digitiser result in different questions. In general the questions are self-explanatory and the defaults usually work quite well.

Configuring the plotter   The procedure is much the same as for selecting the digitiser. You get a list of supported plotters. You can also correct for any scaling errors in the plotter and select the level of optimisation the AutoCAD is to use when generating plots. Finally, you will be given the usual plotting prompts discussed in Chapter 9. This allows you to set up your own defaults for the next plot. Again, selection 2 allows you to specify the communications port being used.

Sometimes it is useful to output plots to ADI (AutoCAD Device Independent) formats (see Hints and Hiccups in Appendix B). The next example could be used to change from a Hewlett-Packard plotter to the ADI.

Enter selection: <0>: **5**
Your current plotter is: Hewlett-Packard
Do you want to select a different one? <N> **Y**

Available plotters:

   1. None
   2. ADI plotter
   etc.

Select device number or ? to repeat list <7>: **2**

The following prompts are specific to ADI. Other devices will have their own set of questions to be answered.

Select output format:

   0.   ASCII file
   1.   Binary file
   2.   AutoCAD DXB file
   3.   Installed INT driver

Output format, 0 to 3 <0>: **2**
Maximum horizontal (X) plot size in drawing units <11.0000>: **297**
Plotter steps per drawing unit <1000.0000>: **100**
Maximum vertical (Y) plot size in drawing units 8.5000: 210

The more plotter steps per unit, the smoother curves will be and the bigger the DXB (Data eXchange Binary) file. The rest of the prompts are common to many plotters.

Do you want to change pens while plotting? <N> <**ENTER**>

If you have previously measured the lengths of a horizontal and a vertical line that were plotted to a specific scale, you may use these measurements to calibrate your plotter.

Would you like to calibrate your plotter? <N> <**ENTER**>

It is worth calibrating your plotter occasionally. Some plotters have their own calibration routine, independent of AutoCAD. It is better to use this latter calibration if other software packages are used with the plotter. The rest of the questions are the same as those that appear when you are actually plotting a drawing (see Chapter 9).

Size units (Inches or Millimeters) <I>: **M**
Plot origin in Millimeters <0.00,0.00>: <**ENTER**>

Enter the Size or Width,Height (in Millimeters) <MAX>: <**ENTER**>
Rotate 2D plots 90 degrees clockwise? <N> <**ENTER**>
Pen width <0.25>: <**ENTER**>
Adjust area fill boundaries for pen width? <N> <**ENTER**>
Remove hidden lines? <N> <**ENTER**>
Specify scale by entering:
Plotted Millimeters=Drawing Units or Fit or ? <F>: **1=1**

The DXB file generated at the next PLOT execution will contain the drawing in terms of lots of short line segments. This can be imported to another AutoCAD drawing with the DXBIN command. Some other software also supports the DXB format and so can import the plot file. When you are finished generating DXB files from drawings you can reconfigure AutoCAD for the original device.

Configuring the printer plotter   This is done by selecting option 6 from the configuration menu. The routine is much the same as for plotters. The ADI printer device allows output in the CAD/camera format for generating 35mm slides. This requires special hardware.

Configuring the system console   There are no console configuration parameters on the IBM PC and compatibles and so option 7 in the menu is redundant.

Configuring the operating parameters   Selecting option 8 from the con-figuration menu gives a further menu for various operating parameters. This allows you to specify the default prototype drawing name, plot filenames. If your computer is in a network you can specify the node name and plot spooler directory. Extra software is required to control the plot spool. This is a queuing system for plotting files.

Selecting sub-option 5 allows you to direct AutoCAD's temporary files to a specific disk drive or directory. When editing large drawings, AutoCAD uses disk space for storing parts of the drawing and information for the UNDO command etc. You can speed up the performance by specifying a RAM disk for the temporary files. However, long editing sessions create lengthy temporary files which can be as big as the drawing itself. The AutoCAD Installation Guide warns that the "Disk almost full" condition cannot be tested if the temporary files are not in the same directory as the drawing file. This results in a fatal "disk full" error if the temporary files disk becomes full. The final option, 7, in the sub-menu gives you the option of enabling or disabling AutoLISP or using extended AutoLISP. Extended AutoLISP can be used if you have an extended memory board fitted in your computer.

Enter selection <0>: **8**

Operating parameter menu

    0.   Exit to configuration menu
    1.   Alarm on error
    2.   Initial drawing setup
    3.   Default plot file name
    4.   Plot spooler directory
    5.   Placement of temporary files
    6.   Network node name
    7.   AutoLISP feature

Enter selection <0>:

Boosting performance

The performance of AutoCAD on your personal computer can be fine tuned. This is usually a trial and error procedure involving the parameters in the CONFIG.SYS and AUTOEXEC.BAT files. The optimum values for the parameters, FILES, BUFFERS, LISPHEAP, LISPSTACK and ACAD-FREERAM depend on the size of drawing file and the speed of your disk drives, processor and the amount of memory available. If you find that the disk is being accessed very frequently then you should achieve some improvement in speed by increasing the size of the I/O buffers. You can free memory by reducing the LISPHEAP and LISPSTACK variables. You know you've reduced the heap too much when you get the message "insufficient node (or string) space" or reduced the stack too much if "LISPSTACK overflow" appears when running a program.

After a few months of use, the hard disk on your PC may become slower to respond. As old files are deleted, small patches of the disk are freed for new files. If the new file is bigger than the old one it will be split between two or more parts of the disk. It takes more time to read such a file than one which is stored in one neat unit. There are a number of relatively inexpensive utility programs (Norton's Utilities Speed Disk, for example) that reorganise the files on the hard disk to optimise its performance. The optimisation process typically takes about 10 to 20 minutes for a congested 30Mb disk drive. The time taken depends on the degree of reorganisation necessary. It is recommended to run a hard disk optimising program at least once every couple of months.

Shelling from AutoCAD

You can use external commands from within the drawing editor as long as AutoCAD knows how much memory is needed. This information is given in a file called ACAD.PGP. The commands included in the PGP file can be typed at AutoCAD's "Command:" prompt and are executed without exiting the drawing editor. Use your wordprocessor or the DOS TYPE command to examine the file. I have included the last line below so that I can use the PCWRITE text editor to write scripts and lisp programs from within AutoCAD.

```
CATALOG,DIR /W,27000,*Files: ,0
DEL,DEL,27000,File to delete: ,0
DIR,DIR,27000,File specification: ,0
EDIT,EDLIN,42000,File to edit: ,0
SH,,27000,*DOS Command: ,0
SHELL,,127000,*DOS Command: ,0
TYPE,TYPE,27000,File to list: ,0
ED,C:\PCWRITE\ED,120000,Enter name of file to edit:,4
```

ACAD.PGP

The first item in each line is the new AutoCAD command name. The second item is the DOS or external command followed by the amount of memory required. Next comes the prompt to appear on the screen when executing the command. The final digit is a numeric code for AutoCAD. "0" does nothing, "4" restores the graphics screen at the end of the command. The other codes

"1" and "2" are used by third party software developers to load DXB files into the drawing.

To calculate the amount of memory required add together the size of the program file and any data files it loads into memory and an extra 4Kb or so. If you don't allow enough memory you will get the message "Not enough memory" when you try to run the command from the drawing editor. If you allow too much memory things will run a bit slow.

Appendix B **HINTS AND HICCUPS**

General

This appendix contains a number of techniques to speed up AutoCAD as well as some of the less pleasant events that may befall the unlucky user. It also includes tips on how to recover from errors and how to avoid them. The list represents some of the more common happenings and some useful techniques. A special section is devoted to plotting drawings and its particular problems.

Hints

The SAVE command stores a complete copy of the drawing. If you want to discard unused layers and blocks from the saved file you normally have to edit the file and execute the PURGE command. To get around this use WBLOCK instead of SAVE. Give a filename but no block name. Then select the objects you wish to save. When the WBLOCKed file has been written you can recover the deleted objects with OOPS. The new file will only contain those layers containing its objects. All frozen and unused layers will be omitted.

Another way to get rid of unused blocks is simply to redefine them to contain nothing. Unlike PURGE this can be done at any time. The block will still appear in the list of defined blocks but it won't take up much memory. It can be purged at a later and more convenient time.

It is not recommended to run AutoCAD without a mouse or similar pointing device but it can be done. The arrow keys can be used to move the cursor up/down and left/right. You can speed up the movement by pressing the Pg Up key and slow it down with the Pg Dn key. When using these keys you can select points with the SPACE bar. Pressing the INS key moves the cursor to the screen menu. Use the up/down arrows to move in the menu and INS to select an item. You can't use pull-down menus with the arrow keys.

Hiccups

Symptom: The graphics screen disappears.
Cause: Many commands force AutoCAD into text mode to display information.
Remedy: Press the F1 key or type "GRAPHSCR" to get back to the graphics screen.

Symptom: Lost in the screen menu system.
Cause: It can happen to the best of us.
Remedy: Pick "AutoCAD" from the top of the menu. This will restore the root menu. If you are in a different menu file or if no menu appears on the screen, type "MENU" at the AutoCAD Command: prompt and give "ACAD" as the menu file name.

Symptom: The pull-down menu won't go away.
Remedy: Press the ESC key or pick EXIT from the menu.

Symptom: Linetypes CENTER, DASHED etc appear solid.
Cause: The LTSCALE setting may be too big or too small.
Remedy: Use ZOOM to get a closer look. If it now appears correctly you should increase the LTSCALE value. If it still looks solid when you have ZOOMed in a few times then you probably need to reduce LTSCALE. If LTSCALE is too large you might fit only one dash on the drawing.

Symptom: ZOOM All causes the drawing to disappear.
Cause: An entity has been created far outside the normal drawing limits.
Remedy: Do a ZOOM All and check the edges of the drawing screen for the offending item(s). Use ERASE to get rid of it/them.

Symptom: Erased object reappears later.
Cause: More than one object had been drawn at that location. If you draw two lines, one directly on top of the other, you will only see one line on the screen. When you pick that line for erasing only the most recent one will be selected and deleted.
Remedy: ERASE Window will select all the lines. If you do a REDRAW you will see if another line existed at the same spot and has not been deleted. If you delete too many objects use OOPS to restore them.

Plotting pitfalls

This is just a short list of some common errors that are made when using plotters.

Symptom: Nothing happens after pressing "RETURN to continue".
Cause: Plotter not switched on.
Remedy: Switch the plotter on. If things go haywire press ^C. If it has a reset button, pressing it might help. If the plot refuses to be cancelled you may have to do a "Control Alt Del" to reboot. If you have already saved the drawing this won't involve too much upset. Replot the drawing.
Other cause: Less traumatic is a simple paper tray empty or paper out situation. The plotter should display a message or warning light if this is the case.
Remedy: Reload the paper tray and things should proceed normally.
Further cause: Plotter cable not connected. The cable may have come loose or you may have a computer with only one serial port which hasn't been switched over to the plotter.
Remedy: Make the connection and the plotter should come to life.

Symptom: Paper crinkles and bubbles.
Causes: This happens sometimes with large flat bed plotters and it can be difficult to keep the paper smoothed flat. The usual cause is temperature and humidity variations between the paper storage location and the plotter room.
Remedy: Paper should be left in the open, in the same location as the plotter for about 30 minutes before use. This allows it to readjust to the ambient conditions. Avoid placing the plotter or paper in direct sunlight.

Symptom: Pen skips part of the drawing.
Cause: Out of ink/ pen clogged.
Remedy: Check all pens before plotting. Regularly clean all ink pens. Depending on how much use is made of the plotter you may have to change the pens daily.
Other cause: Pen–paper–speed mismatch.
Remedy: Consult the pen/paper manufacturer's guidelines. As a general rule, felt tip pens work best on a non-absorbant, glossy, type of paper while roller-ball and ink pens work on a matt surface. Ink pens require slower pen speeds and light pen pressure; felt tips work at high speeds and low pressure; roller-ball pens can work at high speeds with medium pen pressures. In all cases the slower the pen speed the darker the resultant plot. If the pen speed is too slow you may get blotches and ink blobs.
Further cause: Grease on paper. This is easy to recognise as the the skipping is confined to specific areas. It can be caused by the "fat of the hand" if you try to smooth down the paper with the palm of your hand.
Remedy: Replace paper and smooth down new sheet using a dry cloth.

Symptom: Picture plotted with wrong colours.
Cause: Assuming the selections have been made correctly this might result from one of the pens being incorrectly mounted in holder. If this is so, the plotter will think that there is no pen in that holder and use an adjacent one instead.
Remedy: Remove all pens and replace carefully.

There are many other things that can go wrong with plotters. However, even though they are delicate instruments they can be made to operate successfully for many years as long as they are cared for. There are a number of maintenance tasks that should be carried out frequently to ensure that the pens are operating, paper feed works smoothly and other commonsense items are taken care of.

Summary

No doubt you will come up with your own list of hints and hiccups. When you do solve a particular problem it is worth making a note of how you did it. Sharing notes with others can be a very fruitful way of improving your AutoCAD techniques.

AutoCAD help is available through user groups and the independent magazines mentioned in Chapter 12. You can also get help via Autodesk's bulletin board on Compuserve but this requires some knowledge of communications software and hardware.

GLOSSARY

AEC   Architect, Engineer, Constructor – an add-on package for AutoCAD. The term used for the construction industry CAD market.

ASCII   American Standard Code for Information Interchange – method of defining text characters with 8-bit binary numbers.

Atom   Anything that is not a list in AutoLISP. Atom is also the name of an AutoLISP function.

AUI   Advanced User Interface – AutoCAD's pull-down menu system.

AUTOEXEC.BAT   DOS batch file that is automatically run when the computer is switched on.

AutoLISP   Programming language in AutoCAD, based on Common LISP.

BASIC   A high level computer language suitable for mathematical, algorithmical programming.

BAT   DOS batch file extension, eg AUTOEXEC.BAT.

Bezier surface   Mathematical technique for generating smooth surfaces using a number of control points.

Binary   A number system using the base 2.

BOM   Bill of materials – a list of the components necessary to manufacture an item.

British Standard   Also BS – A document published by the British Standards Institute, outlining recommended practices for British manufacturers.

B-spline	A two-dimensional version of the Bezier surface.
CAD	Computer Aided Drafting – use of computers to produce engineering drawings. Also Computer Aided Design – use of computers in the design process.
CADD	Computer aided design and drafting.
CAD/CAM	Computer aided design interfaced with computer aided manufacturing.
Cartesian coordinate system	Definition of points by X,Y, and Z coordinates relative to imaginary axes and origin.
CD	DOS Change Directory command.
CDF	Comma Delimited Format for attribute extraction files. Text items are separated by commas, suitable for use with BASIC programs.
CIM	Computer Integrated Manufacturing.
COM1,COM2	Serial communications ports on computer.
Common LISP	The most widely used standard for the high level language, LISP.
Coplanar points or objects	Points or objects that lie in the same 3D plane
Digitiser	Device for translating movement on a tablet or desk into cursor movements on the screen.
DOS	Disk Operating System, the controlling program for most IBM compatible personal computers.
Dot matrix	Type of printer head that prints using an array of pins to generate the letters etc.
DPI	Dots per inch, a measurement of the resolution of a dot matrix, laser or similar printer.
DWG	File extension for AutoCAD drawings.
DXB	AutoCAD's Drawing interchange format producing binary files.

DXF	AutoCAD's Drawing interchange format producing text files. This is the most common format used in PC-CAD interchange.
EGA	Enhanced Graphics Adapter, an IBM standard for controlling colour monitors.
Entity	In AutoCAD, a single graphical object in a drawing.
Expanded memory	Extra memory between 1 and 16Mb. DOS versions 3 can only address memory up to 640Kb. AutoCAD can use up to 4Mb if it is available.
Extended memory	Extra memory between 1 and 16Mb using a different specification to expanded memory.
FORTRAN	High level computer language suitable for scientific and engineering calculations.
Gland	In mechanical engineering, a device for preventing leakage of lubricant in a shaft assembly.
Hardcopy	Computer output on paper or other long lasting medium.
Heap	Memory where AutoLISP stores all functions and symbols.
Hercules graphics card	Standard circuit for controling monochrome video display units.
Icon	In computing, a graphical symbol depicting a command which when picked executes that command.
IGES	Initial Graphics Exchange Standard – a text format for exchanging drawings from one CAD system to another.
Inkjet printer	Type of printer that prints using tiny jets of fast drying ink. Typically they work at a resolution of 300 dots per inch.
Integer	A whole number, eg 4, −6 etc.
Isometric projection	Graphical construction for showing 3D information on a 2D page or screen. The X and Y axes are drawn at 30 and 150 degrees to the horizontal with the Z axis in the vertical.

Laser printer	High quality printer for graphical and text output. It works similarly to a photocopier to produce output. The image is traced on the paper by a laser source.
LISP	LISt Processing computer language often used for artificial intelligence application.
LPT1, LPT2	Parallel ports on the computer usually used for connecting printers.
LSP	Extension for AutoLISP files.
LST	Extension for printer plot files.
Macro	A program consisting of AutoCAD commands.
Maths coprocessor	A computer chip specially designed to do mathematical operations quickly.
Mesh	A regular assembly of AutoCAD 3D faces.
MNU	Extension for AutoCAD menu files.
Mouse	Input device for computer. The location of the mouse defines the location of the cursor on the screen. Buttons on the mouse can be used to select items and commands.
MS-DOS	Microsoft's version of DOS
OS2	Operating System 2. IBM's replacement for DOS.
Parallel port	Communications port where 8 bits are transmitted simultaneously along eight wires. See LPT1.
Parametric	Complex graphical entity whose dimensions may be manipulated independently.
PATH	DOS command to tell the computer the names of directories to search for program files.
PC-CAD	Computer aided design on a personal computer. Synonymous with the AutoCAD program.
PC-DOS	IBM's version of DOS. Same as MS-DOS.
Perspective	2D graphical representation of 3D objects taking into account the reduction in the size of objects farther away from the viewer.

Pixel	Picture element. The smallest dot on a computer screen or printer output.
Plane	A flat imaginary surface defined by 3 points in space.
PLT	Extension for plot file names.
Polar coordinates	Coordinate system where points are located in space by the length and orientation of a vector from the origin to the point.
Port	Special circuit on computer with socket(s) for connecting other devices.
Postscript	High level printer control language for producing graphical output.
Prototype drawing	The starting point for new AutoCAD drawings.
Pull-down menu	A screen menu that appears when the cursor is positioned in certain parts of the screen.
RAM	Random Access Memory, where the computer stores programs and data while running.
RAM Disk	Part of RAM set up to behave like a very fast disk drive, accepting such DOS commands as DIR, etc.
Real number	Decimal number or one written in scientific notation, eg 3.2456, 45.67E-6.
Script	A list of AutoCAD commands stored in a text file with the extension "SCR".
SDF	Space Delimited Format – see CDF.
Selection set	Set of objects picked using AutoCAD's "Select objects:" routine.
Serial port	Communications port where bits of information are transmitted in series. Usually slower than parallel port but can transmit over longer distances.
SLD	Extension for AutoCAD slide files.
Slide	A raster image file of an AutoCAD drawing. Can be viewed but not edited.

Solid modeller	CAD program that constructs 3D objects from solid primitives such as rectangular blocks and cylinders etc.
Stack	Part of RAM set aside for storing AutoLISP arguments and partially completed computations.
String	A variable containing text characters.
Surface	A 3D shell type object.
TXT	Extension for AutoCAD SDF and CDF text files.
UNIX	Form of multi-user operating system for networked computers.
Wire frame model	CAD representation of 3D objects from their outlines only.
Wordprocesssor	Program to facilitate the generation of text files.
WORM	Write Once Read Many – device for storing large amounts of data on compact laser disc.

SUBJECT INDEX

Page numbers in bold indicate the most important reference